Antonia Clare   JJ Wilson

INTERMEDIATE

Total English

Students' Book

Longman

Contents

LESSON 3	VOCABULARY	COMMUNICATION	FILM BANK
Grammar: Present Perfect Simple and Past Simple/use of *for* and *since* **Vocabulary:** time expressions **Can do:** retell a simple narrative in your own words	Phrasal verbs	The tree of friends	Best friends
Grammar: Past Simple and Past Continuous **Vocabulary:** common collocations **Can do:** describe an important event from your life	In the news	The front page	Breaking news
Grammar: future possibility **Vocabulary:** compound nouns **Can do:** make a formal phone call	Prefixes and suffixes	Your dream house	City or country?
Grammar: First Conditional with *if/when/unless/as soon as* **Vocabulary:** opposites **Can do:** write a short classified advertisement	Confusing words	What a waste!	From rags to riches
Grammar: countable and uncountable nouns **Vocabulary:** food **Can do:** recommend a restaurant	Explaining what you mean	What are you good at?	Favourite films
Grammar: articles **Vocabulary:** describing nature **Can do:** show interest and surprise	Expressions with *get*	London in a day	Dream holidays
Grammar: modals of ability, past and present **Vocabulary:** old age **Can do:** talk about abilities in the past and present	Idioms about learning	School days	Cambridge
Grammar: Third Conditional **Vocabulary:** life changes **Can do:** describe the effect of important decisions	Word building	Time for a change?	From cradle to grave
Grammar: past obligation/permission **Vocabulary:** job requirements **Can do:** state routine job requirements	UK and US English	Job advertisements	The ideal workplace
Grammar: phrasal verbs **Vocabulary:** common phrasal verbs **Can do:** write a thank you letter	The senses	The memory game	Icons

Irregular verb table page 165   Pronunciation bank page 166   Tapescripts page 168

Do you know...?

1 a Do you know these tenses? Match the sentences to the tenses (a-g) below.

1 I've lived here since I was a child.
2 She's studying French at the Sorbonne.
3 We left the office at about 7.00pm.
4 I'd already eaten lunch so I wasn't hungry.
5 He was playing his guitar when the string broke.
6 I'm leaving the company in July.
7 I write about fifteen e-mails a day.

a) Present Simple
b) Present Continuous (for ongoing actions)
c) Present Continuous (for future actions)
d) Present Perfect
e) Past Simple
f) Past Continuous
g) Past Perfect

b Complete the sentences below by writing the name of the correct tense from Ex. 1a.

1 We use the _____ to describe something that started and finished in the past.
2 We use the _____ to describe a future plan.
3 We use the _____ to describe something that started in the past and continues in the present.
4 We use the _____ to describe something that is a state, habit or general truth.
5 We use the _____ to describe a temporary situation that is happening around now.
6 We use the _____ to describe something that happened before another event in the past.
7 We use the _____ to describe something temporary that was in progress at a time in the past.

2 Can you recognise the <u>underlined</u> parts of the sentences? Label them using the headings below.

> prefix (x2)   suffix (x2)   phrasal verb (x2)
> idiom (x2)

1 The story was <u>un</u>believable! _____
2 Can you <u>give me a hand</u> with this? _____
3 She <u>grew up</u> in Ecuador. _____
4 I've <u>given up</u> eating chocolate! _____
5 This meat is <u>over</u>cooked. _____
6 Happi<u>ness</u> is the most important thing. _____
7 This is the poem that I <u>learned by heart</u>. _____
8 I was always use<u>less</u> at Maths. _____

3 a Complete the word webs with words from the box below.

travel   food and drink   home   relationships

> husband   beach   hall   yoghurt   colleague
> vacuum cleaner   stepmother   roof
> vegetable   daughter   island   potato
> sightseeing   coffee   tourist   doorbell

b Underline any /ə/ sounds in the words above.

c Add some more words to each word web.

4 a Complete the table below with the correct verbs, nouns and adjectives.

verb	noun	adjective
educate	(1) _____	*educated*
(2) _____	*improvement*	*improved*
televise	(3) _____	xxx
govern	(4) _____	xxx
xxx	*expense*	(5) _____
xxx	*beauty*	(6) _____
attract	xxx	(7) _____
(8) _____	*application*	xxx

b Mark the main stress in the words above. How many syllables are there?

5 Write the words in the correct order to make useful phrases for the classroom.

1 could a little, speak you please up ?
2 dictionary I could your borrow ?
3 you paper, give some could please me ?
4 these down words write .
5 in do English say you how 'XXX' ?
6 mean does 'XXX' what ?
7 and the between what's 'X' 'Y' difference ?
8 you again say can that ?
9 are page on we what ?

1 Friends

Lead-in

1 Look at the photos. What type of relationships do they show?

2 Put the words/phrases in the box in groups: a) work/school, b) family, c) friends, d) other. Can you add any more words?

> close friend   acquaintance   boss   classmate   husband
> colleague   stranger   ex-girlfriend   best friend   stepmother
> old friend   father-in-law   friend of a friend   team-mate

3 Match the phrases in **bold** in A with the correct definition in B.

A	B
1 Let's **keep in touch**.	a) not stay in contact
2 We **have the same sense of humour**.	b) like to be with him/her
	c) know him/her better
3 We **have a lot in common**.	d) find the same things funny
4 I hope we don't **lose touch**.	e) like/enjoy the same things
5 He's really nice when you **get to know him**.	f) have a friendly relationship
	g) stop being friends
6 I really **enjoy her company**.	h) stay in contact
7 They **fell out** over money.	
8 We **get on** really **well**.	

4 Choose four people from Ex. 2. Describe your relationship with them to a partner.

I don't have a lot in common with my stepmother.

5

Speaking and vocabulary

1 Discuss.

   1 What is/isn't 'normal' about the painting?

   2 Do you like unusual pictures/food/clothes?

   3 Do you have any unusual hobbies/likes/ dislikes? What are they?

2 **a** Complete the questions below using the prepositions from the box.

> about (x3) on (x2) in (x2) for to at

   1 What subjects do you like **reading** _____?

   2 What do you **use** the Internet _____?

   3 What activities and hobbies are you **good** ___?

   4 What do you **spend** most of your money _____?

   5 What do you **worry** _____?

   6 What types of exercise are you **keen** _____?

   7 What do you usually **talk** _____ with friends?

   8 What cultures are you **interested** _____ ?

   9 What clubs do you **belong** _____?

   10 How many languages are you **fluent** _____?

b Work in groups. Choose five of the questions to ask other students.

Listening

3 **a** 〔1.1〕 Listen to the dialogues. Which questions from Ex. 1 do the speakers answer?

b What were their answers? Write one key word in the table below.

	Question?	Answer?	More information
Dialogue 1			
Dialogue 2			
Dialogue 3			
Dialogue 4			
Dialogue 5			

c 〔1.2〕 Listen to the dialogues again. Can you add any more information?

René Magritte, *The Son of Man*

Grammar | auxiliary verbs

4 Complete the Active grammar box with sentences from the conversation below.

   1 A: I'm keen on running.

   2 B: **Do** you do it regularly?

   3 A: Yes, I **do**. Three or four times a week.

   4 B: **Where do** you run?

   5 A: In the park. I **don't** run very fast.

> ### Active grammar
>
> **a)** *Yes/No questions*
>
> Use *do/does* in the present, *did* in the past and *have/has* in the Present Perfect. The order is ASV (auxiliary + subject + verb).
> e.g. sentence: _____
>
> **b)** *Wh- questions*
>
> The question word comes before the auxiliary. The order is QASV (question word + auxiliary + subject + verb).
> e.g. sentence: _____
>
> **c)** **Short answers**
>
> Use the auxiliary verb from the question.
> e.g. sentence: _____
>
> **d)** **Negatives**
>
> Use *don't/doesn't* in the present, *didn't* in the past and *haven't/hasn't* in the Present Perfect.
> e.g. sentence: _____

see Reference page 17

5 Find and correct the mistakes in the sentences/questions.

Where ~~are~~ you come from?
Where do you come from?

1 Use you the Internet a lot?
2 She don't like Maths.
3 I do not keen on football.
4 He doesn't lives here any more.
5 Are they like playing tennis?
6 What you talk about with your friends?
7 Are you from Switzerland? No, I don't.
8 Have you seen the film yet? Yes, I did.
9 Did they stay long? No, they don't.
10 Do you play the violin? No, I doesn't.

6 **a** Make questions for these answers.

Blue. – *What's your favourite colour?*

1 Swimming.
2 With my parents.
3 Yes, I do. He's great.
4 Pasta.
5 No, I haven't. Is it good?
6 No, I don't. It tastes horrible.
7 At ten o'clock.
8 Manchester United.

b Compare your questions with a partner.

Person to person

7 Think of four things that most of the class don't know about you and write one word in each space in the diagram. Work in pairs. Ask questions about your partner's words.

A: *How many sisters do you have?*
B: *Six.*
A: *Really? Are they older or younger?*

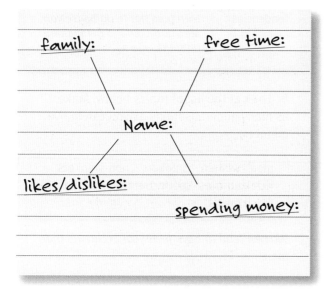

family: free time:

Name:

likes/dislikes:

spending money:

Reading

8 **a** Work with a partner. Do you think these sentences are true or false?

1 Men live longer than women. ☐
2 Women smoke more than men. ☐
3 Most men are happy with their weight. ☐
4 Women watch more TV than men. ☐
5 Sixty-five percent of men do some physical exercise. ☐
6 Men like to talk about relationships. ☐

b Student A: read text A. Find the answers to 1–3. Student B: read text B on page 8. Find the answers to 4–6. Tell your partner which sentences are true.

Text A

Health and wealth

Life, love and death

In the developed world the average man lives until he is 75.4 years old, whereas the average woman lives to 80.2. In general, the illness which causes most deaths is heart disease, and Monday is the most common day for a heart attack! In Europe men don't tend to get married until they are 27, women when they are 25. Couples whose marriage ends in divorce have usually been married for 10.5 years.

Work, habits and body

On average, women who work full-time in the UK earn €580 per week. Men earn €790 per week. Men work for forty hours a week and spend €170 on leisure (hobbies and presents). Seven times a year, British men buy presents for their partners after an argument! Men who smoke have 104 cigarettes a week, fifteen more than women. Also, not surprisingly, men generally eat more – the average man will eat 27,200 kilograms of food during his lifetime – the weight of more than six elephants. And only 36% of men worry about their weight. On the other hand, 90% of women don't like their body, and they try to diet six times in their life.

Text B

Free time and chat

Leisure activities

Men and women are nearly equal in the living room. Every day women watch TV or listen to the radio for two hours 37 minutes, only twenty minutes less than men. On the other hand, women are in the kitchen, or doing the housework, for 2 hours 18 minutes, while men spend just 45 minutes doing housework. For exercise she goes to the gym or does yoga. He goes for a walk or, in 35% of cases, doesn't do anything at all. Men like driving more than women, though 95% of drivers of both sexes consider themselves 'above average'.

Conversation topics

Regarding chat, women tend to talk a lot about relationships and other people, and they say about 7,000 words a day. Men talk about sport and use only 2,000 words a day. Conversations that aren't about sport tend to be about work, politics, economics or abstract ideas, for example 'how the world began'.

9 a What do these numbers refer to? Write sentences and use your own words.

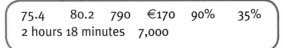

> 75.4   80.2   790   €170   90%   35%
> 2 hours 18 minutes   7,000

On average, men in the developed world live to 75.4 years.

b Discuss.

1 Which facts do you find surprising?
2 In what ways do you think you are 'normal'? Refer to the text.

Pronunciation

10 a 〔1.3〕 Listen and repeat the numbers in the box above.

b Choose the correct answer.

1 How do we say '.'? (a) dot (b) point
2 When do we use *and*? (a) before numbers under 100 (b) before numbers over 100

c 〔1.4〕 Listen and write the numbers you hear.

d Say the numbers aloud.

Speaking

11 a Look at the How to ... box. Tick (✓) the expressions that are in the text.

<table>
<tr><td rowspan="7" style="writing-mode: vertical-lr">HOW TO ...</td><td colspan="2">**make generalisations**</td></tr>
<tr><td>Talk about averages</td><td>*The average man/woman ...*
On average, ...</td></tr>
<tr><td>Make generalisations</td><td>*In general, .../... in general ...*
Generally, .../... generally ...
Usually, .../... usually ...</td></tr>
<tr><td>Talk about/ tendencies</td><td>*Women tend to talk a lot about ...*
Men tend not to do housework.
Men don't tend to get married until they are 27.</td></tr>
</table>

b Look at the list of topics below. Make as many generalisations as you can in five minutes.

> men   women   smokers   non-smokers
> rich countries   poor countries   capital cities
> small towns

Women tend to have fewer car accidents than men.

Speaking and listening

1 **a** Read these quotes about friendship. Tick (✓) the ones you agree with. Compare your ideas with a partner.

> 'To like and dislike the same things. That is a true friendship.'

> 'I have never had better friends than the ones I had when I was twelve.'

> 'Strangers are just friends waiting to happen.'

> 'A real friend is one who walks in when the rest of the world walks out.'

> 'Make new friends and keep the old. One is silver, the other is gold.'

b Complete the sentence with your ideas.

A real friend is ...

c Read your sentences to the class.

2 **a** **1.5** Listen to the dialogues about how people met their friends. Which speaker met their friend:

1 by using a computer?
2 at work?
3 in a car park?
4 in an airport?
5 while studying?

b Listen again. Complete each speaker's words.

Speaker 1: ... we _____ _____ for a while

Speaker 2: Luckily, we've got the same _____ of _____

Speaker 3: ... and I really enjoy _____ _____

Speaker 4: ... we've found that we have a lot _____ _____

Speaker 5: After that trip, we just _____ in _____

3 Discuss.

1 In general, do you have lots of friends you don't see often, or a few friends that you are close to?
2 Where do you go to meet new friends?
3 How did you meet your closest friend?

Vocabulary | using a computer

4 **a** Which of the following can a computer do?

> write poetry   help people become friends
> compose music   recognise voices

b What else can a computer do?

5 **a** One of the collocations is not possible. Which one?

work/print/shop/research **online**

You can work, shop and research online but not print online.

1 *send/receive/forward/catch*   **a message**
2 *access/surf/switch on/use*   **the Internet**
3 *visit/shut/find/join*   **a website**
4 *shut down/repair/work on/stop*   **a computer**
5 *download/delete/save/surf*   **a file**

b Can you add any verbs of your own?

c Which of the things in Ex. 5a have you done in the last week? Which do you do most days?

Reading

6 Read the text about *friendsters.com* and answer the questions.

   1 What is the relationship between Louise and Juanita?

   2 What are the benefits of joining websites like this?

Any friend of yours ...
is a friend of mine.

Louise Henry, a 31-year-old business executive from London, arrives at her desk and turns on her computer. She is happy as she is expecting a message from her new best friend Juanita, a museum worker who lives in Vancouver, Canada.

Louise and Juanita email every day, and by doing this they are part of a new social trend that is spreading around the world. From London to Sydney, New York to Singapore, you don't have to live in the same city to make new friends, or even on the same continent. You can form new friendships on the Internet.

In the past there were pen pals. Now there is *friendsters.com*, which has over 1.5 million members. And a British service, *everyonesconnected. com*, has over 500,000 members and more are joining every day. These new websites are based on the 'small world hypothesis'* developed by an American sociologist, Stanley Milgram, in the 1960s.

The potential for making friends on the Internet is huge, but there are also dangers to meeting people you don't know. Because of this, these websites only accept members who are invited by their real-life friends. Once members are accepted they can put their whole social network on the website. This way, friends can get to know friends' friends, without going out to parties to meet them. Friendsters can chat, meet for a coffee and, of course, become friends.

Louise became friends with Juanita by five steps: her friend Colin, a computer consultant, knew Jess, a secretary, who was friends with Catherine, who went to school with Peter, who worked with Juanita a few years ago. The connections became apparent when they both joined *everyonesconnected*. The two friends have been in touch ever since.

Louise says: 'Juanita and I chat over the Internet all the time, about films, religion and her new flat. Although she lives in Canada, we have a lot in common. We're both doing photography courses at the moment. I'm on the site to meet new people in a society where I don't think it's easy to make new friends.'

*small world hypothesis
Stanley Milgram believed that everyone in the world is connected by no more than six 'degrees' of separation, i.e. by following a path of friends, friends' friends' friends' friends' friends, etc, you can get from one person to any other person in no more than six steps. To test the theory, a team of researchers asked computer users to contact a stranger by emailing acquaintances. So Bruce in the UK was asked to find Olga, in Siberia. Bruce did this through his uncle David, in Uganda, who he knew had computer pen pals across Russia. He completed the task in just four steps.

7 Read the text again and answer the questions.

   1 How often are Louise and Juanita in touch with each other?

   2 Where do they live?

   3 What is the 'new social trend'?

   4 How do people join one of these websites?

   5 According to the article, what is the advantage of meeting your friends' friends on the Internet?

   6 What do Louise and Juanita have in common?

   7 Why does Louise Henry use the Internet site?

   8 What is the main idea of 'the small world hypothesis'?

8 Discuss.

   1 If one of your friends invited you, would you join a website like *friendsters. com*? Why/Why not?

   2 Do you think it's easy to make new friends? Why/Why not?

   3 Have you made any new friends on the Internet?

Grammar | Present Simple and Present Continuous

9 **a** Look at the Active grammar box. Match the example sentences (1–5) to the rules (a–e).

b What is the difference in meaning between the two sentences?

1 What **do** you **think** about our new teacher?

2 What **are** you **thinking** about?

Active grammar

1 We **are** both **doing** photography courses at the moment.

2 She **is expecting** a message.

3 Louise and Juanita **write** every day.

4 She **lives** in Vancouver.

5 There **are** many dangers.

Use the **Present Simple** for:

a) habits/routines, e.g. sentence: _____

b) things that are always true/permanent, e.g. sentence: _____

c) describing a state, e.g. sentence: _____

Use the **Present Continuous** for:

d) things that are happening now at this precise moment, e.g. sentence: _____

e) temporary situations that are happening around now, e.g. sentence: _____

Some verbs are not usually used in the continuous form, e.g. *hate, want, need*.

---

see Reference page 17

10 Put the verbs into the correct form of the Present Simple or Present Continuous.

1 _____ (you/read) that book? Can I see it?

2 Sasha _____ (not work) on Tuesdays so she's at home now.

3 I'm so tired. I _____ (need) a holiday!

4 That looks hard. _____ (you/want) any help?

5 I'm afraid we _____ (not have) any tea because I always drink coffee.

6 Where _____ (you/live) at the moment?

7 _____ (you/understand) this computer manual?

8 You look very happy! Who _____ (you/think) about?

9 I _____ (not/want) to leave too late because I _____ (hate) driving in the dark.

10 What horrible weather! I _____ (stay) inside until the rain stops.

11 Make questions from the prompts using the Present Simple or Present Continuous.

1 What/you/do? (job/occupation)

2 What/you/do/at work (or school)/at the moment?

3 How often/you/go out with friends?

4 What/you/like/do?

5 What films/you/like/watch?

6 What/you/usually/do/at the weekends?

7 You/read/a good book/at the moment?

8 You/play (or watch)/any sports/these days?

9 Why/you/study/English/this year?

10 You/do/any other courses/at the moment?

Person to person

12 Ask your partner the questions in Ex. 11. Tell the class anything interesting you learned.

Writing

13 Find ten mistakes in the email.

Hi,

My name is Stefano and I'm Italian student. I am coming from Rome, which I am thinking is the most beautiful city in the world.

At the moment I studying Engineering at university in Pisa, so I am living in a flat with three other students. We have a lot in common and are sharing the same sense of humour.

Most nights we listen music, and on Saturdays we usually go to a disco and dance all night. All except Marco, who is studying Chemistry. He is very boring and is never going out.

This year I am study English twice a week because I would really like to work for an American company when I am finish my degree.

Look forward to hearing from you soon.

All the best,

Stefano

PS I have attached some photos of me and the Leaning Tower.

14 Read the email and complete the exercises in the Writing bank on pages 162–3. Write an email introducing yourself to a new friend (in the class).

1.3 Brotherly love?

Grammar	Present Perfect Simple and Past Simple
Can do	retell a simple narrative in your own words

Listening and speaking

1 a [1.6] Listen to three people talking about someone who they fell out with. Match the speakers 1–3 to the photos A–C below.

b Listen again and complete the notes.

Speaker	1	2	3
Who do they talk about?		Romina – best friend	
How long have they known/did they know each other?			1 year
Why/When did they fall out?			
How is their relationship now?			

c Check your answers with a partner.

2 Discuss.

1 Do you ever have arguments with your friends?
2 Have you ever fallen out with a close friend? What happened?
3 What do friends/family usually argue about?

Reading

3 a You are going to read about the Dassler brothers. Look at the pictures. What do you think the story is about?

b Read the text on page 13 and put the pictures in order.

Brotherly Love?

Adidas and Puma have been two of the biggest names in sports shoe manufacturing for over half a century.

Since 1928 they have supplied shoes for Olympic athletes, World Cup-winning football heroes, Muhammad Ali, hip hop stars and rock musicians famous all over the world. But the story of these two companies begins in one house in the town of Herzogenaurach, Germany.

Adolph and Rudolph Dassler were the sons of a shoemaker. They loved sport but complained that they could never find comfortable shoes to play in. Rudolph always said, 'You cannot play sports wearing shoes that you'd walk around town with.' So they started making their own. In 1920 Adolph made the first pair of athletics shoes with spikes[1], produced on the Dasslers' kitchen table.

On 1st July 1924 they formed a shoe company, Dassler Brothers Ltd. The company became successful and it provided the shoes for Germany's athletes at the 1928 and 1932 Olympic Games.

But in 1948 the brothers argued. No one knows exactly what happened but family members have suggested that the argument was about money or women. The result was that Adolph left the company. His nickname[2] was Adi, and using this and the first three letters of the family name, Dassler, he founded Adidas.

Rudolph relocated across the River Aurach and founded his own company too. At first he wanted to call it Ruda, but eventually he called it Puma, after the wild cat. The famous Puma logo of the jumping cat has survived until now.

After the big split of 1948 Adolph and Rudolph never spoke to each other again and since then their companies have been in competition. Both companies were for many years the market leaders, though Adidas has always been more successful than Puma. In the 1970s new American companies Nike and Reebok arrived to rival them.

The terrible family argument should really be forgotten, but ever since it happened, over fifty years ago, the town has been split into two. Even now, some Adidas employees and Puma employees don't talk to each other.

Glossary
[1] *spikes* = Sharp metal points that grip the ground
[2] *nickname* = name (not your real name) given to you by friends and family

4 Mark the sentences true (T) or false (F).
1 The Dassler's father was a sportsman. ☐
2 The brothers first made sports shoes at home. ☐
3 They argued about the shoes. ☐
4 They decided to start their own companies. ☐
5 Puma sells more shoes than Adidas. ☐
6 People in the town have now forgotten the argument. ☐

5 What is the significance of the following things in the Dassler story?

a wild cat   a river   a shoemaker   a nickname
the 1932 Olympic Games   an argument

6 Find verbs in the text which mean the following:
1 provided a product (paragraph 1)
2 created (an institution/company, etc.) (paragraph 4)
3 moved permanently to a different place (paragraph 5)
4 be in competition with another person or company (paragraph 6)

7 Take it in turns to retell the story using the words/phrases from Ex. 5, the verbs from Ex. 6 and the pictures to help you.

Grammar | Present Perfect Simple and Past Simple

8 a What tense are the <u>underlined</u> verbs in the sentences below?

Since 1928 they <u>have supplied</u> shoes for Olympic athletes, ...

After the big spilt of 1948 ... their companies <u>have been</u> in competition.

On 1st July, 1924 they <u>formed</u> a shoe company.

Active grammar

1 Use the <u>Past Simple</u>/<u>Present Perfect Simple</u> to describe an action that started in the past and continues in the present.

2 Use the <u>Past Simple</u>/<u>Present Perfect Simple</u> to talk about something that happened in the past but has a result in the present.

3 To include more detailed information (e.g. exact times), use the <u>Past Simple</u>/<u>Present Perfect Simple</u>.

---

b Choose the correct alternatives in the Active grammar box.

c Find two more examples of the Present Perfect Simple in the text on page 13.

see Reference page 17

9 Correct the mistakes in each sentence.

1 Has you bought those expensive shoes yet?
2 These are my favourite trainers. I've bought them last year.
3 I knew him for six years. We're still friends now.
4 Oh! You had a haircut. It's ... nice.
5 I don't have seen him for several weeks.
6 While I was in Italy I've eaten lots of pizza.

10 a Complete the dialogues using the verbs in the box. Use the Present Perfect Simple or the Past Simple.

---

decide (x2) lose have (x2) find see (x2) put

A: *I've decided* to stop smoking.
B: What a great idea! When (1) _____ this?
A: Last Monday. I (2) _____ a cigarette for three days.
B: Congratulations!
A: I (3) _____ a cigar yesterday, though.
B: Oh.

C: (4) _____ my handbag? I can't find it anywhere.
D: Yes, I (5) _____ it on the table a few minutes ago.
C: Ah, here it is. I (6) _____ it! Oh no. Where are the car keys? I (7) _____ the car keys now.
D: They're on the table. I (8) _____ them there for you before breakfast.
C: Oh. Thanks.

b ▶1.7 Listen and check your answers.

Pronunciation

11 a ▶1.7 Listen again. How is *have* pronounced in a) positive sentences? b) negative sentences?

b Practise the dialogues with a partner.

Grammar | *for* and *since*

12 a Read the Active grammar box and choose the correct alternatives to complete rules 1 and 2.

Active grammar

The Present Perfect Simple is often used with *for* and *since*.

*Puma has sold shoes **for** over 50 years.*

*Adidas has sold shoes **since** 1948.*

1 We use *for* + <u>period of</u>/<u>point in</u> time
2 We use *since* + <u>period of</u>/<u>point in</u> time

---

see Reference page 17

b Do the time expressions below go with *for* or *since*?

---

last night   a couple of months   this morning
fifteen years   a while   the moment when ...
last weekend   the day before yesterday

---

c Complete the sentences with *for* or *since*.

1 I've lived in the same house _____ I was born.
2 I've studied English _____ about three years.
3 I've known my best friend _____ I started school.
4 I've had the same hobby _____ over half my life.
5 I've watched four hours of TV _____ last night.
6 I've been at this school _____ a few weeks.

Person to person

13 a Make the sentences in Ex. 12c true for you and add more information after each sentence.

b Compare your sentences with other students.

1 Vocabulary

Phrasal verbs

1 Work with a partner. What is a phrasal verb? What makes it different from other verbs? Check your answers on page 17.

2 Circle the correct alternatives to complete the sentences.

1 I grew *up/down* in Brazil.
2 The children were brought *down/up* by their aunt.
3 My brother always told me *off/on* for borrowing his records.
4 You really take *before/after* your father. You are always complaining.
5 My sister looked *after/before* me when I was ill.
6 I don't get *on/off* very well with my mother.
7 I still look *down/up* to my older brother, and ask him for advice.
8 We carried *off/on* arguing until they left home.

3 Use the sentences in Ex. 2 to help you match the phrasal verbs from A with the definitions from B.

A	B
1 grow up	a) admire and respect someone
2 bring up	b) continue (doing something)
3 tell (someone) off	c) develop from being a child to being an adult
4 take after (someone)	d) take care of (someone or something)
5 look after (someone or something)	e) talk angrily to someone because they have done something wrong
6 get on with (someone)	f) have a friendly relationship with someone
7 look up to (someone)	g) look or behave like another member of your family
8 carry on (doing something)	h) care for children until they are adults

4 Complete the text using the correct form of the phrasal verbs in Ex. 3.

I was _brought up_ in a small town near Paris. My parents are English, so I (1) _____ speaking English and French. A young English student lived with us during the school holidays, and she (2) _____ me when my parents were away on business. I remember my father always (3) _____ us _____ if he heard us speaking in English, because she was studying French. Usually we changed to French for a few minutes, and then (4) _____ in English when he couldn't hear us, because it was easier for both of us. She was an artist, and we (5) _____ very well. I (6)_____ her, and later tried to become a painter myself. Unfortunately, I (7) _____ my father, who wasn't artistic, and so I was never successful.

5 Answer the questions in groups.

1 Where did you **grow up**?
2 When you **bring up** a child, what do you think is the most important thing to teach him/her?
3 As a child, did anyone **tell you off**? Why? Did this make you stop or did you **carry on** anyway?
4 Which member of your family do you **get on with** best?
5 Who in your family do you **take after**?
6 Who **looks after** you when you are ill?
7 As a child, who did you **look up to**?

The tree of friends

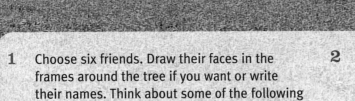

1 Choose six friends. Draw their faces in the frames around the tree if you want or write their names. Think about some of the following questions. Make notes.

1 What was your first impression of each other?
2 Why do you like him/her?
3 What don't you like about him/her?
4 What things do you have in common?
5 What type of character does he/she have?
6 How do you keep in touch?
7 What job does he/she do?
8 What activities/hobbies is he/she keen on?

2 **a** Draw a line between friends who know each other.

b Show your books to a partner. Describe the friends, and who knows who.

c Find out which of your partner's friends would get on with your friends. Why? Find five things they have in common.

3 Write a paragraph describing your relationship with a close friend. Use the questions and your notes to help you. Think about how you met, and how your relationship has developed.

1 | Reference

Auxiliary verbs: *do, be, have*

Use auxiliary verbs *do, be* and *have* to form tenses and make questions, short answers and negatives.

Use the verb *do* as the auxiliary verb with the 'simple' tenses, except if the main verb is *be*.

***Does** he smoke? Yes, he **does**. No, he **doesn't**.*

*I **don't** have breakfast.*

*When **do** you have breakfast?*

***Are** you hungry?* NOT: ~~Do~~ you hungry?

Use the verb *be* with continuous forms.

*I **am (not)** studying German.*

***Are** you studying? Yes, I **am**. No, I'**m** not.*

Use *have* to make perfect verb forms.

*I **have**/**haven't** finished my book.*

***Have** you finished? Yes, I **have**. No, I **haven't**.*

Present Simple vs. Present Continuous

Use the **Present Simple** for:

1 habits/routines

   Seung-Ah starts work at eight o'clock.

2 things that are always true/permanent

   Spain is a hot country.

3 describing a state

   Dimitri is really happy about his new job.

Use the **Present Continuous** for:

1 things that are happening now, at this moment

   Jade is having a shower.

2 temporary situations that are happening around now (but not at this exact moment)

   I am learning Spanish for my job.

! Some verbs are used in the Present Simple and Present Continuous, but their meaning changes.

*We'**re having** a wonderful holiday. (have = action/ experience – **can** be used in the continuous)*

*We **have** a lovely room by the sea. (have = possess – **can't** be used in the continuous)*

The following verbs are not usually used in the continuous form: *like, love, hate, have (possess), need, want, hope, prefer, find, know, think, realise, believe, understand, remember, seem, depend, suppose, mean, see, hear, smell, taste.*

Time expressions

With the Present Simple use *every day, once a month, sometimes, never, often ...*

With the Present Continuous use *now, at the moment, this week, today ...*

Present Perfect Simple and Past Simple

Use the **Present Perfect Simple** to describe:

1 an action that started in the past and continues in the present (unfinished time)

   *I **have known** her since I was a child. (I met her when I was a child and I still know her)*

2 an action that happened in the past but has a result in the present (present result)

   *Tom **has left** his bag at home. (He doesn't have it now)*

Use the **Past Simple** to talk about:
something that happened at a specific time (details)

*My mother **phoned** me yesterday.*

For and *Since*

We often use *for* and *since* with the Present Perfect.

Use *for* + period of time and *since* + point in time.

*I've known her **for** two months/**since** April.*

Phrasal verbs

Form: verb + one or two prepositions (or adverb)

*He **grew up** in France. I **got on** well **with** her.*

One phrasal verb can have more than one meaning.

*Take off. The plane **took off** at 6.00. I **took off** my coat.*

The meaning often has no connection with the verb.

*We **ran out of** money. (= there is none left)*

Phrasal verbs are often informal/spoken English. Often there is a formal word which means the same.

*The bomb will **go off**. (= The bomb will explode.)*

Key vocabulary

Relationships

close/old/best friend   acquaintance   father-in-law
husband   boss   colleague   stranger   ex-girlfriend
stepmother   classmate   friend of a friend   team-mate
keep in touch   have the same sense of humour
have a lot in common   lose touch   fall out   get on well
get to know him/her   enjoy his/her company

Verbs/adjectives + prepositions

read about   use (something) for   good at
spend money on   worry about   keen on   talk about
interested in   belong to   fluent in

Using a computer

work/shop/research online   send/receive/forward a
message   access/surf/use the Internet   visit/find/
join a website   shut down/repair/work on a computer
download/delete/save a file

Phrasal verbs

grow up   bring up   tell ... off   take after ...
look after ...   get on with ...   look up to ...   carry on ...

1 Review and practice

1 Circle the correct auxiliary verb.

Mary *is*/*has* taking a shower.

1 *Does*/*Has* the postman delivered the post yet?
2 They *are*/*do* writing in their journals now.
3 *Had*/*Have* your friends spoken to you today?
4 I *don't*/*haven't* understand this question.
5 *Do*/*Are* we going to the theatre tonight?
6 She *has*/*is* never been to Hawaii before.
7 *Doesn't*/*Don't* his mother live here?
8 *Haven't*/*Didn't* we seen this film already?

2 Complete the dialogues using auxiliary verbs.

1 A: Hi. <u>Do</u> you know many people here?
  B: Yes, a few. Some of us _____ doing an English course together.
2 A: _____ you live near here?
  B: No, we _____. We live in Italy.
3 A: _____ you staying in a nice hotel?
  B: Actually, we _____ like it very much.
4 A: _____ you know this area well?
  B: No, we _____. We _____ never been here before.
5 A: _____ you like the city?
  B: Yes, we _____ enjoying our stay here.
6 A: _____ you worked here long?
  B: No, I _____. Only one year.
7 A: Liz! What _____ you doing here in Rio?!
  B: I _____ travelling around South America!
8 A: _____ we met before?
  B: Yes, we _____. We met in Jakarta.

3 Circle the correct verb tense.

Do you remember/*Are you remembering* your Uncle Mick? He's coming to visit.

1 Usually it *isn't snowing*/*doesn't snow* here.
2 John's in France at the moment. *He's learning*/*He learns* French.
3 Stop! What *are you doing*/*do you do*? You'll break the TV if you continue like that!
4 Blue mixed with yellow *is making*/*makes* green.
5 *Are you knowing*/*Do you know* the way there?
6 *I'm living*/*I live* with Sam until I find a flat.

4 Put the verb in the correct form, Present Simple or Present Continuous.

I'm <u>going out</u> (go out) now. I'll see you later.

1 We can walk. It _____ (not/rain) now.
2 Alexis _____ (have) two older brothers.
3 Olga _____ (stay) at the Palace Hotel.
4 We _____ (want) to go as soon as possible.
5 Is it 5 o'clock already? I _____ (not believe) it.
6 Al is busy. He _____ (work) on a new project.

5 Circle the correct verb form.

The Brontë sisters: Charlotte, Emily and Anne *have written*/*wrote* novels and poems about love in the 19th century.

1 Venus and Serena Williams *have played*/*played* tennis since they were children.
2 Van Gogh *didn't have*/*hasn't had* many friends, but he *was*/*has been* close to his brother.
3 The Wright brothers *have invented*/*invented* the first aeroplane in 1903.
4 Freud's daughter, Anna, studied psychology and *became*/*has become* a psychoanalyst.
5 Brothers Phil and Gary Neville *have played*/*played* football for Manchester United since they were teenagers.
6 Michael Schumacher *has won*/*won* more races than any other Formula 1 driver.

6 Put the verb into the Past Simple or the Present Perfect Simple.

We <u>worked</u> (work) hard last night.

1 I _____ (not call) her yesterday because I was busy.
2 _____ (you ever eat) Thai food? It's delicious.
3 Technology _____ (influence) the way we live now.
4 He _____ (stop) running when he got tired.
5 We _____ (not see) each other since Easter.
6 She _____ (be) a smoker for years.
7 Who is Jo? I _____ (never hear) of her.
8 They _____ (wake up) at 7.00a.m. today.

7 Complete the sentences with a word or phrase which means the same as the words in brackets.

Let me introduce you to my <u>colleague</u> Gustav. (someone you work with)

1 He was a complete _____. (someone you don't know)
2 We get on well because we _____ common. (share similar interests)
3 Barbara is _____ Spanish. (speaks very well)
4 Could you _____ the message to me? (send the message you received)
5 I pressed the wrong button and _____ the file by mistake. (destroyed/erased)
6 I haven't seen Ali for a _____ of months. (two)
7 We're staying in their house for a _____. (some time – not specific)
8 Mike _____ smoking even when he felt ill. (continue)

2 Media

Lead-in

1 Read the text about newspapers in the UK.

Journalists write the stories, but the **editor** controls the contents of the newspaper. He/She decides which stories should go on **the front page.** Editors also write the **headlines** for the **main stories. The Sunday papers** have more **sections** than **the daily papers,** for example they have a **sports section** with **reports** of different sporting events, a **financial section** with **articles** about money and a **review section.** This often has **interviews** with **celebrities** like film stars and singers. Newspapers are cheap in the UK and they make lots of money by including **advertisements. Online news** is one of the fastest growing areas of the media.

2 a Which words in **bold** can you find in the photos?

b Put the words/phrases above in the correct column in the table and underline the stressed syllables.

People	Things you find in a newspaper	Other
journalists	*main stories*	*the Sunday papers*

c ▭ **2.1** Listen and check your answers.

3 Discuss.

1 Is the system of newspapers different in your country? How?
2 Do you read a daily newspaper? What is your favourite section?
3 Would you like to be a journalist or an editor? Why/Why not?

Speaking and reading

1 Discuss.

   1   In what order were the things in the box invented? (See page 145 for answers.)

   2   Which of them have been the most important for a) the world? b) you personally? and c) your country?

> TV   newspapers   the Internet   radio   video

2 **a** Do the quiz in pairs.

   1   What is the world's most popular reality TV show?

   2   Which country makes the most films?

   3   Which search engine is the most popular?

   4   Which film is often voted the greatest ever?

   5   Which quiz show is the most popular?

   6   Which country watches most TV?

   7   Which newspaper sells the most copies?

   b Read the text to check your answers.

ON TOP
OF THE MEDIA

'The mass media is a combination of information, entertainment and complete rubbish.' *D. Yandell*

You may or may not agree with psychologist David Yandell, but most people agree that the media has one key characteristic: it keeps growing and growing. These days, few people can remember life before television. And most of us have been influenced by the constant flow of words and images from screens or newspapers. Some of it is 'complete rubbish' and some of it is wonderful. Here are some of the 'firsts' and 'bests' of the media world.

The No.1 reality TV show: *Big Brother*. Like it or not, *Big Brother* is the most popular show of its kind. It was first shown in Holland in 1999 and it has been broadcast in over twenty countries.

The No.1 film industry: the Indian film industry (nicknamed Bollywood). More films are made in India than in any other country.

The No.1 search engine: Google. Lots of information can be found by searching Google. In fact, it is used for over 250 million searches in 182 languages every day. It was named after Googol, which is the number represented by one + one hundred zeros.

The No.1 film: *Citizen Kane*. In lists of great films it usually comes first. It was made by Orson Welles in 1941 and tells the story of a media tycoon*.

The No.1 quiz show of recent years: *Who wants to be a millionaire?* It started in the UK in 1998 but has now been broadcast all over the world.

The No.1 TV addicts: The US has 805 televisions per 1,000 people, the world's highest number, and in the US they watch TV the most. By the age of sixty-five the average US citizen has spent nine years in front of the TV.

The No.1 selling newspaper: *Yomiuri Shimbun*. It sells ten million copies a day in Japan.

And some firsts ...

- The TV was invented by John Logie Baird. He gave the first public demonstration in 1926.
- Ten years later there were still only 100 TV sets in the world.
- The first TV 'ad' was for a clock, in New York in 1941. They paid nine dollars for the ad.
- The first video recorder (1956) was 1.1 metres high and weighed 665 kilograms, as much as a small car.

> **Glossary**
> * *media tycoon* = a person who owns newspapers, TV stations, etc. They are rich and powerful.

diaphana
Devdas
un film réalisé par
SANJAY LEELA BHANSALI

EVERYBODY'S TALKING ABOUT IT!
It's Terrific!
ORSON WELLES
CITIZEN KANE
JOSEPH C
DOROTHY C
EVERETT
RAY CO
GEORGE CO
AGNES MO
PAUL ST
RUTH WA
ERSKINE S
WILLIAM

Big Brother

3 a Read the text again and mark the sentences true (T), false (F) or no information (NI).

1 According to the article, most people think the media contains a lot of rubbish. ☐

2 People in Holland didn't like *Big Brother*. ☐

3 Googol is a number. ☐

4 Orson Welles was a media tycoon. ☐

5 *Who wants to be a millionaire?* is the most popular quiz show in history. ☐

6 Americans watch more TV than any other nationality. ☐

7 *Yomiuri Shimbun* is a daily newspaper. ☐

8 The first ever TV ad was very successful. ☐

b Tick (✓) any information in the text that you already knew. Write (!) if you were surprised by the information. Compare with a partner.

Grammar | the passive

4 Complete the example sentences in the Active grammar box using examples from the text. Then match the rules (a–c) to the sentences (1–3).

Active grammar

Present Simple	Many films _____ **made** in India.
Past Simple	The TV _____ **invented** by John Logie Baird.
Present Perfect Simple	Big Brother **has** _____ **broadcast** in over twenty countries.
Modal verbs	Lots of information **can** _____ **found** by searching Google.

a) We use the **active** to describe what someone/something does.

b) We use the **passive** to describe what happens to someone/something (often when the person or thing that does the action is not known or not important.)

c) If we want to say who/what does the action in a passive sentence, we often use **by**.

1 *The TV was invented in 1926 by John Logie Baird.*

2 *John Logie Baird invented the TV in 1926.*

3 *The TV was invented in 1926.*

---

see Reference page 31

5 Put the sentences from TV news stories into the Present Simple active or passive.

1 A top politician _____ (remove) from office.

2 The boss of HAW Steel _____ (give) €1,000,000 bonus by company directors.

3 Workers in a car factory in Scotland _____ (stop) work for forty-eight hours.

4 Injured football star _____ (tell) to rest for three weeks.

5 The body of a famous climber _____ (find) in Austrian mountains.

6 Philip Roth _____ (win) the big prize – again.

7 Tesways Supermarkets _____ (open) their doors to Sunday night shoppers.

8 A new health report finds that fewer games _____ (play) at school than ever before.

6 a Add one missing word to each sentence.

1 The story has told many times.

2 Last week's article was written our leading journalist.

3 The magazine sold in twenty countries now.

4 The newspaper will printed at 3.00a.m.

5 'This news report been brought to you by Fox Cable News, USA.'

6 The World Wide Web invented by Tim Berners-Lee.

7 These days, over 10,000 books published every week.

8 The growth of television can't stopped.

b 🔊 **2.2** Listen and check your answers.

Pronunciation

7 a 🔊 **2.2** Listen again to the sentences in Ex. 6. Which verb is stressed, the main verb or the auxiliary verb? Mark the stress.

b Practise saying the sentences.

Person to person

8 a Finish the sentences to make them true for you.

1 The last present I was given was _____.

2 When I was younger I was told _____.

3 I have been helped by _____.

4 Recently I have been taught how to _____.

b Say your sentences to other students. Add at least one piece of information to each sentence. Who has had similar experiences to you?

Listening

9 **a** **2.3** Listen to the first part of an interview with a journalist and answer the question.

Is she talking about ...

a) types of journalist?

b) types of story?

c) types of newspaper?

b **2.4** Listen to the whole interview. The journalist talks about the topics below. Number them in the order she mentions them.

a) Writing about people's private lives. ☐

b) Celebrities who need publicity. ☐

c) Newspapers which write only about celebrities. ☐

d) Famous people who do something wrong. ☐

c Listen again. What does she say about each topic? Make notes and then compare your answers with a partner.

10 Complete the How to ... box by putting the headings below in the correct place.

> Agreeing   Saying it may change (according to what happens)   Giving an opinion   Disagreeing   Asking for an opinion

HOW TO ...

give opinions and (dis)agree

a) _____	*I think ...* *In my opinion ...*
b) _____	*What do you think?* *What's your opinion?*
c) _____	*Definitely* *Me too (to agree with I think ...)* *Me neither (to agree with I don't think ...)*
d) _____	*I'm not sure about that.* *I don't think so.*
e) _____	*It depends (on ...)* *It depends (who, when ...)*

11 **a** **2.5** Listen to some statements. Decide if you agree or disagree with them.

b Listen again and write a response using a phrase from the How to ... box.

c Discuss your opinions with your partner.

Lifelong learning

Using the media!

A great way to improve your English is to interact with the language outside the classroom. Make a list of:

• the magazines that you read in English

• the books that you have read and enjoyed in English

• the websites that you read in English

• the TV programmes that you watch in English

• all the places you can read/listen to English.

Bring English language articles from the Internet/magazines/newspapers to class.

A

B

Vocabulary | TV programmes

1 Discuss.

   1 What type of TV programme can you see in the photos? Do you enjoy these types of programmes?

   2 What other programmes do you watch?

2 a Look at the words in the box below and find:

   1 five people who work in television.

   2 four types of TV programme.

   3 two pieces of television equipment.

   4 a person who goes to a TV studio to appear on a programme.

   5 a programme which goes 'on air' at the time of the recording.

   6 the people who watch a programme in a TV studio.

> cameraman   microphone   producer   audience
> contestant   newsreader   live performance
> quiz show   presenter   documentary   actress
> chat show   TV camera   soap

b Use words in the box to describe the photos above.

3 Discuss.

People who work in TV say 'Never work with children or animals'. Why do you think they say this? What can go wrong on a live TV show?

Listening

4 a 🔊 **2.6** Listen to four people talking about what can go wrong on a live TV show. Write the number of the speaker next to the problems they talk about.

   1 Technical problems: *speaker one*

   2 Reading bad news

   3 Forgetting to take off the microphone

   4 Problems with furniture

   5 People laughing

   6 People getting nervous

   7 Problems with names of places

   8 People forgetting their words

b Listen again to check. What do they say about each thing? Make notes and compare with a partner.

5 Complete the How to ... box by putting the phrases/expressions below in the correct place.

> is broken   deal with   out of order
> What's the matter

HOW TO ... deal with problems

Ask what the problem is	*What's the problem?* (1) _____?
Explain the problem	*The photocopier is* (2) _____ /*isn't* **working** *(properly).* (3) *It* _____ /*keeps* **breaking** *(down).* *My boss* **keeps** *shouting at me.*
Offer a solution	(4) *I'll* _____ /*fix it.* *Shall I ... call the engineers?* *Try turning it off.*

23

6 **a** Look at the pictures of people having problems at work. Complete the dialogues and match them to the pictures.

1 **A:** What's the (1) _____?
   B: The printer's (2) _____, again.
   A: Oh dear. Shall I (3) _____ the engineers?

2 **A:** Oh no! My computer (4)_____ freezing!
   B: (5)_____ turning it off and on again.
   A: Thanks.

3 **A:** What's the matter?
   B: The photocopier isn't (6) _____. I think the paper's run out.
   A: Don't worry. I'll (7)_____ it.

A

B

C

b **2.7** Listen and check your answers.

c Practise the dialogues in pairs.

Speaking

7 **a** Work in pairs.

Student A: You are having a bad day at work/school. Everything is going wrong. Think of three problems you are having and then use the How to ... box on page 23 to tell Student B about them.

Student B: Student A is having problems. Use the How to ... box on page 23 to offer help.

b Now change roles.

Reading

8 **a** Discuss.

Do you think it is possible to cheat on a TV quiz show? How?

b Work in pairs. **Student A:** read the text below. **Student B:** read the text on page 147.

Answer the questions.

1 What was the TV programme?
2 What did the contestants win?
3 Why was there a scandal?
4 Who was involved in the scandal?
5 What happened in the end?

Who wants to be a millionaire?

Since making its debut in September 1998, *Who wants to be a millionaire?* has become a worldwide hit. Four people have become millionaires (legally), seven have walked away with £500,000 and seven have walked away with nothing.

On 10th September 2001 Charles Ingram became one of those lucky (and intelligent) people who won the big prize – a million pounds. So why, when he returned to the dressing room, did he have an argument with his wife? Why did he not celebrate? It was because they cheated, and they were nervous about being caught.

When the truth was revealed, nineteen months later, they *were* caught. During the show which Ingram won, viewers heard someone coughing regularly. It was a college lecturer friend of theirs, Tecwen Whittock. He was in the studio, and every time he heard the correct answer, he coughed. Ingram never admitted cheating, but viewers who saw the show said that the cheating was obvious. On some occasions Ingram actually changed his answer after coughs from Whittock told him he was wrong. A doctor later said that Whittock suffered from an allergy that was making him cough. But the 15.1 million people who watched a replay of the show on a later documentary, had other ideas.

Charles, his wife, and his friend were all found guilty of cheating and ordered to pay fines totalling £40,000. Luckily for them, when they were sentenced, they were not sent to prison because of their young families and good jobs.

c Tell your partner about your story. Use your notes to help you.

9 Discuss.

Do you think people who cheat on quiz shows should be punished? How?

Grammar | defining relative clauses

10 a Complete the extracts from the texts using the words in the box.

> who   where   which   whose   when   that

1   Ingram became one of those lucky people _____ won the big prize.
2   During the show _____ Ingram won, viewers heard someone coughing regularly.
3   He nervously looked around the studio _____ he was being filmed.
4   The man _____ fame meant that he received 500 letters a day ...
5   Whittock suffered from an allergy _____ was making him cough.
6   _____ the truth was revealed, nineteen months later, they were caught.

b Use the sentences in Ex. 10a to complete the Active grammar box.

Active grammar

Ingram became one of those lucky people who won the big prize...

... who won the big prize ... is an example of a defining relative clause; it defines exactly who or what we are talking about. This is essential information about a person, a place or a thing.

Use *who* or _____ for people
Use _____ or _____ for things or animals
Use _____ for places
Use _____ for possessions
Use _____ for time

In spoken English we often use *that* instead of *who* or *which*.
*The actress **that** stars in that film has beautiful eyes ...*

We can leave out the pronouns *who*, *which* or *that* if they are the object of the relative clause.
Quiz shows are programmes I never watch.

---

see Reference page 31

11 a Add *who, which* or *where* to each sentence.

1   That's the studio the last Bond film was made.
2   He's the man helps the director.
3   I've seen the film won an award at Cannes.
4   The quiz show host is the same woman reads the news.
5   Did she like the camera you bought her?
6   Here's the house I grew up.

b Which sentence in Ex. 11a doesn't need a relative pronoun?

12 Link the two sentences by using *who, where, which, whose, when* or *that*. There may be more than one possible answer.

That's the road. The accident happened there.
That's the road where the accident happened.

1   Last year I met a boy. His father is a pilot.
2   She loves the city. She was born there.
3   This is her new novel. It has already sold 500,000 copies.
4   We work for a small company. You haven't heard of the company.
5   I like the start of spring. Flowers begin to grow.
6   He's an actor. I have never seen him perform.
7   We met the artist. His exhibition was in town.
8   The children like to stay on the beach. On the beach they can play.
9   I had a great time. My cousins from New Zealand stayed with us.
10 That's the man. He won the big prize.

Speaking

13 a Play *Who wants to be a millionaire?*. Work in two groups. **Group A:** Look at page 145 and **Group B:** Look at page 148. Complete the quiz questions.

b Now work with someone from a different group. Ask your questions. If your partner answers all the questions correctly he/she wins €1 million. Count his/her score. Who is the quiz champion in the class?

Speaking

1 Discuss.

1 Do you believe everything you read in the news? Why/Why not?

2 Are some newspapers more believable than others? Which ones?

2 **a** Complete the headlines using the words below.

saves inherits takes escapes deliver survives

1 Traffic police officer in Bangkok helps to _____ baby in car

2 Lost driver _____ a wrong turn for 5,000 miles

3 Circus monkey _____ and destroys a restaurant

4 Top chef _____ giant lobster from cooking pot

5 Sailor _____ four months at sea

6 Cat _____ £350,000 house and £100,000 from owner

b Match the headlines to the pictures. In pairs, describe what you think happened in each situation.

A

B

C

D

E

F

Reading

3 **a** Read the texts (A–F) quickly. Write the headlines from Ex. 2a above the correct story.

b Write the number of the story next to the topics below.

1 restaurants: *stories B, D* 5 food or drink

2 travel 6 babies or pets

3 animals 7 survival

4 people getting lost

c Compare your answers with a partner.

4 Read the texts again. Answer the questions.

1 a) Where did Mrs Bright want to go?
b) Why didn't she ask for directions?

2 What did Parn Hung Kuk eat for four months?

3 Why is Pooker the cat famous?

4 What damage did Lala the monkey do?

5 a) Why didn't the chef cook the lobster?
b) What did the chef do with the lobster?

6 a) What special skills does Sergeant Sakchai Kodayan have?
b) Why did the taxi driver ask for help?

A

_____

A nervous driver who went on a day-trip to Calais ended up in Gibraltar after a five-day mystery tour. Mrs Bright was planning to go to France to buy some wine. However, as she was driving around Calais looking for the supermarket, she took a wrong turn and lost her way. Without a map, and unable to speak French, she was too embarrassed to ask for directions and eventually she found herself in Gibraltar.

B

_____

A giant lobster, saved from the cooking pot by a top chef, has been returned to the sea. Chef Anton Gretzky said he was planning to serve the lobster at his expensive restaurant, but decided he couldn't boil such a fine creature. Staff from the Aquarium Restaurant in Victoria, Australia, took the lobster, named Billy, to the coast to free him. Gretzky said: 'He has been on this Earth much longer than I have.'

C

_____

Pooker, a grey and white cat, has become Britain's most famous pet. The eight-year-old cat inherited a £350,000 house and £100,000 after its owner, Mrs Rafaella Barese, died. Mrs Barese's neighbours will use the £100,000 to buy food for the lucky cat. The rich and famous always seem to make new friends easily. After just one day, two local cats were trying to move in with Pooker.

5 **a** Use the verbs below to complete the collocations (1–7) from the texts. Then match them to the correct definitions (a–g).

> take   return   give   take   move   cause   get

COLLOCATION	DEFINITION
1 _____ a wrong turn (story A)	a) stop working for a short time
2 _____ lost (story E)	b) go to live in the same house
3 _____ in with someone (story C)	c) go/give back to
4 _____ damage (story D)	d) help someone when they have an injury
5 _____ to the sea (story B)	e) not know where you are
6 _____ first aid (story F)	f) drive in the wrong direction
7 _____ a break (story F)	g) break something by physically attacking it

b Cover the texts. Use the phrases above to retell the stories.

c Discuss.

1 Which stories did you find most interesting? Unbelievable? Funny?

2 What interesting stories have you heard/seen/read about recently?

D

A monkey, who escaped from a local circus, caused €10,000 of damage to a pizzeria after the owner of the restaurant tried to feed it bread and salad. The monkey, named Lala, was sitting in the restaurant bathroom when the owner found her. Lala dropped a vase, then started throwing paper towels around, and finally turned on the water taps and flooded the restaurant in Lehre, Germany.

E

'He was eating a seagull when we found him,' said a member of the South African navy team that rescued Vietnamese immigrant, Parn Hung Kuk from the Atlantic Ocean. Kuk took a day-trip from Cape Town in his boat. After getting lost in a storm, he was rescued four months later. 'He was living on seagulls, a turtle and rain water. It's a miracle he's still alive,' said the rescue ship's captain.

F

Bangkok traffic police helped to deliver another baby yesterday. Sergeant Sakchai Kodayan is one of 130 members of the city traffic police whose special skills include giving first aid to motorists and helping mothers as they give birth. 'I was taking a break in a café by the road when a taxi driver shouted for help,' said Sakchai. 'His passenger was having a baby. It was a boy. The woman said she would call it Sakchai as a way to say thank you.' Sakchai has so far assisted with the birth of twenty-eight babies.

6 **a** Answer the questions.

1 What are the past forms of the verbs in the headlines in Ex. 2a?

2 Which verb is irregular?

3 Here are some more irregular verbs. Why are they in these groups?

> **Group 1:** know, fly, grow
> **Group 2:** get, lose, shoot
> **Group 3:** bring, teach, fight
> **Group 4:** hit, put, cost
> **Group 5:** wake, speak, choose

4 Add the verbs in the box below to the correct group.

> buy cut think let draw forget blow break catch hurt shut write

b Test your partner.

A: *Forget?*

B: *Forgot.*

A: *That's right. Your turn.*

Pronunciation

7 **a** [2.8] Listen to the past tenses of these regular verbs. Practise saying them.

/t/	/d/	/ɪd/
escaped	saved	inherited
placed	delivered	decided
washed	survived	waited

b Choose the correct answer. We pronounce the past ending /ɪd/ for:
a) verbs ending in *t* or *d*
b) verbs ending in *p*.

c [2.9] Listen and write the sentences. Practise saying the sentences.

Grammar | Past Simple / Continuous

8 **a** Read the Active grammar box and answer question 1.

b Read rules a) + b) and find more examples of the Past Continuous in the texts on pages 26–27. Answer question 2.

Active grammar

*Mrs Bright was planning to go to France ...
She was driving around Calais ...*

1 Do the <u>underlined</u> verbs describe something complete or something temporary and in progress?

a) Use the Past Continuous and Past Simple together to say that something happened in the middle of a longer action.

*I **was taking a break** in a café by the road when a taxi driver **shouted** for help.*

b) The Past Continuous is often used to set the scene at the beginning of an article or story.

*This happened about eight years ago when I **was studying** for my degree. I **was feeling** a bit tired and ...*

2 Which verbs are not normally used in the continuous form?

---

see Reference page 31

9 Put the verbs in brackets into the Past Simple or Past Continuous.

They *were watching* (watch) a film in the cinema so they *didn't realise* (not realise) it *was snowing* (snow) outside.

1 I _____ (work) in a school in Prague when I _____ (meet) my boyfriend.

2 When I _____ (be) a child, I _____ (like) swimming.

3 My sister _____ (arrive) just as I _____ (cook) some lunch.

4 I _____ (know) I wanted to marry him the first time I _____ (meet) him.

5 He _____ (not break) his arm while he _____ (play) rugby. He _____ (fall) down the stairs.

6 I _____ (check) on the children and both of them _____ (sleep).

7 The phone rang while I _____ (listen) to my Discman and I _____ (not hear) it.

8 I think I _____ (see) you yesterday in the station. _____ (wear) a blue shirt?

10 The picture shows the beginning of a story. Write the first four sentences of the story.

It was raining hard.

11 Complete the story below by inserting verbs/ verb phrases from the box in the correct place.

fell didn't know ~~was staying~~ hoping
was expecting was visited was having

I remember when my little sister was born. I was ten years old, and I *was staying* in London with my parents. I knew my mother a baby, but I how soon it would arrive. I was really for a girl. It happened when I at a friend's house. It was her birthday and so she a party. My grandmother came to collect me, but when she told me the news I was so excited that I ran down the stairs, and I and broke my arm. I my mother and sister in hospital, and I had to spend the night there with my arm in plaster too.

Speaking and writing

12 **a** Choose one of the events in the box below and think about these questions. Make notes.

What **were** you **doing**	
Where **were** you **living/staying**	when it happened?
What **were** you **hoping for**	
What **were** you **thinking about**	

someone was born
you received some good news
you received your exam results
something important happened in your country
an important/interesting event in your life

b Tell other students about your event.

13 Write a short text describing your event.

2 Vocabulary

In the news

1 Find the odd one out.

Go on a) strike ✓ (b) holiday ✓ (c) work ✗

You can go to work, but not go on work.

1 Make (a) a job (b) a discovery (c) a profit
2 Come into (a) fashion (b) money (c) movement
3 Win (a) a team (b) a race (c) a competition
4 Commit (a) a crime (b) business (c) suicide
5 Develop (a) news (b) an idea (c) a product
6 Have (a) a duty (b) death (c) plastic surgery
7 Perform (a) a match (b) a song (c) a play
8 Cause (a) trouble (b) an accident (c) time
9 Break (a) a price (b) a record (c) a promise

2 On which newspaper pages might you find the collocations from Ex. 1? Choose from the words and phrases in the box.

go on strike, go on holiday = from general news and current affairs

> sports pages   arts section   business section   science section
> gossip   general home or international news and current affairs

3 Now read these sentences from newspaper articles and complete the sentences with expressions from Ex. 1. Use the correct tense.

1 Yesterday The Rolling Stones _____ that did the most to make them famous: *I Can't Get No Satisfaction*.
2 When his father died, Paul Getty _____ billions of dollars.
3 Marie Curie _____ that changed the world: she found radium.
4 When a food or drinks company _____ for the international market, it takes years to test it.
5 Many ageing celebrities _____ in order to look young, but it doesn't guarantee everlasting beauty!
6 In the UK there is a 45% possibility that criminals will _____ after their release from prison.
7 Ice on the roads _____ yesterday but luckily no one was hurt.

4 a Write the name of a famous person who:

1 has had plastic surgery.
   _____
2 won a race recently.
   _____
3 developed an important idea. _____
4 performs songs on TV.
   _____
5 won a competition.
   _____
6 went on strike.
   _____
7 committed a crime.
   _____
8 came into lots of money.
   _____
9 causes trouble regularly.
   _____
10 has broken a record.
   _____

b Compare your answers with a partner.

5 a Work in groups. Read the first line of a newspaper report below. Continue the story, using as many of the expressions in Ex. 1 as possible. Then write a headline for your report.

On Thursday night, actor William Begley committed a terrible crime …

b Read the other groups' reports. Which is the best?

2 Communication

The front page

1 Work in groups.

You are one of the editors of a Sunday newspaper.

Students A: read your role on page 145

Students B: read your role on page 146

Students C: read your role on page 148

2 **a** In your groups (As, Bs, Cs) choose six stories from the list below to go on the front page of this week's paper.

1 **Skirts for men come into fashion.**

2 **Doctors discover a cure for AIDS.**

3 Brad Pitt stars in world's most expensive film.

4 **Talking mouse created by scientists.**

5 Princess Diana's 'lost' jewellery raises $500,000 for charity.

6 **Healthy chocolate developed by food scientists**

7 **Freak storm kills 1,000 in southern Africa.**

8 **Computer virus likely to crash all computers worldwide.**

9 *Ancient city in Asia discovered by archaeologists.*

10 **Bill Gates pays off all Third World debts.**

b Look at the How to ... box on page 22 to help you give your opinions for choosing these stories.

What do you think?

I'm not sure about that.

In my opinion ...

3 Now work in groups of three (one student A, one student B and one student C).

You are in an editors' meeting. Discuss which stories are to go on the front page. Don't forget your role! When you have decided, write the headlines on the front page.

4 Return to your original groups. Compare your front pages. How similar are they?

The passive

Form: the verb *to be* + past participle.

*James **is paid** a lot of money.*

*Are you **being followed**?*

*We **were given** a new car to drive.*

*She **has been told** this before.*

In **active sentences,** the person (or thing) who does the action comes first.

*The man **kissed** the baby.*

In **passive sentences,** the person (or thing) affected by the action comes first and is the main focus.

*The baby **was kissed** by the man.*

The person (or thing) who did the action is often not known or not important.

*The programme **has been shown** since 1959.* (It isn't important <u>who</u> has shown it.)

Use *by* to include the person (or thing) who did the action in a passive sentence.

*The book **was written** by Faulks.*

The passive often sounds 'impersonal'. It is used in formal English and often in the news.

*The President **was asked** to resign.* (It isn't important who asked him to resign.)

Defining relative clauses

A 'clause' is part of a sentence. A defining relative clause makes it clear who or what you are talking about in a sentence. It gives essential information.

*The man **who lives next door** had an accident.*

Relative clauses begin with relative pronouns:

who for people   *where* for locations

when for time   *whose* for possessions

which for things and animals

! Don't use *what* as a relative pronoun.

*The vase **that** I broke was very expensive.* (NOT: ~~The vase what I broke was very expensive.~~)

In less formal English we often use *that* instead of *who* or *which*.

*The police caught the man **that** robbed the bank.*

When the verb after the relative pronoun has a different subject, we can omit *who* and *which*.

The film which I saw was called Jaws. (The subject of *saw* is *I* not *the film*)

The film I saw was called Jaws.

The boy who she met was nice. (The subject of *met* is *she* not *the boy*)

The boy she met was nice.

Past Simple and Past Continuous

The Past Continuous form: *was/were +___ing*

Use the **Past Continuous** to talk about what was happening at a particular moment in the past.

*What **were** you **doing** at 10 o'clock last night?*

It is often used at the beginning of stories to explain the situation.

*This happened several years ago. I **was staying** by the sea with friends. We **were having** lunch on the beach ...*

Use the **Past Simple** for complete, finished actions in the past.

When the Past Simple and Past Continuous are used together, the Past Continuous refers to the longer, background action or situation. The Past Simple refers to the shorter action or main event that happened to interrupt it.

*I **was walking** through the park when the storm **began**.*

Use the **Past Continuous** for temporary actions and situations.

*I **was living** in Barcelona last summer.*

Use the **Past Simple** for longer or permanent situations.

*I **lived** in Berlin for ten years when I was a child.*

Key vocabulary

Media

journalist   editor   the front page   headlines main stories   the Sunday papers   the daily papers reports   articles   review/sports/financial section interviews   celebrities   advertisements online news

Giving opinions

definitely   me too/neither   It depends on ...

TV programmes/studio

cameraman   microphone   producer   audience contestant   newsreader   quiz show   TV camera live performance   presenter   documentary   actress chat show   soap

Dealing with problems

What's the problem?   What's the matter? It isn't working properly.   It's out of order.

News collocations

go on strike/on holiday   make a discovery/a profit come into fashion/into money   win a race/a competition   commit a crime/suicide   develop an idea/a product   have a duty/plastic surgery cause trouble/an accident   perform a song/a play break a record/a promise

1 Complete the sentences with the verbs from the box below. Decide if you need the active or the passive and which tense.

> give call show sell ~~read~~ make record
> employ invent speak send

It's a funny book, and it can _be read_ by children or adults.

1 Wine _____ from grapes.

2 She _____ three CDs already, and has a fourth CD coming out next month.

3 Since 2002 we _____ over $40,000 by the government to improve our services.

4 When they find him, the thief _____ to prison.

5 After the accident, somebody _____ an ambulance, and the girl went to hospital.

6 Two thousand people _____ in this company at the moment.

7 Yesterday we _____ this painting to an art gallery for $1,000,000!

8 The old cinema is now a nightclub. Films _____ there any more.

9 Paper _____ by the Chinese over 2,000 years ago.

10 Four languages _____ in Switzerland.

2 **a** Complete the text with the correct relative pronoun from the box.

> who where which when whose

7.30	**Brothers in Arms:** Marlon is a lawyer <u>whose</u> brother has escaped from prison. He faces a dilemma (1)_____ he realises Eddie wants to live with him.
8.00	**Home Questions:** The quiz show (2)_____ asks contestants questions about the place (3)_____ they were born.
8.30	**Big Year:** Roy Johns speaks to the people (4)_____ have made history this year. Guests include Milly Cheiz, a doctor (5)_____ anti-cancer treatment is being tested in Australia, and Moses Kenui, an athlete (6)_____ shocked the world (7)_____ he broke four athletics records in one year.
9.30	**News**
10.00	**Restaurant:** Follows the progress of two restaurants (8)_____ famous chefs have visited. They both opened last year – one in Clydehead, a town (9)_____ there is 60% unemployment, and one in Tindell, a city (10)_____ the rich are happy to pay €350 for dinner.
11.00	**Fright Kids:** Comedy horror film about a woman (11)_____ has twins.

b In which two sentences can you omit the relative pronoun? In which sentences can you use _that_?

3 Choose the correct alternatives.

We first (met)/were meeting Irina when we travelled/(were travelling) across Russia.

1 I was/was being at school when I started/was starting learning French.

2 We watched/were watching TV when we heard/were hearing about the Twin Towers.

3 A: What did you do/were you doing this time yesterday?
B: I read/was reading a novel.

4 When I last saw/was seeing my sister, she looked/was looking for a flat in Madrid.

5 I crashed/was crashing into the car because I wasn't looking where I went/was going.

6 A: Did they win/Were they winning when you left the match?
B: No. They lost/were losing 2 – 1 but there were still twenty minutes left.

7 While I studied/was studying yesterday I found/was finding this great website.

8 A: Did you see/Were you seeing our new boss at the conference?
B: Yes. He wore/was wearing a white suit. Didn't you notice/Were you noticing him?

4 Complete the sentences with the words/phrases below.

> sections record contestant article
> profit accidents documentary
> plastic surgery performance the front page

1 Did you read about the fire? It was on _____ of all the newspapers.

2 I saw an interesting _____ about Ancient Egypt on TV yesterday.

3 I'm sure that actor's had _____. He looks twenty years younger!

4 Which _____ of the paper do you read? I like the sports pages.

5 The company made a _____ of €50,000 this year.

6 One _____ on _Who wants to be a millionaire?_ cheated!

7 Speeding drivers cause a lot of _____.

8 George Michael gave a live _____ on MTV. He sang brilliantly.

9 Asafa Powell broke the _____ for the 100 metres. He ran it in 9.77 seconds.

10 There's an _____ about immigration in the newspaper today.

3 Lifestyle

Lead-in

1 **a** What does home mean to you? Write notes about: favourite rooms, smells, views, special objects, feelings about home.

    b Compare your ideas with other students.

2 **a** Check you understand the words and expressions.

HOUSE	AREA/NEIGHBOURHOOD	LIFESTYLE
I live in ... a (semi-) detached/ terraced house a block of flats an apartment a cottage	**I live in ...** the suburbs a residential area the centre/outskirts of town	**I prefer ...** country life city life
It's got ... a lift an attic a cellar a balcony a good view a gate a fireplace high ceilings a drive wooden floors stairs	**It's got ...** shops and restaurants cinemas and theatres a park and a playground **It is ...** quiet lively	**I have a/an ...** **lifestyle.** hectic quiet exciting boring healthy unhealthy **I enjoy ...** staying in clubbing reading sport
It is ... spacious cramped modern old-fashioned		

    b Add any other words you already know to each section.

3 **a** Work in pairs. Take it in turns to describe the houses in the photos using the expressions from Ex. 2

    b Describe where you live and your lifestyle.

    I live in a block of flats. It's quite modern. It has a ...

Reading and speaking

1   Describe the photos and then answer the questions.

  1   How are the houses/rooms similar and how are they different?

  2   Which style of house/room do you prefer?

2   *Yourhome-Myhome.com* is a website where families can exchange homes with other families for a holiday. Read the property descriptions below and match them to the photos.

3   **a** Read the property descriptions again and write 'property 1' or 'property 2' next to each question.

Which property:

  1   is near the old centre? *property 1*

  2   has outside space? _____

  3   has one big bathroom? _____

  4   is good for dinner parties? _____

  5   has restaurants near the house? _____

  6   is near public transport? _____

b Which of the two properties would you prefer to live in for one month? Why?

Yourhome-Myhome.com

Property 1

A beautiful apartment in the centre of Seville. It is on the third floor and is very quiet all day. All you can hear is the sound of the church bells. The apartment is light and sunny with large windows. The kitchen is new and opens onto the balcony. The bathroom is spacious. There are two bedrooms, one double and one single, and there is a sofa bed in the living room.

The area

The apartment is in the historical centre of Seville, two minutes' walk from the cathedral and fifty metres from the commercial centre. There are plenty of local bars and restaurants serving 'tapas' (typical Spanish dishes).

Yourhome-Myhome.com

Property 2

We have a large semi-detached house with a garden, one hour from the centre of London. The house has four bedrooms, each with an en-suite bathroom, a large kitchen/eating area, a sitting room, a formal dining room and a study. The house is old and has a sense of history, and that makes it special.

The area

There is a daily market and a high street full of shops just ten minutes walk from the house. We are also close to a tube station, which can take you into central London, where you will find all the museums, theatres, shops and restaurants you could wish for.

Listening

4 **a** **3.1** Listen to two families talk about their plans for a home exchange. Write 1 (Dos Santos) or 2 (Armitage) next to the activities they mention.

1 visit museums	4 go shopping
2 see cathedrals	5 visit friends
3 enjoy the local cuisine	6 sit outside and enjoy the sun

The Armitage family

The Dos Santos family

b Listen again and choose the correct alternatives.

1 **Miriam:** ... we (1) *will spend/'re spending* more than one month in London. We've never been there before.

2 **Interviewer:** I'm sure you (2) *'ll love/'re loving* it.

3 **Miriam:** And I (3) *'m going to/'m doing* do lots and lots of shopping.

4 **Interviewer:** Great. There are some wonderful shops in London. I (4) *'ll give/am giving* you the address of a great shoe shop.

5 **Jeremy:** Spain has such a rich culture ... We (5) *'ll/'re going to* see the cathedrals ...

6 **Jeremy:** Sarah and I (6) *will/are going to* enjoy the Spanish culture. And the girls (7) *will/are going to* sit outside and enjoy the sun.

7 **Jeremy:** I really hope this (8) *'ll be/is being* the holiday of a lifetime for us all.

Grammar | talking about the future

5 Match sentences 1–7 in Ex. 4b to the rules (a–d) in the Active grammar box.

Active grammar

We can use the **Present Continous**, *going to* or *will* to talk about future plans.

a) Use *going to* to talk about something **you've decided to do.** Plans can be general.
e.g sentences: _____

b) Use *will* for a **decision made at the time of speaking,** or an **offer.**
e.g sentence: _____

c) Use the Present Continuous to talk about **arrangements** (plans that you have already organised i.e. you have arranged the dates.)
e.g sentence: _____

d) Use either *will* or *going to* for **predictions.**
e.g sentences: _____

---

see Reference page 45

6 Complete the texts with words and phrases from the box below.

---
is going (x2)   'm starting   'll (x2)
're going   won't   we'll   's moving

Sarah and Jeremy

I _____ a new job in June and it's in Oxford, so I think we _____ need to move house. We'd like to buy somewhere in the countryside, so we _____ to look at some of the small villages outside the city. Unfortunately, it's very expensive around there so I'm not sure if _____ have enough money.

Miriam and Carlos

My mother _____ in with us next year, because she's old and doesn't want to stay on her own. She _____ to sell her house, which I hope _____ be too difficult. She _____ to share a room with our son for the moment. Carlos isn't too happy about this plan, but I think it _____ be great because I'll have some help with looking after the baby.

7 Correct the mistakes in the sentences. There may be more than one correct answer.

1 I'm sorry, I have to leave early. I will play squash this evening.

2 Tomorrow I go on a trip to Cambridge.

3 **A:** That's the telephone.
   B: OK. I get it.

4 Hurry up, or we're being late again!

5 **A:** Would you like a drink?
   B: Yes, I'm having a glass of water, please.

6 Will you staying here for long?

7 When I grow up, I be a firefighter.

8 We are get married in August.

9 **A:** How do I get to the airport from here?
   B: Don't worry, I'm showing you.

Person to person

8 a Write three or four questions to ask other students about their plans for:

> this evening   this weekend   their home
> their education/career   their (family's) future
> their next holiday

b In groups, ask and answer the questions about your future plans.

A: *Katia, what are you planning for the weekend?*

B: *I'm going to visit my aunt. She's having a party to celebrate her ...*

Listening

9 a Look at pictures of Jeremy and Miriam during their home exchange. What do you think the problems were? Discuss in pairs.

A

B

C

D

b [3.2] Listen and check your ideas.

c Listen again and make notes. Describe what happened.

Reading and speaking

10 Read Miriam's letter of complaint to *Yourhome-Myhome.com*. Underline the problems she talks about.

> Dear Sir/Madam,
>
> I am writing to complain about the home exchange organised by your company. I stayed in a London house, owned by Jeremy Armitage between 10 May and 6 June.
>
> According to the information I received, the house was near the city centre. In fact, it took over two hours to get there. In addition to this, the directions for finding the house were difficult to follow and sometimes incorrect.
>
> Unfortunately, this was not the only problem. When we arrived, the house was in a terrible mess. There were dirty dishes and cups everywhere, the bathroom was filthy, and there were no clean sheets or towels as promised. Also, the central heating wasn't working, so the house was freezing, and there was no hot water!
>
> When I phoned your London office to explain the problems, the man who answered was very rude and unhelpful. He said that it was not possible to do anything until the house owners returned.
>
> I am very disappointed with the standard of the house, the organisation, and the service I received in London. I expect to receive a full refund of the agency fee, and I would also like to remove my own apartment from your website.
>
> I look forward to receiving a satisfactory reply.
>
> Your faithfully,
>
> *Miriam Dos Santos*
>
> Miriam Dos Santos

11 Work in pairs. You are going to have a meeting between Miriam and a representative from *Yourhome-Myhome.com*.

Student A: You are Miriam. Read page 145.

Student B: You are the representative. Read page 147.

When you are ready, begin like this:

Representative: *Hello, Mrs Dos Santos. Please come in. I understand there were some problems with your home exchange.*

Writing

12 a Read the letter in the Writing bank on page 161 and do the exercises.

b Write a letter of complaint from Jeremy to *Yourhome-Myhome.com*. Use the pictures in Ex. 9a to help you.

Listening and speaking

1 **a** **3.3** What do you think 'Homeward bound' means? Listen to the song and check.

Homeward Bound

I'm sitting in the railway station,
Got a ticket for my destination
On a tour of one-night stands[1],
My suitcase and guitar in hand
And every stop is neatly planned
For a poet and a one-man band

CHORUS
Homeward bound,
I wish I was homeward bound,
Home – where my thought's escaping,
Home – where my music's playing,
Home – where my love lies waiting
silently for me

Every day's an endless stream[2]
Of cigarettes and magazines
And each town looks the same to me,
The movies and the factories,
And every stranger's face I see
Reminds me that I long to be ...

(CHORUS)

Tonight I'll sing my songs again,
I'll play the game and pretend,
But all my words come back to me
In shades of mediocrity[3]
Like emptiness in harmony[4]
I need someone to comfort me

(CHORUS)

Glossary

[1] *a tour of one-night stands* = a different place to play music every night

[2] *an endless stream* = a continuous series of events, people and objects

[3] *all my words come back to me in shades of mediocrity* = his words are 'mediocre' (not very good)

[4] *Like emptiness in harmony* = even though the music sounds good, he feels empty

b Discuss.

1 Is it a sad or happy song?
2 Who is it about?
3 What does he do every day/night?

2 **3.3** Read and listen again. Which is the best summary?

1 He is a musician. He doesn't like his life because he thinks his songs aren't good enough. He wants to work in the movies or a factory.

2 He is a musician. He is sad because his girlfriend left him. Now he feels empty and he doesn't want to sing his songs any more.

3 He is a musician. He travels around playing his songs in different cities every night. He is tired of travelling and wants to go home to see his girlfriend.

3 **a** Discuss.

1 Do you think 'each town looks the same' when you travel? Why might the singer think this?

2 What do you enjoy about seeing different towns and cities?

b Work in pairs. Write a list of what makes a city good or bad to live in. Then compare your list with other students.

Good – beautiful views   *Bad – dirty.*

Which cities do you think are good to live in?

Vocabulary | adjectives describing places

4 **a** The words in the box can be used to describe cities. Find pairs of words that mean the opposite.

> ~~unspoilt~~ modern ugly tiny clean noisy peaceful
> dull enormous ~~touristy~~ picturesque lively historical polluted

unspoilt – touristy

b Think of a town or city for each adjective.

Tokyo is enormous.

Reading

5 Read the text about top cities. Does it mention any of the cities you thought of in Ex. 4b?

Top Cities

Have you ever walked around a city and thought, 'this is Paradise'? Or maybe, 'this is the ugliest, most polluted, dangerous, frightening place I've ever been to and I can't wait to get out'?

Most of us have. And that's why most of us like to know about the place before we go there. One thing we can do is read a good guide book. Another is to look at a new survey conducted by William Mercer, one of the world's largest Human Resources consultancies.

Mercer decided to judge some of the world's great cities. They produced their results by giving marks for various criteria. These included political, economic and social environment, healthcare, educational provision, recreation and transport infrastructure.

So, which are the best cities to live in, and which should we avoid? In joint first place were Vancouver, Berne, Vienna and Zurich while Sydney, Geneva, Auckland and Copenhagen came second. Swiss cities occupied three of the top ten

places, making it the single most successful country of all those surveyed.

New York was used as the base city with a score of 100, which put it in 50th place. Overall, US cities suffered because of high crime rates. The highest ranked US city was Honolulu with 104 points.

For Londoners, the news was not too bad. London was slightly ahead of New York with 101.5. The report named London's good international relations as a positive point. Its poorest scores – six

out of ten – were awarded for its climate and traffic. Bottom of the list was Brazzaville, in the Congo, where there has been a civil war for many years.

Ken Livingstone, Mayor of London, last night said it was unfair to compare large international cities with small cities since the smaller ones were far easier to run. 'You have to look at cities of five million people plus. On that basis we're much better than Tokyo and New York,' said Mr Livingstone.

6
a Read the text again and answer the questions.

1 Who or what is William Mercer?
2 How did Mercer compare the cities?
3 Where did Zurich come in the results?
4 Which country did best in the survey?
5 What particular problem do US cities have, according to the survey?
6 What problems does London have?
7 Which city came bottom of the list and why?
8 Why is the survey unfair, according to Ken Livingstone?

b Discuss.

1 Are you surprised by any of the results?
2 Do you think the survey is unfair?
3 Have you been to any of the cities in the list? What did you think of them?

Listening

7 **3.4** Listen to John and Simona discussing the survey. Which cities do they mention?

8 **3.4** Listen again. Mark the sentences true (T) or false (F).

1 She says you can't compare big cities and small cities. ☐

2 She says that people don't usually like the city where they live. ☐

3 She doesn't like San Francisco. ☐

4 She thinks Tokyo is well-organised. ☐

Grammar | comparatives and superlatives

9 **a** Look at the tapescript on page 170 and find examples of comparatives and superlatives.

b Match the rules (a–e) in the Active grammar box to the sentences (1–6).

Active grammar

	Comparatives	Superlatives
a) One syllable adjectives	+ -er than	+ the -est
b) Two (or more) syllable adjectives	more + adjective + than	the most + adjective
c) Two syllable adjectives ending in -y	remove -y and add -ier than	the -iest
d) Irregular adjectives: e.g. bad	worse than	the worst
e) For negative comparatives	not as + adjective + as	

1 *Zurich is **the nicest** city.* <u>Rule a) superlative</u>

2 *Vancouver is a **better** place to live **than** Amsterdam.* ___

3 *Small cities are **easier** to run **than** big ones.* ___

4 *London **isn't as organised as** Tokyo.* ___

5 *Vienna is **more beautiful than** most cities.* ___

6 *Brazzaville was **the most dangerous** city.* ___

---

see Reference page 45

10 Correct the mistake in each sentence.

1 Lagos is largest than Milan.

2 Cape Town is small than Mexico City.

3 Auckland is windier to Sydney.

4 Cairo is most important city in Egypt.

5 Rio de Janeiro is the more picturesque than Brasilia.

6 Katowice isn't as historical than Krakow.

7 Prague is more prettier than Kolin.

8 The food in Madrid is more better than the food in Edinburgh.

11 Use the words in brackets to make comparative or superlative sentences.

— Web log —

Day 24:
Just finished my tour of Russia, which is
(1) _____ _____ (big) country in the
world and one of (2) _____ _____ _____
(interesting) too. My flight was much
(3) _____ _____ (comfortable) this time
– big seats! Also, the service was
(4) _____ _____ (good) last time – free food
and drink! When I arrived in Warsaw, the
people at Customs were (5) _____ _____
(friendly) before (on my first trip I waited
an hour while they checked my passport!).
Fortunately, Poland isn't (6) _____ _____
(cold) as Moscow, which was freezing!

This afternoon I had (7) _____ _____
_____ (delicious) lunch of my trip so far: a
Polish speciality called pieczeń in a great
restaurant in (8) _____ _____ (old) part of
the city.

12 Write sentences about cities you have been to. Compare them using the words/ phrases from Ex. 4a and the box below .

> beautiful warm bad
> easy to live in
> frightening lovely

Speaking

13 a Choose one category of things you are interested in (e.g. music, countries, food, cars). Write your own Top Five for the category.

*Films: 1 American Beauty
2 Citizen Kane 3 Casablanca
4 Alien 5 The Jungle Book*

b Tell other students why you chose your category. Explain how you chose your number one.

The Jungle Book is at number 5. It's funnier than the other films on the list – actually I think it's the funniest film ever. However Alien is much more exciting ...

Vocabulary | compound nouns

1 a Match a noun from A with a noun from B to make compound nouns.

A	B
1 answer	a) conditioner
2 washing	b) clock
3 air	c) phone
4 central	d) alarm
5 mobile	e) player
6 burglar	f) heating
7 DVD	g) phone
8 alarm	h) machine

b Match the items to their functions in the box below.

> clean clothes   stay warm
> speak to people   stay cool
> leave messages   watch films
> wake up on time
> keep the home safe

Pronunciation

2 a `3.5` Compound nouns usually have the stress on the first word. If the first word is an *-ing* word, it is *always* stressed. Listen to the words in Ex. 1 and mark the stress.

b Listen again and repeat.

Speaking

3 Discuss.
1 Which of the items in Ex. 1a above have you got?
2 Would life be easier with/ without any of these? Why?
3 Which are the most/least important to you?

Reading

4 a Apart from phone calls and texting, what can you use mobile phones for?

b Read the text and choose the best title.
1 New reasons to phone home.
2 Mobile phones in Europe.
3 How phone technology stops crime.

First they changed our lives by allowing us to make phone calls while travelling. Then teenagers used them to send secret text messages. But in the future, mobile phones will allow us to control our lives and homes.

Imagine you want to go home early but your house is still cold. Your mobile will let you switch on your central heating. You <u>might</u> accidentally leave the door of the fridge open. Don't worry – your mobile phone will send you a warning message. Burglars may try to enter your house when you are on holiday. No problem! Your phone will tell you.

These ideas <u>will probably</u> be reality very soon. At Japan's Combined Exhibition of Advanced Technologies, companies including Toshiba, Panasonic and Mitsubishi say they are going to use the mobile phone to create 'intelligent homes'.

Panasonic's 'Echonet' is already on sale. This piece of technology is the same size as a book. You put it on the kitchen wall and it allows you to communicate with your fridge, air conditioner, washing machine, oven and burglar alarm. It doesn't matter where you are in a train, on the street, or at the airport; if you have your mobile phone you can control everything at home.

Mitsubishi plans to develop technology for forgetful shoppers. For example, if you want to know how many eggs or tomatoes you have left in your fridge, you will be able to use your phone to find out. It will ask your fridge to send you a picture and you will be able to view the picture on your mobile phone.

This technology <u>probably won't</u> be available in the next two years, but it <u>will certainly</u> arrive eventually. All these new developments come from Japan. The Japanese love technology in a way many Western countries can't understand. Why? Because 'Japanese consumers always want something new,' says Fumo Ohtsubo, the Director of Panasonic. And in terms of technology, where Japan leads the world follows.

5 **a** Answer the questions.

1 How did mobile phones change our lives, according to the text?

2 When will Echonet be available?

3 What will Echonet allow you to do?

4 Who is Mitsubishi's new technology for?

b Read the text again and mark the sentences true (T) or false (F).

1 You will be able to control your central heating with your mobile phone. ☐

2 If you leave your fridge door open, your phone will close it. ☐

3 If burglars come into your house, your phone will call the police. ☐

4 Echonet is a large piece of technology for the kitchen. ☐

5 When you are shopping, your phone will communicate with your fridge. ☐

c Correct the false sentences.

6 **a** How useful do you think these changes will be? Write 1–5 next to each change in the text (1 = not useful, 5 = very useful).

b Discuss your opinions with other students.

Grammar | future possibility

7 Complete the Active grammar box using the underlined words from the text.

> **Active grammar**
>
> **Certain**
>
> ⊕ New technology _____ _____ / **definitely** change our lives.
>
> ⊖ New technology **certainly/definitely won't** solve all our problems.
>
> **Probable**
>
> ⊕ It _____ _____ arrive in Japan first.
>
> ⊖ It _____ _____ be cheap.
>
> **Possible**
>
> ⊕ Customers **may/_____/could** find it difficult to use.
>
> ⊖ They **may not/might not** understand it.

see Reference page 45

8 Choose the correct alternatives.

1 She *might/definitely/may to* arrive tomorrow. It depends on her work.

2 *I'll probably/Probably I will/I won't probably* see you later. My class has been cancelled.

3 I *mayn't/may not/could not* be able to check my emails. I'm having some problems with my computer.

4 Real Madrid will *win probably/win definitely/probably win* the competition again. They have a strong team.

5 David *won't probably/probably won't/will not probably* come to the party. He's sleeping as usual.

6 They *may come/may to come/come may* to the cinema with us if they have time.

9 Decide if these things will certainly, probably or possibly happen in the next twenty years. Then complete the sentences.

Computers *will definitely* get faster.

1 People _____ stop using CDs and DVDs. They _____ download all music and films from the Internet.

2 Mobile phones _____ become smaller.

3 People _____ get bored with new technology.

4 There _____ be robots in every house.

5 People _____ be able to take holidays in space.

6 China's economy _____ become much bigger.

Person to person

10 **a** Write seven predictions for people in your class. Don't write their names.

She'll probably move to the USA.

He might become a famous musician.

b Exchange your predictions with other students. Guess who the predictions are about.

Speaking and listening

11 a Discuss.

1 What is difficult about speaking on the phone in English?

2 Have you ever made a phone call in English? Who to? What was it about?

b Complete the How to ... box using the words below.

> message   through   back   take
> like   calling   this

HOW TO ... make formal phone calls

Person answering: First words	*Hello. Smith and Son. Tracy speaking.*
	Hello. Tracy Brown.
Caller: Say who you want to speak to	*Hello. Is ... there, please?*
	Hello. I'd _____ to speak to ...
Person answering: Find out who is speaking	*(May I ask) who's _____, please?*
	Can I take your name?
Caller: Say who you are and why you are calling	*_____ is John Fox. I'm calling about ...*
Person answering: Continue the call	*I'll put you _____. One moment.*
	I'm afraid he's not here at the moment. Would you like to call back later?
	Can I _____ a message?
Caller: Continue the call	*Could he call me _____? My number is ...*
	Can I leave a _____?

12 a 3.6 Listen to three telephone conversations. Complete the table.

	Call 1	Call 2	Call 3
Caller's name			
Message			
Caller's phone/ fax number			

b Listen again and check your answers.

c Look at the tapescripts on page 170 and practise the phone calls with a partner.

13 a Put the words in order.

a) I'll that Yes, do . __

b) *Johnson and Johnson.* you help may I How ? _1_

c) afraid the not I'm office in moment at she's the . __

d) is Brown Mr This. Hello. like please Cardusio to Maria I'd to speak . __

e) course Yes, of . __

f) Can call her to back ask you me ? __

g) Oh. I Can message leave a ? __

h) you Thank. Goodbye . __

b Now put the sentences in order to make a telephone conversation.

14 Work in pairs.

Student A: look at the role cards below.
Student B: look at page 148. Roleplay the telephone conversations.

Student A

ANSWER THE PHONE.

1 You work in an office (Smith and Co). Your manager is on holiday.

2 You work in a private bank (Jeeves Bank). Mr Jones is in a meeting.

3 You work at hotel reception (Hotel Paradiso). The line is engaged.

PHONE YOUR PARTNER.

1 Your partner works in a computer shop (Bust Computers). Ask for an engineer (your computer isn't working).

2 Your partner works in an office (Lula Incorporated). Ask to speak to Lula (about an invoice).

3 Your partner works in a school (Cool School of English). Ask to speak to the school director (about doing a course).

3 | Vocabulary

Prefixes and suffixes

1 **a** Which parts of the words in the box are prefixes? Which are suffixes? What do you think the prefixes and suffixes mean?

> forgetful   unfair   successful   endless
> touristy   unspoilt

b Add some more examples to the prefix table below. Use a dictionary or ask your teacher to help you.

PREFIXES	EXAMPLES	YOUR EXAMPLES
un = not	*uninteresting* *unusual*	un_____
re = again	*rearrange* *review*	re_____
ex = former/ previous	*ex-boyfriend* *ex-Prime Minister*	ex-_____
mis = wrong	*mispronounced* *misheard*	mis_____
dis = not	*dislike* *disappear*	dis_____

2 **a** Add prefixes from the table above to the words in the box. Each prefix is used once.

> understanding   wife   usual   visit   agree

b Complete the sentences with the new words. Change the verb tense where necessary.

1 We decided to _____ the area before buying our house there.
2 We always _____ about what to watch on TV.
3 The film was like most Hollywood films: a good guy, a bad guy and a beautiful girl – nothing _____ at all.
4 I think there has been a _____. These are the wrong tickets.
5 I'm having dinner with my _____ tomorrow.

Lifelong learning

One word in six words!

When you learn a new word, find out if it uses prefixes and suffixes, and if it has other forms (for example, the noun can change to a verb). This will help you to increase your vocabulary.

3 **a** Which adjectives in the table below have been formed from a noun and which from a verb by using a suffix?

b Add some more examples to the table.

SUFFIXES	EXAMPLE ADJECTIVES	YOUR EXAMPLES
ive	*creative, attractive, ...*	_____ ive
(l)y	*dirty, friendly, ...*	_____ y/ly
ful	*careful, helpful, ...*	_____ ful
less	*useless, careless, ...*	_____ less
able/ible	*enjoyable, comprehensible, ...*	_____ able _____ ible

4 Read the advertisements and change the base words in **bold** to complete the gaps.

FLAT TO RENT

Airy flat (60 square metres)   air
in _____ area of London. Two   peace
bedrooms, sitting room, bathroom.
_____ neighbours.   friend
_____ rent – £680.   week
Call **Mr Johnson** on **0207 93167**

Home needed!

Extremely _____ cat, Musa,   **attract**
soon to be _____   **home**
needs _____ owner   **response**
with large, _____ garden.   **sun**

Please call Luke on **01823 273305**

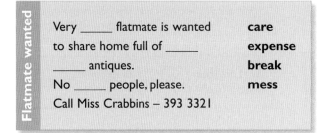

Flatmate wanted

Very _____ flatmate is wanted   **care**
to share home full of _____   **expense**
_____ antiques.   **break**
No _____ people, please.   **mess**
Call Miss Crabbins – 393 3321

Writing

5 Write a short advertisement for one of these: a flat to rent, a flatmate, a partner, a new person for a team or club, or anything else. Try to include at least three words with prefixes or suffixes.

1 Read the advertisement for a competition.
What can you win? What do you have to do?

Would you like to stay in one of these houses for a year COMPLETELY FREE?!
New Lifestyle magazine is giving you the opportunity.

It's simple. Just tell us:

1 why you want to stay here

2 what you will do during the year

3 which house you prefer and why.

The person with the best answers wins the house for a year.

2 **a** **3·7** Listen to two people trying to win the competition and complete the notes in the first two columns of the table.

	SPEAKER 1	SPEAKER 2	ME
Where do you live now?	*in the suburbs of the city*	*in a (6) _____*	
What type of lifestyle do you have?	*(1) _____*	*it's boring and quiet*	
Where would you like to spend the year?	*in the (2) _____*	*in the (7) _____*	
What are you going to do?	*stop working and study (3) _____*	*find a job, meet people from different (8) _____, join a (9) _____ and go clubbing a lot*	
What will you learn?	*the names of birds, trees, plants. Practical skills: how to grow vegetables and make (4) _____*	*(10) _____ _____*	
What are your long-term plans?	*to return to (5) _____*	*might (11) _____ in the city*	

b Listen again and check.

c Work in groups. Should Speaker 1 or Speaker 2 win the competition? Why?

3 **a** You are going to enter the competition. Prepare what you will say. Make notes in the table.

b Work in groups of six: three speakers and three judges.
Speakers: make a short speech explaining why you should win the house/apartment for a year.
Judges: ask questions to find out more information. Then, change roles.

c Tell the class who won and why.

Future forms for personal plans

Use **going to** to talk about plans for the future or intentions (things you have already decided to do).

I am going to take a holiday in March.

Sue isn't going to buy that car.

With the verbs *go* and *come* we often use the Present Continuous.

Use the **Present Continuous** to talk about fixed future arrangements (usually involving another person).

I am meeting Sam at 2p.m. (I called him this morning to arrange it)

Are you coming to the dinner this evening? (You have been invited)

In many cases you can use either *going to* or the Present Continuous.

I am playing rugby tomorrow.

I am going to play rugby.

Use **will** for unplanned decisions (made while speaking), offers or promises.

I'll/won't tell her I saw you.

Will you carry this box for me?

For general predictions you can use *will* or *going to*.

I think Brazil will/are going to win the next World Cup.

Future possibility

Use *will/won't* + adverb to say how likely something is in the future. *Will* comes before the adverb in affirmative sentences and after the adverb in negative sentences.

I will definitely go. (you are certain)

I certainly won't go. (you are certain)

I will probably stay. (quite certain)

I probably won't stay. (quite certain)

Use *may/might/could* when you are not certain. Do not use *could* in the negative.

Alice may meet us later for a drink.

The shop might not be open.

With modal verbs (*will, may, might, could*) use the infinitive without *to*.

Comparatives and superlatives

One syllable adjectives, or two syllable adjectives ending in -y

Adjective	Comparative	Superlative	Notes
old	older	oldest	Add -er, -est
big	bigger	biggest	With short vowels (/ɪ/, /e/, /ɒ/,/æ/), double the consonant
large	larger	largest	If the adjective ends in -e, just add -r, -st
friendly	friendlier	friendliest	If the adjective ends in -y, change it to -i and add -er

Two syllable, and longer adjectives

Adjective	Comparative	Superlative	Notes
useful	more/less useful (than)	(the) most/least useful	Add more (+), or less (–), (the) most (++), or (the) least (– –)
dangerous	more/less dangerous (than)	(the) most/least dangerous	

Irregular adjectives

good – better (than) – (the) best

bad – worse (than) – (the) worst

far – further (than) – (the) furthest or *(far/farther/farthest)*

(not) as + adjective + as

If two things are the same, use *as* + adjective + *as*.

*The train is **as expensive as** flying.*

For negative comparisons, use *not as* + adjective + *as*.

*It's **not as warm as** last week.*

Key vocabulary

Home

(semi-) detached house   terraced house   block of flats   apartment cottage   lift   attic   cellar   balcony   view   fireplace   ceiling   floor   stairs gate   drive   suburbs   residential area   outskirts of town   centre of town

Lifestyle

country/city life   hectic   quiet   exciting   boring   healthy   unhealthy

Compound nouns

answer phone   washing machine   air conditioner   central heating mobile phone   burglar alarm   DVD player   alarm clock

Describing places

spacious   cramped   modern   old-fashioned   unspoilt   touristy   ugly picturesque   tiny   enormous   clean   polluted   noisy   peaceful   dull quiet   lively   historical   frightening   easy to live in

1 **Choose the correct verb form.**

There is a great programme on tonight. *Will you/* ~~*Are you going to*~~ watch it?

1 I *am thinking/will think* of moving house soon.

2 *Will you go/Are you going* out tonight?

3 We would love to come and see you at the weekend, but Lorenzo *is working/will work*.

4 **A:** Who is that at the door?
   B: *I'll go/I am going to go* and see.

5 What *will you/are you going to* wear to the theatre tonight?

6 I can't see you on Sunday because I *am playing/will play* football with some friends.

7 I am too tired to finish my homework now. I think I*'ll do/am doing* it in the morning.

8 What *are you doing/will you do* after class?

2 **Rewrite the sentences using the phrases in brackets so that the meaning stays the same.**

I don't know if I'll finish my essay on time.

(might not) *I might not finish my essay on time.*

1 I think I'll stay at home and watch TV.
   (probably) _____

2 I don't think Mark will be able to come to lunch.
   (probably won't) _____

3 Australia have a good chance of winning the next Rugby World Cup.
   (might) _____

4 I am working late tomorrow so it's possible that I won't see you.
   (might not)_____

5 I'm almost certain we'll buy a flat next year.
   (probably) _____

6 It's possible that my father won't come home for another two months.
   (may not) _____

3 **Rewrite the sentences so that they have the same meaning. Use the words in brackets.**

The blue car and red car both cost €900. (cheap)

The blue car is *as cheap as* the red car.

1 He's 1.7 metres tall. I'm 1.6 metres tall. (than)
   He's _____ me.

2 No mountains are higher than Everest. (the)
   Everest is _____ in the world.

3 I found her first book very interesting, but not her second. (interesting)
   Her first book was _____ her second.

4 Hospitals were more efficient in the past. (as)
   Hospitals are not _____ they were in the past.

5 She earns twice as much money as me. (much)
   She earns _____ than me.

4 **Complete the sentences using a comparative form of the words in the box. Use *than* if necessary.**

> ~~quick~~ easy old-fashioned picturesque
> far cold crowded polluted quiet

It takes such a long time to drive to Scotland. We usually fly because it's *quicker*.

1 Bangkok is such a noisy city. I'd prefer to live somewhere _____.

2 There were so many people on the train. It was _____ usual.

3 We saw them a lot when they lived in Paris, but now they have moved _____ away.

4 Our old apartment was much _____ our new one, which is really modern.

5 Look at all the snow! It's much _____ today _____ it was yesterday.

6 Cities are so ugly. I prefer living in the countryside where the views are _____.

7 Some parts of the city are _____ others because of all the traffic.

8 It's _____ to find your way around New York streets _____ in London because in New York the streets have numbers.

5 **Make the opposite meaning by changing the underlined words.**

Dear Juliana,

I'm here in El Paso for six months. I'm staying in a house in the <u>modern</u> (historical) part of town. The part of town where I'm staying is really (1) <u>clean</u> and (2) <u>unspoilt</u>, and the house is (3) <u>spacious</u>. My room is (4) <u>enormous</u> and very (5) <u>tidy</u>. During the day it's very (6) <u>peaceful</u>. The city centre is very (7) <u>lively</u> at night and I go for a walk with friends most evenings. My landlady is quite (8) <u>helpful</u>.

See you next week.

Clara

4 Wealth

Lead-in

1 **a** Read the quotations below. Are any reflected in the photos?

'Money never made a man happy.'

'Happiness comes from spiritual wealth, not material wealth.'

'Time is money.'

b Which quotations do you agree/disagree with?

2 **a** Put the verbs/phrases from the box in the correct column.

> run out of ~~spend~~ lend It's not worth the good value for
> make use your ... wisely save earn have got ... to spare
> waste not have enough inherit steal invest ... in

MONEY	MONEY AND TIME
	spend

b Can you add any more words or phrases?

3 **a** Write down one thing that ...

1 is a waste of money/good value for money.

2 you'd like to do but you don't have enough time to do.

3 you do to use your time wisely.

4 you spend a lot of money on.

5 you would do today if you had lots of money to spare.

6 you'd like to invest in.

b Compare your ideas with other students.

Reading and listening

1 **a** What do you think is the connection between the three photos?

b These words and phrases are in the text. What do you think the text is about?

> good-looking trickster cheated mystery
> charm illegally pretended prison
> $3 million consultant egotistical

c Read the text. Match the headings to the correct paragraph.

1 Childhood and tricks
2 Frank today
3 Wanted all over the world
4 The FBI's opinion of Frank
5 ~~Three top jobs and five happy years~~

The true story of a real fake

(a) Three top jobs and five happy years

Frank Abagnale, a good-looking American boy with more dreams than money, pretended to be first a pilot, then a doctor and then a lawyer.

For five years he travelled the world for free, stayed in expensive hotels and had relationships with beautiful women. By the age of twenty-one he had tricked and cheated his way to $2.5 million.

(b) _____

In the golden age of James Bond, Abagnale really was an international man of mystery. He was wanted by the FBI and Interpol (International Police) in twenty-six countries. His good looks and greying hair helped him, but his charm was his most important tool. He dressed well and everybody believed the stories he made up. Leonardo DiCaprio, who plays Frank Abagnale in the film *Catch me if you can* said, 'Frank Abagnale is one of the greatest actors who has walked the earth.'

(c) _____

Abagnale was a lonely child. When his mother, who was French, broke up with his father, a New York shopkeeper, Abagnale had to choose which parent to live with. Instead, aged sixteen, he dropped out of school, ran away from home and began his life as an international trickster. He used magnetic ink to change bank code numbers illegally. He managed to steal $40,000 of other customers' money before the banks worked out what he was doing. He also got a Pan Am pilot's uniform by saying that his

was lost at the dry cleaner's and that he had an urgent flight. This allowed him to stay in any hotel he wanted; Pan Am always paid the bill. He even pretended to be a doctor and worked as a hospital administrator for a year. With no formal training, he picked up the skills by reading medical books and watching other doctors at work.

(d) _____

Abagnale broke the law repeatedly. He ran out of luck in France, where he spent time in prison, before the FBI finally caught up with him in the USA. Despite his crimes, Abagnale never had any enemies. Joseph Shea, the FBI man who arrested him and later became his friend, said, 'I think Frank is close to genius. What he did as a teenager is incredible. His crimes weren't physical. There were no guns, no knives, he just used his brain. He's charming and I admire him. I think he's a good man and a moral character, but like anybody he wants to better himself and in this country, money is the way to do it. He makes $3 million a year and that's a lot more than I ever made.'

(e) _____

These days Abagnale doesn't need to trick anybody: he is a successful consultant. He advises companies on security, and he also lectures – for free – at the FBI Academy. It is ironic that he has ended up working for the people who were trying to catch him for so long! He wrote his autobiography in the 1970s and sold the film rights for $250,000. Abagnale says, 'When I was twenty-eight I thought it would be great to have a movie about my life, but when I was twenty-eight, like when I was sixteen, I was egotistical and self-centred. We all grow up.' That's true. But not many people grow up like Frank Abagnale.

Vocabulary | phrasal verbs

4 Underline phrasal verbs in the text and put them in the correct place in the diagrams.

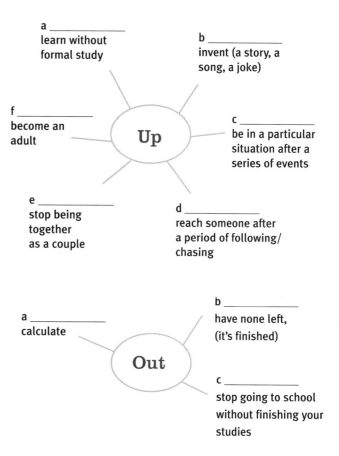

a _____
learn without
formal study

b _____
invent (a story, a
song, a joke)

f _____
become an
adult

Up

c _____
be in a particular
situation after a
series of events

e _____
stop being
together
as a couple

d _____
reach someone after
a period of following/
chasing

a _____
calculate

b _____
have none left,
(it's finished)

Out

c _____
stop going to school
without finishing your
studies

2 a Answer the questions.

1 How old was Frank when he left home?

2 What did he look like?

3 How did he get his first $40,000?

4 How did he get a pilot's uniform?

5 Who was Joseph Shea? What type of person do you think he was?

6 What does Frank do now?

7 How does Frank feel about his past?

b **4.1** Close your books and listen to a summary of Frank's story. Find seven more differences between the text and the summary.

1 *Frank Abagnale wasn't English. He was American.*

3 Discuss.

1 Joseph Shea said, 'I think he's a good man and a moral character.' What do *you* think of Frank?

2 Frank says, 'I thought it would be great to have a movie about my life.' Would you like a movie about *your* life? Why/Why not? Which actor would you choose to act as you?

5 One of the sentence endings is not possible. Which one?

He dropped out of (a) ~~his exams~~ (b) *school* (c) *university.*
You can drop out of school and university but not exams.

1 I broke up with (a) *my girlfriend* (b) *my relationship* (c) *my husband.*

2 They made up (a) *stories* (b) *an excuse* (c) *acting.*

3 We worked out (a) *what the problem was* (b) *the answer* (c) *wrong.*

4 She picked up (a) *Spanish very quickly* (b) *some information* (c) *a new haircut.*

5 We ran out of (a) *enough milk* (b) *money* (c) *things to do.*

6 I caught up with (a) *my studies* (b) *myself* (c) *you easily.*

7 She ended up (a) *living with me* (b) *work as a doctor* (c) *in Warsaw.*

Speaking

6 In pairs, retell Abagnale's story using the phrases below.

… his mother **broke up with** …

… he **dropped out of** …

… he made $40,000 … the banks **worked out** what he was doing

… he pretended to be … he **picked up** the skills by reading medical books

… he **ran out of** luck in France …

… the FBI finally **caught up with** him …

… he **ended up** working for …

Grammar | question tags

7 **a** Read the dialogues. What words go in the gaps?

1 **Mr Charming:** What a beautiful dress! Haven't I seen you before? You work in fashion, ___ you?
Woman: Yes, I ___. We met at a fashion show.

2 **Mr Charming:** I've read all your books. You've just written a new one, ___ you?
Man: Yes, I ___. It's about a film star.

3 **Mr Charming:** I love lobster! The food is delicious here, ___ it?
Woman: Yes, it ___. But I prefer caviar.

4 **Mr Charming:** You're Sarah, ___ you? No, you're Judy! Anyway, can I get you a drink?
Sarah: *I'm* Sarah!
Judy: And I'd love a drink!

5 **Mr Charming:** You were at the last party here, ___ you? Would you like something to eat?
Dog: Woof woof!
Mr Charming: Yes, you ___!

b [4.2] Listen and check your answers. Then practise the dialogues in pairs.

8 Read the Active grammar box and choose the correct alternatives to complete the rules (1–4).

Active grammar

When we want to confirm information, we often use question tags.

You **are** a singer, **aren't** you?*	Yes, I **am**.
You **aren't** Spanish, **are** you?*	No, I**'m not**.
You work full time, **don't** you?	Yes, I **do**.
You lived in Paris, **didn't** you?	Yes, I **did**.
They **have** arrived, **haven't** they?	Yes, they **have**.
You **can** go today, **can't** you?	Yes, I **can**.
You **would** like to see her **wouldn't** you?	Yes, I **would**.

1 To make question tags, we repeat the main verb /the auxiliary verb. *

2 If the question is in the positive, the question tag is negative /positive.

3 If the question is in the negative, the question tag is negative /positive.

4 If there is no auxiliary verb, the question tag uses the main verb /uses *do, does* or *did.**

*the verb *to be* acts as an auxiliary verb in question tags

see Reference page 59

9 Add the correct tags to these questions.

1 You can speak several languages, ___?
2 You work in a big company, ___?
3 It's warm in here, ___?
4 You have been to the US, ___?
5 We didn't meet last year, ___?
6 You don't like champagne, ___?
7 You're looking for a new job, ___?
8 You will be here tomorrow, ___?
9 They would like a break, ___?
10 This isn't a very good film, ___?

10 Think about your answers to the questions in Ex. 9. Imagine you are making small talk at a party. Ask other students some of the questions.

Ophrah Winfrey

Stella McCartney

Richard Branson

Paul Newman

Speaking

1 Discuss.

1 Think of as many ways as possible to get rich quickly. Which are legal?

2 What do you know about the people in the photos? How did they become rich?

3 Can you name any other famous multimillionaires? What type of reputation do they have? Do people like and admire them?

Vocabulary | qualities

2 **a** In pairs, check you understand the expressions in the box.

> be ambitious
> be confident
> be good with figures
> be good with people
> be extravagant
> be mean
> have a sense of humour
> be generous
> be tolerant
> work long hours
> be flexible
> know your strengths and weaknesses

b Discuss.

1 For which jobs do you need the qualities in the box? Compare your answers with other students.

2 Which qualities do you think you have?

3 What qualities and habits do you think are necessary to be a successful entrepreneur?

work hard

entrepreneur /ˌɑːntrəprəˈnɜːr/
someone who starts a company and arranges business deals

Listening

3 **a** `4.3` Listen to the first part of a seminar and answer the questions.

1 Who is the seminar for?

2 What is the topic?

b `4.4` Listen to the rest of the seminar. Which of the expressions in Ex. 2 does the speaker mention?

c Listen again and complete the notes below.

> How to be an entrepreneur
>
> 1 Be mean. You **shouldn't** _____
>
> 2 You **should** start _____
>
> 3 You **mustn't** _____ your money
>
> Bill Gates doesn't care about looking good because he **doesn't have to** _____
>
> 4 Be confident. You **must** _____ in yourself
>
> 5 You **have to** work _____

4 **a** Work with a partner. How are the words in the box connected to the seminar?

> payphone mice suit five o'clock

b Do you think you would be a good entrepreneur? Why/Why not?

Grammar | modals of obligation and prohibition

5 Put the words in **bold** from Ex. 3c into the correct column in the Active grammar box. Then answer the questions.

> ### Active grammar
>
> | It is an obligation (you have no choice). *must* / _____ | It is a good idea (but you have a choice). _____ | |
> |---|---|---|
> | It is prohibited (you have no choice). _____ | It isn't a good idea (but you have a choice). _____ | It is not necessary. You can do it if you want to (you have a choice). *don't* / _____ |
>
> Look at these examples:
>
> 1 *You mustn't smoke on an aeroplane.*
>
> 2 *You don't have to eat the food on an aeroplane.*
>
> a) In which sentence do you have a choice? *sentence:* _____
>
> b) In which sentence is something prohibited? *sentence:* _____

see Reference page 59

6 Complete the sentences using the words in brackets.

It's a good idea to take an aspirin if you have a headache. (take)
You *should take* an aspirin if you have a headache.

1 It's not necessary to wear a suit to work. (have)
You _____ wear a suit to work.

2 It's a good idea to get the tickets early. (buy)
We _____ our tickets in advance.

3 He can't go home until he has switched off all the lights. (to)
He _____ all the lights before he can go home.

4 A passport is necessary to enter the country. (get)
You _____ if you want to enter the country.

5 Smoking is forbidden in the waiting room. (smoke)
You _____ in the waiting room.

6 It isn't a good idea to wash your hair now. It's cold outside. (wash)
You _____ now. It's cold outside.

Pronunciation

7 **a** **4.5** Listen to these sentences. Mark the stress.

1 You have to buy a ticket.
2 You don't have to pay.
3 You should send a card.
4 I must remember.
5 You mustn't smoke.

b How is *to* pronounced in (*don't*) *have to*?

c Are the 't's pronounced in *don't/must/mustn't* in sentences 2, 4 and 5 in Ex. 7a?

d Listen again and repeat.

8 **a** Change the modal verbs to make true sentences.

1 You have to pay by credit card when you go shopping in the supermarket.
2 You mustn't bring some identification when you open a bank account.
3 You should pay for English lessons.
4 You mustn't carry a lot of money with you late at night in dangerous areas.
5 You shouldn't pay to go to the library.
6 You don't have to buy a ticket to see a film at the cinema.

b Compare your answers with other students.

Speaking

9 **a** Work in pairs. Think about how to be:

1 a good public speaker.
2 a good student OR a good teacher.
3 a good employer OR a good employee.

You should be good with people. You have to be well-prepared. You mustn't be mean.

b Make a list. Compare your ideas with another pair.

Writing

10 Read the letters/emails and answer the questions.

1 What is the purpose of each letter/email?

2 What type of work do you think Maria Pesaro and Paul Sharp do?

3 Are the letters/emails formal or informal? How do you know?

> Hi Sophie,
>
> How are you? I'm having a party on Saturday 6th at my place, around 8.00. I've attached a map in case you can't remember how to get there! Hope you can come.   Gavin
> xxx

> Hi Gavin,
>
> I'd love to come. Hope it's OK if I bring a friend. See you on Saturday.
>
> S. x

INTRA SOLUTIONS

Garden Place,
London NE3 8AJ,

Dear Mr Sharp,

I am writing to invite you to speak at our conference, *Entrepreneurs for the New Millennium*. Our company, Intra Solutions, helps young businessmen and businesswomen to develop their plans for the future.

The conference will take place at The Great Hall, 15 Queen's Street, London SW6, on Friday 14th July. We would like you to speak for one hour. I have enclosed the conference timetable and our brochure.

We look forward to hearing from you.

Yours sincerely,

Maria Pesaro

Maria Pesaro

Paul Sharp, EXTON LTD, London NW5 7EF, 0207 566 7463, extonltd.co.uk

Dear Ms Pesaro,

Thank you for the invitation to speak at your conference, *Entrepreneurs for the New Millennium*. I will be pleased to attend on the 14th. Could you send me more information about the audience numbers and equipment available? I will also need confirmation of expenses and fees.

Yours sincerely,

Paul Sharp

11 Put the words in the box below in the correct place in the How to ... box.

> writing   will   like   am   can't   enclosed

HOW TO ... write/respond to an invitation

Inviting	Informal: *I'm having a party on Saturday 21st June. Would you _____ to come?* Formal: *I am _____ to invite you to ...*
More information	*I have _____ /attached a map/programme.* *Can you give me confirmation of ...*
Accepting	Informal: *I'd love to come.* Formal: *I _____ be pleased to attend.*
Refusing	Informal: *Sorry, I _____ make it because ...* Formal: *I am afraid I _____ unable to attend due to ...*

12 a You are going to write a letter inviting one of the people in the photos below to give a talk at your school. Answer the questions in groups.

1 Who will you choose? Why?

2 When will they come?

3 What will they talk about and for how long?

b Write your letter. Use the How to ... box to help you.

c Exchange letters with another group. How can you improve the letters?

d Write a final version.

Kylie Minogue

Dalai Lama

Hillary Clinton

Johnny Depp

Venus Williams

Prince William

Reading and speaking

1 Discuss in pairs.

1 What are these advertisements for? Do you think they work?

2 Do you think (a) you (b) people in general spend more because of advertisements?

3 How do supermarkets/salespeople make us spend more?

2 Decide what information could complete the sentences.

Did you know...?

1 People in the UK buy _____% of their food in supermarkets.

2 Supermarkets often _____ _____ to help us relax.

3 Supermarkets became very successful after introducing _____ _____ in the 1950s.

4 Advertisements which use _____ are 10% more effective.

5 Advertisements are more memorable if they are _____.

6 Chocolate adverts should make your _____ _____.

7 Good salespeople can sell _____, to _____, at _____ _____.

8 Most salespeople will get to know their client by asking questions about _____, _____ and _____.

9 Salespeople may try to 'mirror' the _____ _____ of a buyer.

3 Read the texts to find the answers.

Student A: read about advertising on this page.
Student B: read about supermarkets on page 146.
Student C: read about salespeople on page 149.

4 **a** Work together (A + B + C) to check your answers to Ex. 2.

b Does any of the information surprise you?

5 Discuss.

1 What are your favourite/least favourite advertisements? Why?

2 Do you prefer shopping at supermarkets or small, specialised shops? Why?

3 Have you ever bought something that you didn't really want because of a good salesperson? What happened?

TAKE SPORT. ADD MUSIC.

Nike
www.nikewomen.com

The Samsung D600 is lead
60 minutes of video recordi
Samsung D5

How you are persuaded to spend more by ...

Advertising

Adverts focus either on what products do, or how the products make us feel. Our emotional response to a product is very important. If the advertisement makes us feel good, i.e. it has images which we enjoy and remember, then we start to associate good feelings with the product.

We respond well to adverts which demonstrate a lifestyle we would like to have. Famous people are often used in adverts because of their successful lifestyle. Footballers advertise sports drinks. We buy the drink, and sense the success. A survey of 4,000 adverts found that adverts with celebrities were 10 percent more effective than adverts without.

Humour is also used, as funny adverts are remembered for longer. In addition, advert makers appeal to our senses. Unless your mouth waters, a chocolate advert is probably a failure. They want you to want their product.

Warning signs:

• High price: If a product costs a lot of money, it won't necessarily be good quality. It might be just part of its image.

• Famous people: Advertisers want you to believe that if you buy their product, you can start to live the lifestyle of the celebrity who advertises it.

• Reward and Punishment: 'If you buy this, you will stay young' (the reward), also means 'Unless you buy this, you will look old' (the punishment).

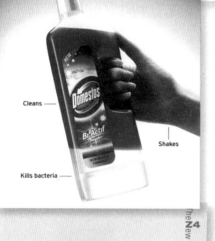

Land Shark.

Vocabulary | opposites

6 **a** Many of the words below are from the texts. Write the opposites using the words in the box.

> punishment sell response success ~~fail~~
> respond consumer reward buyer produce

Verbs
succeed / *fail*
(1) _____ / punish
buy / (2) _____
(3) _____ / consume (a product)
advertise / (4) _____ (to an advert)

Nouns
(5)_____ / failure
reward / (6)_____
(7)_____ / seller
producer / (8) _____
(9) advertisement / _____ (to an advert)

b Complete the sentences with a suitable word from Ex. 6a.

1 I called the train company, but there was no _____.

2 I love the _____ for that new car, where a woman drives through the Italian countryside.

3 Well done. You can have a present as a _____ for passing your exams.

4 Teachers sometimes _____ students by giving them extra work to do.

5 The new advertising campaign was a complete _____, sales have been terrible.

6 His new book has been a great _____. It sold over a million copies in the first month.

7 I don't think cigarette companies should _____ as their products are bad for you.

8 Countries like the USA _____ a lot of pollution.

Pronunciation | word stress

7 **a** **4.6** Listen to the words from Ex. 6a and mark the main stress.
      succ**ė**ed

b Listen and repeat the words.

> ### Lifelong learning
>
> *Mark the stress!*
>
> Write main stress on new words in your vocabulary records.

c **4.7** Listen and answer the questions.

8 Discuss.

1 What is your greatest success?

2 Have you ever been punished for anything?

3 Do you think companies should advertise products that are bad for your health?

4 Are you a better buyer or seller?

5 What products do you enjoy buying?

6 What products do you consume too much of?

Grammar | First Conditional with *if/when* *unless/as soon as*

9 **a** Read the example sentences (1–5) below. Complete the rules (a–e) in the Active grammar box by choosing the correct alternatives.

1 *If customers think of the salesperson as a friend, they will probably keep coming back to the same man or woman.*

2 *If I buy lots now, I won't have to come back later.*

3 *Supermarkets will usually offer these **when** a fruit and vegetable is in season.*

4 *As soon as you walk into the shop, you can smell bread and coffee.*

5 *Unless you buy this (face cream), you will look old.*

Active grammar

First Conditional

a) Use *if* + Present Simple + *will* to talk about <u>real possibilities</u> /<u>imaginary situations</u> in the future.

First Conditionals can also describe events that are always true.

b) Use *if* /*when* for events in the future that are certain.

c) Use *if* /*when* for events in the future that are not certain.

! For general present events, *if* and *when* have the same meaning.

If an advert is good, you want to buy the product.

***When** an advert is good, you want to buy the product.*

d) Use <u>as soon as</u> /<u>unless</u> to emphasise that an event happens immediately.

e) *Unless* + positive verb means the same as *if* /<u>if not</u>.

*I will call you **unless** it **is** too late.*

*I will call you **if** it **is not** too late.*

---

b <u>Underline</u> six more examples of the First Conditional in the three texts on pages 54, 146 and 149.

see Reference page 59

10 Match the beginnings (1–6) of the sentences in A with the endings (a–f) in B.

A	B
1 I will miss everyone	a) we might make fewer mistakes.
2 I will be home by six	b) unless it rains.
3 If we study hard,	c) when I leave my job.
4 I will show my friends around the city	d) when they arrive.
5 I will buy a new suit	e) as soon as I get paid.
6 I am going to have a barbecue	f) unless the train is delayed.

11 Complete the sentences using the Present Simple of the verb and *will* + verb.

1 If they _____ (offer) me the job, I _____ (take) it.

2 When I _____ (see) Tom, I _____ (tell) him.

3 If you _____ (not pay) the bill on time, you _____ (get) a fine.

4 I'm sure he _____ (not phone) us, unless there _____ (be) something urgent to discuss.

5 Unless Sandro _____ (find) an apartment soon, he _____ (have to) live at home.

6 I _____ (buy) a new car as soon as I _____ (can) afford it.

Person to person

12 **a** Make the sentences true for you.
I'll study tonight if *I have time*.

1 I will buy a new ... as soon as ...

2 I will ... next weekend if ...

3 If there is enough time ..., I will ...

4 I'll go on holiday ... unless ...

5 I'll change my ... when ...

b Discuss your sentences with a partner.

Writing

13 Write an advertisement for an object you want to sell. Give details (price, benefits, etc).

A/An _____. Only € _____. If you buy this, _____

4 Vocabulary

Confusing words

1 Choose the correct word
1   **A** Hurry up. We're going to <u>lose</u>/<u>miss</u> the bus.
    B I have <u>lost</u>/<u>missed</u> my wallet. I can't find it anywhere.
2   **A** Did you have a good <u>travel</u>/<u>trip</u>?
    B I enjoy <u>travel</u>/<u>trip</u> so much.
3   **A** Yes, I enjoyed the picnic. It was <u>fun</u>/<u>funny</u>.
    B Charlie Chaplin films are so <u>fun</u>/<u>funny</u> that I laugh out loud.
4   **A** He <u>said</u>/<u>told</u> me to come at 11.00.
    B He <u>said</u>/<u>told</u> the train was late.
5   **A** She found a good <u>work</u>/<u>job</u> in a bank.
    B She is lazy and doesn't like <u>work</u>/<u>job</u>.
6   **A** She is going to <u>lend</u>/<u>borrow</u> me another book.
    B Can I <u>borrow</u>/<u>lend</u> your pen?
7   **A** Can you <u>remember</u>/<u>remind</u> me to call Giovanni tomorrow?
    B I can never <u>remember</u>/<u>remind</u> his name!
8   **A** The National Bank was <u>robbed</u>/<u>stolen</u> last week.
    B $200 million was <u>robbed</u>/<u>stolen</u>.

2 Look at the notes below. Write similar notes for the other <u>underlined</u> words in Ex. 1.

---

rob/steal

You **steal** something from someone/somewhere but you **rob** a place, e.g. a bank.

travel/trip

Travel is a general word for talking about moving from one place to another. **Trip** refers to a specific journey and the time you spend there, e.g. business trip.

fun/funny

Use **fun** to talk about activities you enjoy doing. **Funny** describes something that makes you laugh.

say/tell

You **say** something (to someone) but you **tell** someone something, or tell someone to do something.

---

3 Cover the words in Ex. 1. Complete the sentences with an appropriate word.
1   Am I too early? You _____ me the shop opens at 8a.m.
2   I can _____ you ten Euros. Can you pay me back soon?
3   I can never _____ which verbs are regular or irregular. It's a real problem for me.
4   I have come to report a crime. My bag was _____ last night.
5   On my last holiday I went on a _____ to India.
6   That's great! Jenny got the new _____ she applied for.
7   Do you think the Mr Bean films are _____? I always laugh when I watch them.
8   I'm sorry I'm late. I _____ the train.

4 **a** From information you know already complete the sentences about a few of your classmates.
Marco has an *enjoyable* job.
1   _____ needs someone to remind him/her to ...
2   _____ thinks ... is a waste of time.
3   Yesterday _____ felt ...
4   _____ thinks ... is fun.
5   _____ hopes to get the opportunity to ...
6   _____ wants to go on a trip to ...
7   _____ would like to borrow ...
8   _____ doesn't want to lend ...

b Read out some of your sentences to the class to check the information.

A | CHANEL B

C

D

1 a What do you think is happening in the photos? How much money do think was spent on each activity/thing? Match the figures to the photos.

1 $39.9 million
2 $3.71 million
3 $15 million
4 $2.2 billion

b Read the text to check your answers.

2 a Work in groups.

Group A: Choose three facts from the text. Explain why you think these are a terrible waste of money. How do you think this money should be spent?

Group B: Choose three facts from the text. Think of reasons why it is/was a good idea to spend this money.

b Work with a student from the other group. Discuss your facts and why you think they were a waste of money/worth spending money on.

c Do you know any other ways in which governments, big companies or famous people waste money?

3 a Are you a money-waster or a money-saver? In groups, write a short questionnaire (5 or 6 questions) to decide if someone is a waster or a saver.

If someone gives you some money for your birthday, what do you do with it?

Do you think you should try to save some money every month?

b Ask and answer your questions with students from another group.

The Millennium Bug: Around the world, over $600 billion was spent on updating computer systems to prepare for the new millennium. Everyone thought that the new date would cause computers to crash. No major problems were reported.

Man on the moon: It cost the US approximately $2.2 billion (which is around $40–50 billion in today's money) to send a man to the moon.

Film: The most expensive film ever made was *Titanic*. It cost $200 million (£118.9 million).

Painting: *The Sunflowers* by Vincent Van Gogh was sold for $39.9 million (£22.7 million) at Christie's, in London, in March 1987.

Cars: The Meitec Corporation of Japan paid $15 million for a 1931 Bugatti Type 41 'Royale' Sports Coupe in 1990.

SETI: Paul Allen, co-founder of Microsoft, donated $11.5 million to SETI (Search for Extraterrestrial Intelligence) for a new, powerful telescope to look for aliens. In the 1980s the US government spent around $2 million a year to fund SETI.

Advertising: Actress Nicole Kidman was paid $3.71 million (£2 million) for a 4-minute Chanel No. 5 advertisement in 2004.

Phone number: The phone number 8888 8888 was bought by Sichuan Airlines Co. Ltd (China) for $280,723 (£177,209). Why? The number eight is a lucky number in China.

Course: The Ivor Spencer International Finishing School for Young Ladies and Gentlemen, London. A one-month finishing course cost £77,500 ($126,000) in 1998. Students stay at a top London hotel, and have lessons in how to appreciate ballet, opera, food, wine and style.

Restaurants: The biggest restaurant bill ever recorded in London cost £44,007 ($80,000) for six people. The diners, who were bankers at Barclays, drank Chateau Petrus wine, which costs up to £12,300 ($22,000) a bottle.

First Conditional with *if/when/ unless/as soon as*

To talk about real possibilities in the future we can use **If** + **Present Simple** + *will/can/should/may* (and other modal verbs).

*If it **rains**, I **will** stay at home.*
*If he **stays** here, he **should** learn the language.*
*If it rains I **won't** go out. If it **doesn't** rain, I **will** go out.*

Unless means **if not**.
Unless it rains, I will go out.

We use **when** to show the situation is 100% certain.
When I wake up tomorrow I will make breakfast. (it is certain that I will wake up tomorrow).

We use **as soon as** to emphasise that an event happens immediately.
*I'll tell him **as soon as** I see him.*

! We don't usually use *if* + *will* in conditional sentences.

First Conditionals can also describe events that are always true.
If trolleys are large, people will buy more. (fact)

We also often use Zero Conditionals: **If** + **Present Simple** + **Present Simple** to talk about things that are always true.
*If I **have** time, I **go** to the gym. (a fact)*
*If you **don't drink** for a month, you **die**.* (scientific fact)

Modals of obligation and prohibition

Obligation

Have to is often used for rules/regulations.
*You **have to** show your passport at Customs.* (it's a law)

Must is often used when the obligation comes from the speaker. *Must* is never followed by *to*.
*I **must** stop smoking.* (I think this)

Prohibition

Mustn't means it is prohibited/not allowed.
*You **mustn't** leave your luggage unattended.*

No obligation

Don't have to means you have a choice.
*You **don't have to** wear a suit to work.* (it's not necessary but you can if you want to)

Recommendation

*You **should** go.* (it's a good idea)
*We **shouldn't** stay late.* (it's not a good idea)

Question tags

Use question tags in spoken English to check information and to keep the conversation going.

To make question tags, repeat the auxiliary verb, not the main verb. If the main verb is *to be*, repeat that.

Affirmative statements use a negative tag.
*It's cold in here, **isn't** it?*
*They **are** French, **aren't** they?*
*We **have** been there, **haven't** we?*
Use this structure when you think the answer is *yes*.

Negative statements use an affirmative tag.
*We **don't** have to pay, **do** we?*
*I **won't** be needed, **will** I?*
Use this structure when you think the answer is *no*.

If there is no auxiliary verb, use *do*, *does* or *did*, or their negatives.
*She **went** home, **didn't** she?*
*I **know** you, **don't** I?*

For short answers, we also use the auxiliary verb.
A: *She **doesn't** eat meat, **does** she?*
B: *No, she **doesn't**.*
A: *We **have** finished the bread, **haven't** we?*
B: *Yes, we **have**.*

Key vocabulary

Time and money
run out of   spend   lend   it's not worth the
good value for   make   use your ... wisely   save   earn
have got ... to spare   waste   inherit
not have enough   steal   invest ... in

Phrasal verbs
drop out of   break up with   make up   work out
pick up   run out of   catch up with   end up   grow up

Personal qualities
ambitious   good with figures   good with people
have a sense of humour   confident   generous
mean   extravagant   work long hours   tolerant
know your strengths and weaknesses   flexible

Word building – opposites
succeed/fail   reward/punish   buy/sell
buyer/seller   produce/consume (a product)
reward/punishment   producer/consumer
advertise/respond (to an advert)   success/failure
advertisement/response (to an advert)

Easily confused words
rob/steal   travel/trip   fun/funny   lend/borrow
remember/remind   work/job   say/tell   miss/lose

1 Complete using the correct question tag.

1 I can't park here, _____?
2 I need to phone him, _____?
3 The guests will be here soon, _____?
4 She had a headache, _____?
5 This match is boring, _____?
6 I'm a genius, _____?
7 We're going out later, _____?
8 They haven't called yet, _____?
9 I shouldn't give her the money, _____?
10 You woke up early this morning, _____?

2 Match the questions above to these answers.

a) No, they haven't.
b) Yes, we are.
c) No, you can't.
d) No, you shouldn't.
e) Yes, it is.
f) No, you're not.
g) Yes, you do.
h) Yes, I did.
i) Yes, they will.
j) Yes, she did.

3 Some lines have one extra, incorrect word. Write the extra word in the space. Tick (✓) if there is no extra word.

Memo to: all staff   From: management
At the meeting we agreed on some rules.   ✓
All staff should look smart ~~to~~   _to_
at all times but workers don't never have   ___
to wear a suit unless requested. Staff   ___
must to go outside to smoke and should   ___
try not to blow smoke in through the   ___
windows. Workers mustn't not leave dirty   ___
cups in the workspaces and food must not   ___
to be consumed in the office. Staff do   ___
not have to be eat in the canteen, but   ___
lunch breaks must not have exceed 1 hour.   ___

4 Choose the correct alternative.

1 Children under 16 *don't have to/mustn't* smoke in England. It's illegal.
2 You *don't have to/mustn't* eat if you don't want to. It's your choice.
3 You *don't have to/mustn't* be late for work.
4 Ken's so rich he *doesn't have to/mustn't* work.
5 We *don't have to/mustn't* miss the last bus.
6 Markus *doesn't have to/mustn't* work on Sundays but he often goes into the office.

5 Complete the sentences with *if, when* or *unless*.

1 We haven't booked our accommodation. We'll find a hotel _____ we arrive.
2 _____ the weather's nice it's not worth going to the park.
3 _____ you like action films, you'll love *The Matrix*. The fight scenes are incredible.
4 I'll go home _____ you're late again tonight. I'm tired of waiting for you.
5 She'll never pass the exam _____ she starts working hard.
6 We'll talk about the new products _____ the conference finishes.
7 You won't feel good _____ you do some exercise every week.
8 I'm leaving early. I'll call you _____ I get there.

6 Correct the mistake in each sentence.

1 If I will see you tomorrow, I will give you the book.
2 She won't act in the film unless that she receives her normal salary.
3 We'll go as soon the taxi arrives.
4 If I drink another cup of coffee, I will be not able to sleep tonight.
5 I can't hear you unless you don't shout.
6 When I next go shopping, I'll to buy some milk.
7 Unless you drive carefully, you won't crash.
8 As soon as you will see him, call me.

7 Complete the sentences with the words in the box.

advert run picked value trip up
success figures

1 I can't even buy you a coffee because I've _____ out of money.
2 This computer only cost me $400. Do you think that is good _____ for money?
3 A: What's wrong with Joe?
   B: He's just broken _____ with his girlfriend.
4 A: I didn't know you could speak Russian.
   B: Yes, I _____ it up when I was living there.
5 My wife deals with the money for the business, because I'm not very good with _____.
6 The show was a great _____. More than 600 people came to see it.
7 We need to find a new flatmate, so we're putting an _____ in the local paper.
8 A: I'm flying to Paris in the morning.
   B: Have a good _____!

5 Spare time

Lead-in

1 Do you do any of the activities in the photos in your spare time? What kind of person likes these activities?

2 **a** Put the activities/equipment in the box into the correct columns.

> ~~cards~~ fishing squash skiing aerobics exercise reading
> jogging swimming dancing chess gardening athletics sailing
> surfing computer games cycling karate painting volleyball
> cooking a musical instrument drawing football photography

PLAY	GO	DO	NO VERB
• cards			

b **5.1** Listen and check your answers. Mark the word stress.

3 Choose three activities you enjoy. What do you need for them?
Equipment: *a pack of cards,* _____
People: *a partner,* _____
Place: *a gym,* _____

4 **a** Discuss in pairs.

1 Which activities do you do now/did you do when you were younger?
2 Which activities are/were you good at/hopeless at?
3 When/Why did you start (or stop) doing these activities?
4 Why do you/did you like them?

b Tell other students.

5.1 Are you creative?

Grammar	Present Perfect Simple vs. Present Perfect Continuous
Can do	suggest and respond to ideas

Rudolf Nureyev and Margot Fonteyn

Louis Armstrong

Boris Spassky

Stephen Hawking

Salvador Dali

The Brontë sisters

1 Discuss.

1 Do you do anything creative in your spare time?

2 Do you know any creative people?

3 What do you know about the people in the photos?
   How do they/did they show their creativity?

4 Which other creative people do you admire?

5 Can creativity help you learn English? How?

2 **a** Tick (✓) the activities that you have done in your life:

1 written a poem/song

2 invented and told a story

3 thought of an original solution to a problem

4 made something with your hands

5 painted a picture

6 thought of an idea to improve conditions at work

7 decorated a room

8 changed the rules of a game in order to improve it

9 invented a new recipe

10 entertained young children for several hours

b Find someone in your class who has done these. Ask follow-up questions:

When did you do it?

Where were you?

c Tell other students what you discovered.

Listening

3 **a** **5.2** Listen to three people talking about their own creativity. Which things from Ex. 2 do they mention?

b Listen again. Who says these phrases? Speaker 1, 2 or 3?

1 I've made lots of beautiful things. ___

2 I've been playing with my three children. That's why the room's a mess. ___

3 I've made up lots of my own recipes. ___

4 We've invented a new game. ___

5 I've been taking classes ... for three months. ___

6 I've been trying to open my own restaurant for the last few years. ___

Grammar | Present Perfect Simple vs. Present Perfect Continuous

4 **a** Look at the sentences in Ex. 3b. Which ones are Present Perfect Simple and which ones are Present Perfect Continuous?

b Read and complete the Active grammar box by choosing the correct alternatives.

Active grammar

We use the Present Perfect tenses for actions which began in the past and continue now.

We use the **Present Perfect Continuous:**

1 To emphasise that the action is /isn't finished.

I've been trying to start my own business. (I'm still trying now)

2 To talk about a recently started /finished activity with present results. We can see the results.

We've been running. (I'm hot and tired)

3 To emphasise the activity (not the result), often with *How long ...?*

*How long **have** you **been reading** this book?* (focus on the activity)

*How many chapters **have** you **read**?* (focus on the result)

Present Perfect Continuous form: *have* or *has* + *been*/*being* + *-ing*

---

c Look at sentences 2 and 6 in Ex. 3b. Which rules (1, 2 or 3) do they fit?

see Reference page 73

5 Complete the sentences using the Present Perfect Simple or Present Perfect Continuous form of the verbs in brackets.

1 Oh no! You (break) the window!

2 I (not wash) the dishes yet. I'll do them later.

3 She (write) her novel this afternoon.

4 How long you (wait) for the bus?

5 I (not see) Marta this morning. Maybe she's ill.

6 you (run)? You look tired.

7 Those children (eat) chocolate all day. That's why they feel sick!

8 How long you (have) your mobile phone?

6 The sentences below use the wrong verb tenses. Work in pairs and say why the <u>underlined</u> tenses are wrong.

1 A: Why are you so tired?
   B: <u>I've read</u> *Underworld* this morning.

2 A: Why is your hair wet?
   B: <u>I've swum</u>.

3 A: Does she know Dave?
   B: Yes, <u>she's been knowing</u> him all her life.

4 A: How many exams <u>have you been taking</u>?
   B: Two. I have one more next week.

5 A: <u>I've been giving up</u> smoking!
   B: That's great. Do you feel healthier?

6 A: How long <u>have you learned</u> Chinese?
   B: About two months.

Pronunciation

7 [5·3] Listen to the answers. Notice the contracted verb forms of *have*. Listen and repeat.

Person to person

8 **a** Complete these sentences so they are true for you.

I've been working for ...

I've been living in ... since ...

I've been studying English for ...

I've been coming to this school since ...

I've been playing ... for ...

I've been (doing my hobby) since ...

b Use Ex. 8a to ask and answer questions with your partner.

A: *What's your hobby?*

B: *Squash.*

A: *Really? How long have you been playing squash?*

Reading

9 Discuss.

1 Is everyone imaginative?

2 Which is more important for artists: hard work or inspiration?

3 Are there any techniques which can help us to develop our imagination?

4 Are children more creative than adults?

10 a Read the first paragraph of the text. Which of the questions in Ex. 9 does it discuss?

b Read the rest of the text and put the paragraph headings in the correct place.

a) No limits!

b) Be someone else!

c) Making connections

Three ways to become (more) creative

Most people believe they don't have much imagination. They are wrong. Everyone has imagination, but most of us, once we become adults, forget how to access it. Creativity isn't always connected with great works of art or ideas. People at work and in their free time routinely think of creative ways to solve problems. Maybe you have a goal to achieve, a tricky question to answer or you just want to expand your mind! Here are three techniques to help you.

1 _____

This technique involves taking unrelated ideas and trying to find links between them. First, think about the problem you have to solve or the job you need to do. Then find an image, word, idea or object, for example, a candle. Write down all the ideas/words associated with candles: light, fire, matches, wax, night, silence, etc. Think of as many as you can. The next stage is to relate the ideas to the job you have to do. So imagine you want to buy a friend an original present; you could buy him tickets to a match or take him out for the night.

2 _____

Imagine that normal limitations don't exist. You have as much time/space/money, etc. as you want. Think about your goal and the new possibilities. If, for example, your goal is to learn to ski, you can now practise skiing every day of your life (because you have the time and the money). Now adapt this to reality. Maybe you can practise skiing every day in December, or every Monday in January.

3 _____

Look at the situation from a different point of view. Good negotiators use this technique in business, and so do writers. Fiction writers often imagine they are the characters in their books. They ask questions: What does this character want? Why can't she get it? What changes must she make to get what she wants? What does she dream about? If your goal involves other people, put yourself 'in their shoes'. The best fishermen think like fish!

11 Answer the questions.

1 Which statement is true?

a) Most people aren't imaginative.

b) Only children are imaginative.

c) We are all imaginative.

2 How does the first technique work?

a) You link your problem with an image or word.

b) You link your problem with the word 'match'.

c) You have to think of a present for a friend.

3 In the second technique, what must you imagine?

a) That you are rich.

b) That you aren't limited in any way.

c) That you can ski.

4 What do you do in the third technique?

a) Imagine you are a negotiator.

b) Imagine you are a different person.

c) Imagine you are a fiction writer.

5 In the third technique, what type of questions should you ask?

a) Questions about other people's shoes.

b) Questions about business techniques.

c) Questions about motivation and making changes.

Speaking

12 Complete the sentences in the How to ... box using the words from the box below.

> with   wouldn't   idea   don't   sure

HOW TO ...	suggest and respond to ideas	
Presenting an idea	*Why _____ we do this?* *Shall we try this?*	
Accepting	*That's a good _____ .* *OK, let's go _____ that.*	
Rejecting	*The problem with that is ...* *I'm not _____ about that.*	
Presenting an alternative	*_____ it be better to do this?* *Or we could do this.*	

13 a Work in groups to solve the problems on page 145.

b Tell another group what you discussed, what creativity techniques you used, and what solutions you found.

c Read the solutions to the problems on page 149.

Grammar	verb patterns with *-ing* or infinitive
Can do	describe a film/book

Vocabulary | describing books and films

1 Discuss.

1 Do you recognise the characters in the photos? What films/books were they in?

2 Have you seen any of the films or read the books? What did you think of them?

3 Is there a book/film you read or watch again and again? Why?

4 Do you prefer reading or watching films?

2 a Are these statements about a book, a film or both? Which book/film? What do the words and phrases in **bold** mean?

'I liked the **plot**, especially the bit about the ring.'
book, film – The Lord of the Rings. *Plot = story.*

1 'The first **chapter** introduces us to Gandalf.'

2 'The **soundtrack** was excellent – rock and roll, which is very strange for a Shakespeare play.'

3 'The **main character** is Don Vito Corleone, a mafia boss.'

4 'It **was written by** JRR Tolkien in 1954.'

5 'The **descriptions** of the imaginary place called Middle Earth were beautiful.'

6 'It **is set in** Verona in Italy and **is about** two young lovers.'

7 'It **was directed by** Francis Ford Coppola. He also directed a **sequel**, *The Godfather Part II*.'

8 'It **was dubbed** badly. I couldn't understand what the non-human creatures were saying.'

9 'It **stars** Marlon Brando as the Godfather. He won an Oscar for his **performance** as the boss.'

b Put each word in **bold** in the correct place and say if it's a noun (n), verb (v) or adjective (adj.).

FILM OR BOOK	FILM	BOOK
plot (n)	stars (n), (v)	chapter (n)

Speaking

3 Choose a favourite film or book. Complete the sentences in the How to ... box below. Describe your book or film to other students.

HOW TO ...

describe a film/book

The basics	It's called ... It's set in ... It's about ...
The people	It stars ... The main characters are ... It was directed/written by ...
Talk about particular things you liked/disliked	The soundtrack was ... The final chapter is ... The descriptions of her dreams are ...
Recommend it	I would really recommend this film/book. It's not really worth seeing/reading.

Pronunciation

4 **a** What type of film does the picture show? Find as many objects as you can which have the sounds /æ/ as in apple, /e/ as in hen and /ɑː/ as in car. Write the words in the correct column below.

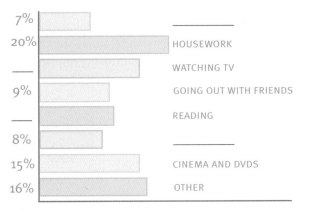

/æ/	/e/	/ɑː/

b Compare with a partner.

5 **a** **5.4** Listen and tick (✓) the sentences you hear.

1 a) I saw the man.
   b) I saw the men.
2 a) She has a warm heart.
   b) She has a warm hat.
3 a) I like the rat.
   b) I like the red.
4 a) He ran after the car.
   b) He ran after the cat.
5 a) That's my pet you've taken.
   b) That's my part you've taken.
6 a) I got a ten last week.
   b) I got a tan last week.
7 a) Is that a bar in the picture?
   b) Is that a bear in the picture?
8 a) It's been said already.
   b) It's been sad already.

b Listen again and repeat.

c Now try and say these sentences fast!

1 I put a can of ham and a leg of lamb in the bag.
2 The ten mad men went to bed in a red tent.
3 The cat's legs, head and heart are in the cart.
4 The fat man's hat is in the red car.

Listening

6 **a** How much of your free time do you think you spend doing the following?

> housework   going to the cinema   reading
> watching TV or DVDs   going out with friends
> eating   shopping   something else

b What would you like to do more/less of?

7 **a** Hannah Cheung is a film-maker. In September 2003 she timed everything she did for one month for a film she is planning to make. Look at the diagram to see how she spends her free time.

b **5.5** Listen to an interview with Hannah. Complete the information in the diagram.

7%	_____
20%	HOUSEWORK
___	WATCHING TV
9%	GOING OUT WITH FRIENDS
___	READING
8%	_____
15%	CINEMA AND DVDS
16%	OTHER

8 a 5.5 Listen again and complete the notes.

> Hannah says:
>
> I didn't **expect** to see these results …
>
> I **can't stand** (1) _____ .
>
> I **don't mind** (2) _____ the housework but it's not very interesting …
>
> I'd **prefer** (3) _____ less of that kind of thing.
>
> I **enjoy** reading …
>
> I always **look forward to** (4) _____ a new book.
>
> I **love** cooking …
>
> I **try** (5) _____ a proper meal at least four nights a week.
>
> I often **invite** (6) _____ over _____ dinner …
>
> I never **manage** (7) _____ much exercise.
>
> I never **seem** to find the time.
>
> That's one thing I'd **like** (8) _____ .

b Look at the tapescript on page 171 to check.

Grammar | gerunds and infinitives

9 a Read the Active grammar box and put the words in **bold** from Ex. 8a in the correct column.

Active grammar

When one verb follows another, the second verb is either a **gerund** (-*ing* form) or an **infinitive** (*to* + verb).

1 Verbs always followed by the **gerund**.
I can't stand shopping.

2 Verbs followed by the **infinitive**.
*I didn't **expect to see** these results.*

3 Verbs followed by **object + infinitive**.
*I **told her to call** me.*

Verb + -*ing*	Verb + infinitive	Verb + object + infinitive
can't stand	expect	tell

! Some verbs can be followed by a **gerund or infinitive**. The meaning usually changes.
A: *I **tried to call** him but he was out.*
B: *Have you **tried sending** him an email?*

b Do the same with the verbs below.

> remind   forget   agree   hate   refuse
> finish   adore   advise

see Reference page 73

10 Choose the correct alternative.

1 What hobbies would you love *to do/do* in the future?

2 Are there any activities you'd advise your classmates *doing/to do*?

3 What hobbies do you enjoy *doing/to do* in a big group? Alone?

4 Is there anything you sometimes forget *to do/do*?

5 What do you expect *doing/to do* in your free time when you are old?

6 Is there any housework that you can't stand *doing/to do*?

11 Rewrite the advertisement using the correct form of the words in brackets. Use the Present Simple.

BOOK WORLD

Would _____ (like/be) a member of a book club?
Would you like to be a member of a book club?

We (1) _____ (invite/join) BookWorld.

If (2) _____ (enjoy/read), BookWorld is for you.

You can (3) _____ (expect/receive) six free books when you join.

If (4) _____ (want/choose) your own books, we can offer great discounts, but we (5) _____ (advise/join) immediately for our special discount membership.

When you (6) _____ (finish/read) the books, you can return them!

Don't (7) _____ (forget/include) your email address. Please write in BLOCK CAPITALS.

Person to person

12 a Ask and answer the questions in Ex. 10 in groups.

b Tell other students what you found out.

Vocabulary | food

1 Discuss.

1 What are the worst/best meals you have ever had?

2 Do you like food from other countries? What types of food do you like best?

2 a What is the difference between:

1 meal/dish? 3 dessert/side dish?

2 service/tip? 4 tablecloth/napkin?

b Check your answers on page 146.

Reading

3 a You are going to read about a strange restaurant experience. Match these words from the text.

1 long	a) café
2 hungry	b) existed
3 roadside	c) road
4 delicious	d) soup
5 never	e) imagination
6 wonderful	f) and tired

b Work in pairs. What do you think happens in the story? Use the phrases in Ex. 3a and photos to help you.

4 Now read the story to check your ideas. Why do you think the man never found the café again?

5 Find eight factual mistakes in the following summary, and correct them.

While two engineers, who were hungry, were driving through a busy area in Iran, they stopped in a small city. They found a little café. The owner of the café, who spoke a little English, offered to serve the men a meal. The meal, which was delicious, was surprisingly expensive. After they had finished eating, the restaurant owner asked the engineers to recommend his restaurant to their friends. They did this, but the engineer's friends didn't believe it was possible to find such a poor restaurant in such a remote area. In the end, the engineer returned to the village with his wife. However, when they arrived, they couldn't find the train station. Eventually, they asked a local man about the restaurant. He said he had never heard of it, and he had been there for thirty years.

The world's best restaurant

When I was working as a civil engineer in Iran I had to visit a factory in Marinjab – the centre of a recent earthquake. Marinjab is about 150 miles from Tehran and is a quiet and isolated place. As we drove back along the long road, my colleague and I were both hungry and tired. We didn't have much hope of finding anything to eat, however, as the next town was 80 km ahead. Our only hope was of finding a small roadside café, where you are unlikely to get more than some weak tea and a little sugar to eat.

Just then we came to a village made of small huts with flat roofs. Outside one of the many huts was a sign, 'ghahvehkhaneh' (café) so we went in. It was cool inside, and there were men sitting around smoking pipes. The owner, a proud man, came in from the back and greeted us. 'Good afternoon,' he said, in perfect English. 'My name is Hosseini. My wife is Russian. We do not usually get any foreigners here. It will be a pleasure and an honour to prepare a meal for you.'

A pale-faced lady appeared with a tablecloth, and some knives and forks, shortly followed by Mr H himself, carrying a couple of bowls of soup. Made with spinach and yoghurt, and served hot, it was the most delicious soup I have ever eaten. Soon, the next course arrived – Dolmas, stuffed vine leaves. These were so delicious I asked Mr H for the recipe. He replied, 'vine leaves and rice'. It is not an Iranian dish.

The next course was a Chelo kebab – the national dish of Iran. The meat was marinated in yoghurt and spices. We ate in silence, and finished with Turkish coffee. There was something almost unreal about the atmosphere of the place. When it was time to go, we asked Mr H how much it cost, and I can tell you the price was astonishingly cheap. It was a fantastic meal – the best I have ever had, and I told him so. Mr H blushed. 'I am glad,' he said. 'As I told you, we do not see many foreigners here. Do come again, and tell your friends.'

I told a lot of friends about the meal I had, yet no one believed me. 'How could you get such a meal in such a remote place?', an English engineer friend asked me.

A few months later, I returned on exactly the same route, with this engineer friend and was determined to show him my special restaurant. We reached the village – I recognised the flat roofs – but there was no sign of the café. It was as if the building had never existed. I asked a villager. 'ghahvehkhaneh?' he said. 'There has never been one here in all the time I have been here. And that is forty years.' We drove away disappointed. Naturally, my companion laughed at me. 'You have a wonderful imagination,' he said. I don't have any explanation. I only know that I definitely had a meal in this village, in a café which, ever since, I have called 'the world's best restaurant'.

Grammar | countable and uncountable nouns

6 Complete the headings (a–e) in the Active grammar box using the words/phrases below.

> A small amount   Uncountable nouns   None
> Countable nouns   A large amount

Active grammar

These are common countable and uncountable nouns.

a) _____   b) _____

village café	sugar water money rice
meal restaurant	coffee soup tea luggage
	information news advice
	paper furniture weather

Some uncountable nouns are often treated as countable nouns because we understand how much someone is talking about.

A: *Can I have **a coffee**, please?*
B: *Sure. Do you take **one sugar** or two?*

Some of the most common nouns that can be both countable and uncountable are:
sugar water coffee tea chocolate ice cream

Quantity	c) _____	d) _____	e) _____
Countable		a few a couple	many
Uncountable		not much a little	much
Countable and uncountable	not any	some	lots of / a lot of

Any, much and *many* are usually used in negatives and questions.

see Reference page 73

7 Add *a*, *an* or nothing depending on whether the nouns are countable or uncountable.

Would you like chocolate? They're delicious.

Would you like a chocolate? They're delicious.

1 Do you like chocolate?
2 That was terrible meal!
3 When he gives advice, you should listen carefully.
4 Mummy, can I have ice cream? They're only 50p.
5 That's great news!
6 Let's go to café for breakfast.
7 Do you have luggage to carry?
8 That's useful information. Thanks for telling me.
9 I live in village in Santa Catarina.
10 He spends money very quickly!

8 Choose the correct quantifier(s).

1 Do you drink *some/a lot of/ a couple of* coffee?
2 How *many/much/little* vegetables can you name? Which ones do you eat most often?
3 Do you eat *much/a few/lots* meat? Why/Why not?
4 Do you eat *much/little/few* fish or seafood?
5 How *much/some/lots of* water do you drink every day?
6 Do you eat *many/few/a lot of* fruit?
7 Do you like pasta *a lot/a little/a few*? Do you prefer *some/any/no quantifier* rice?
8 Do you go out to *a lot of/ much/a little* restaurants?

Person to person

9 Discuss the questions in Ex. 8 with a partner.

Listening and speaking

10 **5.6** Listen to someone describing a restaurant. Tick (✓) the correct summary.

   a) The speaker asks her friend about a new Chinese restaurant.

   b) The speaker thinks the Argentinian restaurant is good, but her friend wouldn't like it.

   c) The speaker tells her friend about a new vegetarian restaurant which she thinks her friend would like.

   d) The speaker is recommending a new Argentinian restaurant to her friend.

11 **5.6** Listen again and tick any expressions in the How to ... box that the speaker uses.

HOW TO ...

recommend a restaurant

Location	*It's on the river/on the main square/on a small street... It's near ...*
Atmosphere	*Very lively/busy/noisy/ romantic It has a bar/live music ...*
Menu	*It specialises in ... The menu is varied/ traditional. The (food) is fresh/good- quality/beautifully prepared.*
Service	*The service is a little slow. The waiters are very friendly/ efficient.*
Prices	*The prices are reasonable. It's quite expensive.*
Recommendation	*If you are in (the area), you must go. It's worth a visit. You'd love it.*

12 **a** Think about a restaurant you like and would recommend to someone else. Use the How to ... box to plan what you want to say.

   b When you are ready, tell your group about the restaurant.

Writing

13 **a** Look back at Ex. 5 and read the summary again. <u>Underline</u> the linking words used to specify time and sequence, e.g., *where*, *after*, *finally*, *eventually*.

   b Look at the Writing bank on page 164 and do the exercises.

   c Write a summary of *Babette's Feast* in 100 words.

5 Vocabulary

Explaining what you mean

1 **a** Think of situations in which you need to explain something:

1 to visitors.

2 to family/friends.

3 to colleagues.

4 to other students.

b Tell other students your ideas.

In a restaurant, I sometimes have to explain the local dishes to visitors to my country.

2 **a** Read the descriptions below. What are the speakers describing? The answers are at the bottom of this page.

1 '**It's a type of** sport which you do in the sea. You need a board and big waves. It can be dangerous, but it's really exciting.'

2 '**It's a kind of** meal you get in Indian restaurants. It's hot and spicy and usually has meat in it. You eat it with rice.'

3 '**It's the stuff you find** under the grass. It's brown. You see it when it rains.'

4 '**It's something you use for** cleaning the house. It's a machine that picks up dust and small pieces of dirt.'

5 '**They are** usually **made of** wood. They are a useful **thing** to have in the house, because you can put your books on them.'

b Answer the questions below.

1 When do we use the expressions in **bold**?

2 Which word, *thing* or *stuff*, do we use for countable nouns and which do we use for uncountable nouns?

3 Put the words in order to make sentences. Then match the descriptions to the pictures.

1 It's in windows something find of you front

2 It's you a pasta type cheese which on of put

3 It's you opening wine use bottles something for

4 It's Spain kind a dish of from rice

5 It's your for use stuff you hair washing the

6 It's large made stone figure of a

4 **a** Work in groups. Complete the notes below. Which group can finish first?

SHAPE – draw something that's:
rectangular
oval
round
square

WEIGHT – name an animal that's:
heavy
light

SIZE – name something that's:
enormous/huge – The Grand Canyon,
tiny
wide
narrow

TEXTURE – name a type of material or a thing that's:
smooth – soap
rough
sticky
soft
hard

b **5.7** Listen to the sentences. Do they mention the same things as you?

c **5.8** Listen and repeat the words in Ex. 4a.

5 Work in pairs. Give your partner clues to finish a crossword.
Student A: turn to page 146.
Student B: turn to page 148.

Lifelong learning

Explain yourself!

You will not always know the words you need in English. But you need to be able to communicate your meaning by using **alternative words**, like *type of, sort of, stuff* and *thing*. Try to develop strategies for explaining. You can also use **synonyms.**

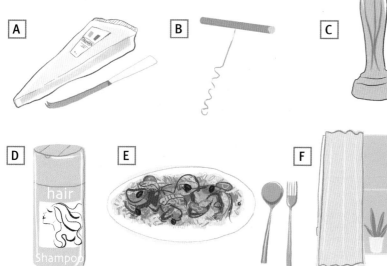

A · B · C · D · E · F

(1) surfing (2) curry (3) mud/earth (4) vacuum cleaner/Hoover (5) bookshelves

5 Communication

What are you good at?

1 **a** What are the people in the photo doing?

   b **5·9** Listen to Pedro talking about Capoeira. Tick (✓) the expressions in the diagram below as you hear them.

2 Choose a skill (it could be anything you enjoy or are good at) and prepare to tell other students about it. Use the diagram to help you plan your ideas.

3 As you listen to the other students, think of one or two questions you can ask when they finish.

Background information

Capoeira originated ... in Brazil. ☐
It was started by ... the African slaves. ☐
It is a kind of ... martial art, which is also like a dance. ☐

Personal qualities necessary

You need to be ... very fit and strong. ☐
You should ... have good control of your body. ☐
You have to ... use your hands to balance. ☐

Main actions/activity

Everyone ... sits around in a circle, singing and playing music. Two people fight in the centre. ☐
As soon as ... you see the other person's hand or foot coming towards you, you have to move away quickly. ☐
You **must** be careful the other person doesn't kick you. ☐
If ... the other person kicks you, **then** ... you lose. ☐

Other information/future plans

I have been doing ... for __ years. ☐
I have improved ... a lot since I first started. ☐
I would like to ... become a trainer, and teach other people about this beautiful sport. ☐

Afterwards

You can ... relax and talk about the fight. ☐
We often ... spend the evening together, listening to music. ☐

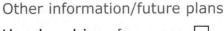

Capoeira

Present Perfect Simple vs. Present Perfect Continuous

Use the **Present Perfect Continuous** to talk about:

1 Unfinished actions which started in the past and continue in the present. The Present Perfect Continuous emphasises the continuation of the activity.

I've been reading your novel. (I haven't finished)
BUT *I've read your novel.* (I've finished it)

2 Recently finished activity with present results. Often we can see these results.

A: *Why are you hot?*
B: *I've been running.* NOT: ~~I've run~~.

3 Situations where we focus on the activity not the result.

I've been studying. (this is why I haven't seen you)
BUT *I've finished* my work. (this is the result)

4 Same as above, particularly using *How long* to focus on the activity. We often use *How much/ many* to focus on the result.

How long have you *been saving* money? (want to know about the activity)

How much money *have* you *saved?* (want to know about the result)

! We don't use the Present Perfect Continuous with 'state' verbs: *know, be, like,* etc.

Verb patterns with infinitive or *-ing*

1 Verbs followed by *-ing*:

verbs of feeling, e.g. *can't stand, like, love, enjoy, don't mind*

2 Verbs followed by the infinitive:

agree, promise, want, choose, decide

3 Many verbs can use the pattern: verb + somebody + *to* + infinitive:

allow, help, want, remind, would like, advise, invite, tell

4 Some verbs can be followed by both forms:

begin, start, continue, stop, remember

Sometimes the meaning changes.

I stopped smoking. = I gave up the habit.
I stopped to smoke. = I had a break from what I was doing in order to have a cigarette.
I remembered to call her. = I called her (I didn't forget) because it was my responsibility.
I remember calling her. = I have a memory of this past action.

Countable/uncountable nouns

Countable

A countable noun can be singular or plural. We can count countable nouns (1 apple, 2 apples, etc.)
*She eats **an apple** a day. I love eating **apples**.*
With singular countable nouns we can use *a* or *an*.

Uncountable

Uncountable nouns have only one form, no singular or plural. We cannot count uncountable nouns.
***some** rice/**a kilo of** rice* NOT: ~~one rice, two rices~~
*In Asia people eat **rice** with every meal.*
We cannot say *a rice*, so we specify *a ... of ...*
***A cup of** coffee, **a bottle of** water...*
Uncountable nouns are generally not used in the plural, e.g. *information, news, hair, advice, paper.*
Can I have some information? NOT: ~~informations~~

Some uncountable nouns are used only in plural form, e.g. *scissors, jeans*
I bought some jeans/a pair of jeans. NOT: ~~a jeans~~

Quantifiers

Countable	Uncountable
some/(not) any	*some/(not) any*
many	*much*
a few/a couple of	*a little*
lots of/a lot of	*lots of/a lot of*

Key vocabulary

Leisure activities

fishing squash skiing aerobics exercise cards
reading jogging swimming dancing chess
gardening athletics sailing surfing football
computer games cycling karate painting drawing
photography volleyball cooking
a musical instrument

Equipment, people, places

a pack of cards   a partner   a gym

Film or book

plot chapter soundtrack main character stars
performance description sequel was written by
is set in was directed by was dubbed is about

In a restaurant

meal dish side dish dessert tablecloth napkin
service tip

Explaining what you mean

it's a type of/kind of ...   it's the stuff you find ...
it's something you use for *-ing*   it's made of ...

5 Review and practice

1 Choose the correct alternatives.

1 I haven't bought your present yet because I've *worked/been working* all morning.

2 How long have you *known/been knowing* Sally?

3 Why are you looking so happy?! I've *danced/been dancing*.

4 Hi. I don't think we've *met/been meeting*. I'm Tim.

5 Have you *finished/been finishing* the report already?

6 How long have you *learned/been learning* to play golf?

7 How many matches have you *played/been playing* this season?

8 I've *come/been coming* to this beach since I was twelve but I've never *seen/been seeing* you here before.

9 Molly hasn't done her homework. She's *watched/been watching* TV all afternoon.

10 I've *cleaned/been cleaning* the bathroom but I haven't *been cleaning/cleaned* the kitchen yet.

2 Complete the dialogues with the correct form of the verbs in brackets.

1 A: You look exhausted. What _____ you _____ (do)?

B: I _____ (play) squash.

2 A: You're late! I _____ (wait) for nearly an hour.

B: I'm sorry. I _____ (work) late in the office.

3 A: I'm really hungry. I _____ (not eat) all day.

B: Sit down. I _____ just _____ (finish) making dinner.

4 A: I haven't seen you for hours. What _____ (do)?

B: I _____ (play) with the dog.

5 A: _____ you _____ (speak) to Alexander yet?

B: No, I haven't . I _____ (try) to phone him all week.

6 A: _____ you _____ (leave) any messages for him?

B: Yes, I _____ (leave) four messages.

7 A: There's paint on your clothes! _____ you _____ (decorate)?

B: Yes, I _____ (paint) the living room. It's nearly finished.

8 A: How many countries _____ you _____ (visit) this year?

9 B: This year? I _____ (visit) four countries.

3 Read the email and write the verbs in brackets in the correct form.

Hi Virginia,

I'd like to *check* (check) a few things with you about next week. I am really looking forward to (1) ____(see) you here in NY. The good news is that my flatmate, Matt, has agreed (2) _____(give) you his room for the week. He said he would prefer (3) ____(stay) at his girlfriend's place because he can't stand (4) _____ (listen) to us talking about university all night!

The other thing is that on Thursday I have been invited (5) ____(go) to dinner with a new colleague from work. I am sure you can manage (6) _____ (entertain) yourself for one night. There is a lot you can do around here if you don't mind (7) _____(go out) on your own. Remember (8) _____(bring) your mobile phone, so you can contact me if you get lost. I forgot (9) ____(ask) you what time your train arrives. Let me know and I'll try (10) ____(leave) work early so I can meet you. Speak soon
Love Felipa

PS I need to warn you (11)_____(bring) some warm clothes with you because it is freezing here!

4 Correct the mistakes in the following sentences. (There may be more than one mistake, and more than one way to correct it.)

We went to buy a furniture.

We went to buy *some/a piece of furniture.*

1 In the evening I love listening to a music.

2 We went out to lovely restaurant.

3 Hurry up! We don't have many time.

4 I don't think I can come to the theatre, because I only have a few money.

5 Would you like a milk in your coffee? Yes, little.

6 The show was cancelled. That's a very bad news.

7 I'm going to the market to buy some breads.

8 I don't like a salt on my food.

5 Circle the correct alternative.

The film is *directed/set/published* in Paris in 2001.

1 Claudio loves *playing/going/doing* fishing.

2 I'd love *to play/to go/going* surfing this summer.

3 I'm very unfit. I need to start *doing/do/going* aerobics again.

4 I've been *play/doing/playing* the guitar for years, but I'm not very good.

5 I've just bought the CD of the *dubbed/soundtrack* of that film. It's brilliant.

6 The first film was a great success, so they're making the *sequel/chapter/performance*.

7 We had to wait for ages because the *service/tip/dish* was very slow.

8 The taxi driver was really helpful, so we left him a big *service/tip/bill*.

6 Holidays

Lead-in

1 **a** What type of holidays do the photos show?

> adventure holiday   package holiday   safari   beach holiday
> sightseeing tour   (river) cruise   camping holiday   sailing holiday

b Which of these holidays are: romantic? convenient? dangerous? expensive? relaxing?

2 **a** Read the texts about tourists and travellers. Check the meaning of the words in **bold**.

Tourists ... are not so interested in **new experiences** and **sensations**. When they **go abroad**, they either **go sightseeing** to see **famous landmarks** like St Mark's Square in Venice, or to **sandy beaches** where they do nothing but sunbathe. Many tourists prefer **package holidays**, which include travel, accommodation, and sometimes even food. Tourists just want to **have fun and relax**.

Travellers ... go to the **cultural** and **historical capitals**, just like tourists. However, travellers also explore **tropical rainforests**, **barren deserts** and other places where tourists never go. Travellers try to experience the **local culture** and meet the local people. They prefer **independent travel** to package tours and hope to experience an **unforgettable journey**.

b Complete the sentences for you. Compare with a partner.

1 I prefer *independent travel/package holidays* because ...

2 I'd rather spend a week *on a sandy beach/in a historical capital/in the tropical rainforest* because ...

3 When I'm on holiday I want to *have an unforgettable journey/have fun and relax* because ...

4 I prefer to *go sightseeing/experience the local culture* because ...

Reading

1 **a** Use the words in the box to complete the phrases.

> ~~home~~ souvenirs diary photos emails

phone *home*

1 keep a _____
2 take _____
3 buy _____
4 send postcards/letters/_____

b Do you do any of these things when you travel?

2 Have you been/would you like to go to Africa? Why/Why not? What would you expect to see/experience there?

3 Read the extract from *Travels Across Africa*, by Sophie Van Ranst, and answer the questions.

1 Where are Sophie and Daniel?
2 Do they experience the things you talked about in Ex. 2?
3 How do they like to remember their travels?

4 Read the text again. Write true (T), false (F) or don't know (DK) next to each sentence.

1 They drove slowly through the busy desert.
2 Sophie wrote about her experiences in a notebook.
3 Daniel took photos of the Victoria Falls.
4 They had seen a lot of things, and heard many stories.
5 Daniel was driving when they saw the horses.
6 They had seen other animals, but they hadn't seen wild horses before.
7 The horses didn't come near the car.
8 Sophie woke Daniel so that he could take photos of the horses.

Travels Across Africa

1   For six hours we shot through the barren landscape of the Karoo desert in South Africa. Just rocks and sand and baking sun. Knowing our journey was ending, Daniel and I just wanted to remember all we had seen and done. He used a camera. I
5 used words. I had already finished three notebooks and was into the fourth, a beautiful leather notebook I'd bought in a market in Mozambique.

Southern Africa was full of stories. And visions. We were almost drunk on sensations. The roaring of the water at Victoria Falls,
10 the impossible silence of the Okavango Delta in Botswana. And then the other things: dogs in the streets, whole families in Soweto living in one room, a kilometre from clean water.

As we drove towards the setting sun, a quietness fell over us. The road was empty – we hadn't seen another car for hours. And as
15 I drove, something caught my eye, something moving next to me. I glanced in the mirror of the car; I glanced sideways to the right, and that was when I saw them. Next to us, by the side of the road, thirty, forty wild horses were racing the car, a cloud of dust rising behind them – brown, muscular horses almost close

20 enough to touch them, to smell their hot breath. I didn't know how long they had been there next to us.

I shouted to Dan: 'Look!' but he was in a deep sleep, his camera lying useless by his feet. They
25 raced the car for a few seconds, then disappeared far behind us, a memory of heroic forms in the red landscape.

When Daniel woke up an hour later I told him what had happened.

30 'Wild horses?' he said. 'Why didn't you wake me up?'

'I tried. But they were gone after a few seconds.'

'Are you sure you didn't dream it?'

'You were the one who was sleeping!'

35 'Typical,' he said. 'The best photos are the ones we never take.'

We checked into a dusty hotel and slept the sleep of the dead.

> For six hours we shot through the barren landscape of the Karoo desert in South Africa.

Vocabulary | descriptive language

5 Look at the descriptive language from the text. Choose the correct meanings and answer the questions.

We shot through the barren landscape (line 1)

This means we moved very fast. Normally we use the word 'shoot' when guns are involved – 'He shot someone!'

1 drunk on sensations (line 9)

This means that you have seen and heard so much that you feel *incredible/bored*.
What normally makes people drunk?

2 roaring of the water (line 9)

This means the water *makes a loud noise/is quiet*. What animal normally roars?

3 quietness fell over us (line 13)

This means that as they drove *they had a small accident/it became very quiet*.
What usually 'falls'?

4 caught my eye (line 15)

This means that she *had something in her eye/noticed something and looked at it*.
Usually you 'catch' a _____.

5 slept the sleep of the dead (line 37)

What does 'sleep of the dead' suggest?
They slept *very well/badly*.

Grammar | Past Perfect Simple

6 **a** Look at the Active Grammar box and choose the correct alternatives.

> ### Active grammar
>
> We **wanted** to remember all we **had seen** ...
> (Past Simple)   (Past Perfect Simple)
>
> Which action happened first?
> a) We saw things
> b) We wanted to remember (the experience)
>
> Use the <u>Past Perfect</u> /<u>Past Simple</u> to show that one event happened before another one in the past.
>
> | We had seen | we wanted to | now |
> | things | remember | |
> | ✗ | ✗ | ✗ |
>
> We make the Past Perfect Simple using *had/ hadn't* + <u>past participle</u>/<u>infinitive</u>

see Reference page 87

b Find other examples of the Past Perfect Simple in the text.

7 Put the verbs in brackets into the correct tense.

1 I felt sick. Later, I realised I _____ (eat) some bad food.

2 She didn't know the area because she _____ (not live) there since she was a child.

3 First, I spoke to Sam. Then, I _____ (meet) Jo.

4 I was sad when I heard that my old teacher _____ (die) two years earlier.

5 We arrived at 8.oo but he _____ (already leave).

6 We were thirsty. We _____ (not drink) anything since 1.oo p.m.

7 Where _____ (you go) after dinner yesterday?

8 I love cycling holidays. I _____ (get) my first bike when I was seven.

8 Match the sentence beginnings in A with endings in B. Change a verb to the Past Perfect Simple in each sentence.

A	B
1 I got lost in the city because	a) I spend a lot of time studying before it.
2 The evening went well because	b) I hear it was good.
3 I went to see the film because	c) I not be there before.
4 I was qualified for the job because	d) I not be able to sleep the night before.
5 I found the exam easy because	e) I plan it carefully.
6 It was a big day but I was tired because	f) I study the subject at university.

Pronunciation

9 **a** [6.1] Listen to the answers to Ex. 8. How is *had* pronounced in the Past Perfect Simple affirmative? In the negative?

b Listen again and repeat the sentences.

Person to person

10 Have you ever been in any of the situations in Ex. 8? Tell your partner.

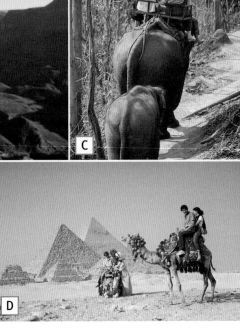

A

C

E

D

B

12 a 〔6.2〕 Listen to three people describing the photos. Which photos do they talk about?

b Complete the notes in the table.

	1 Which place?	2 When did they take the photo?	3 What had they heard about the place?
Speaker 1			
Speaker 2			
Speaker 3			

c Listen again. Tick (✓) the phrases you hear in the How to ... box.

Listening and speaking

11 With a partner, describe the photos. Answer the questions.

1 What can you see in the photos?
2 Where were the photos taken?
3 What do you think the people who took the photos had done earlier that day?
4 How do you think they are feeling?

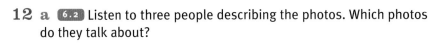

HOW TO ...

describe a memorable photo

Say when and where the photo was taken	*This photo shows ...* *It is/was ...*
Describe what you can see in the photo	*In the background/foreground, you can see ...* *On the left/right there is ...* *I think this is ...*
Give background information/talk about the people in the photo	*I/We had been (there) for ...* *I was staying ...* *I/We had heard ...* *Afterwards, we ...* *We felt happy/sad ...* *I was very excited ...* *We had always wanted to see ...*

13 Use the phrases in the How to ... box to describe a photo you remember well to another student. Try to talk for about a minute. Or, describe a photo from page 149.

Vocabulary | places to visit in a city

1 **a** What are the differences between the pairs of words and phrases?

1 a castle/a palace
2 a museum/an art gallery
3 a pub/a café
4 a park/a garden
5 a lake/a fountain
6 a bookshop/a library
7 a shop/a market

A palace is a large building where a king or queen lives (or lived), but a castle is an old building, built to defend people from attack.

b Tell a partner your top three choices of things to do when you visit a new city.

Number 1 for me is visiting markets, because the atmosphere is usually very friendly. You can meet local people and buy presents too.

Listening

2 **6.3** Stefan and Karina are travelling around Ireland. Listen to their conversations. Where are they? Choose the correct answer.

1 a) at a train station b) on a bus c) in an airport
2 a) in a museum b) on a bus c) in the street
3 a) in a post office b) in the street c) in a taxi
4 a) at an airport b) at a bus stop c) at a train station
5 a) in a restaurant b) in a café c) in a museum

3 Listen to the conversations again. What is the problem in each dialogue?

Conversation 1 – train delay

Pronunciation

4 **a** **6.4** Listen and complete the sentences in the How to ... box.

HOW TO ...

get around a new place

Ask about places in a town	*What time does the _____ ?* *Is there a ____ near here?* *Can you ____ a good restaurant?*
Ask for travel information	*How much is a ____ city centre?* *____ this bus go to the airport?*
Sound polite	*Excuse me. Could you tell me what time the ____ ?* *Excuse me. Do you know ____ ?*
Ask/Give directions	*Can you tell me the way ____ ?* *Just go straight on. It's on ___.*

b **6.5** Listen to these questions. Why does the intonation start high?

Can you tell me what time the park closes?
Do you know if there's a post office near here?

c Listen and repeat.

Speaking

5 **Student A:** look at the role cards below.
Student B: turn to page 147.
Ask and answer questions to find out the information you/your partner needs. Try to use expressions from the How to ... box.

Student A

Situation 1: In a train station:
You work in the ticket office.

Tickets for Cambridge cost:
Adult single: £7.50 Adult return: £10
Child single: £4.50 Child return: £8.50

Trains to Cambridge leave on the hour, and at half past every hour. There are delays today. Trains leave from platform 4.

Situation 2: In a tourist office:
You would like to see the Picasso exhibition at the Tate Gallery.
Find out:
1 how to get to the Tate Gallery.
2 what time it opens/closes.
3 how much the exhibition costs.

Reading and speaking

6 **a** What do you know about Dublin? Are the
following statements true (T) or false (F)?

  1 Dublin is the capital city of Ireland.
  2 Many famous writers were born in Dublin.
  3 Molly Malone was the Queen of Ireland.
  4 Dublin is divided into two parts, north and
south, by the River Liffey.
  5 There is often live music in Irish pubs.

  b Read the Quick Guide to check your
answers.

Dublin
A Quick Guide

Dublin, a city over a 1,000 years
old, is the cultural and historical
capital of Ireland and the birthplace
of many of the world's most popular
writers and musicians. James Joyce
and Oscar Wilde were both born
here. But what's it like?

It has always had a reputation as a vibrant and
lively city, but since the economic boom of the
1990s, Dublin has got even better. Almost as
famous for its lively nightlife as for its history,
Dublin now looks more like other European
cities, and has, in fact, become one of Europe's
most popular destinations.

So, what can you do there?

The first place to go is Temple Bar. It has a great
atmosphere, with shops, bars and cafés full of
stylish young Europeans.

One of the best things to see is the Book of Kells.
This is one of the oldest books in the world (over
1,200 years old!) and you can see it in the Trinity
College Library, at the University of Dublin.

Also, you mustn't miss the statue of Molly Malone, the city's heroine.
She was a beautiful, young fishmonger who died in 1636. Nobody
knows how she died, but a famous song was written about her,
and many say you can still hear the sound of her ghost walking the
streets.

If you enjoy history, make sure you go to Dublin Castle. This castle,
built between 1208 and 1220, lies in the heart of the city, and is
surrounded by beautiful gardens.

Don't leave without throwing a coin into the River Liffey. Walk
across Ha'penny Bridge, which joins the north and south sides of
the city, and throw a coin into the river to bring you good luck.

And finally, you must listen to some live Irish music in Ireland's
famous pubs. A lot of pubs have music several nights a
week. What's it like? It's fast, exciting and beautiful.
Whatever you do in Ireland, you'll certainly
'enjoy the craic', as they say in Ireland,
(meaning have a good time).

7 **a** Which of the places/objects in the photos does the text talk about?

  b Now cover the text. Can you remember what the article says about
each place? Read the text again to check.

  c Which of the places in the text would you like to visit yourself? Tell
another student.

Grammar | uses of *like*

8 Match the sentences (a–e) to the correct meaning (1–5) in the Active grammar box.

a) *What would you like to do?*

b) *It tastes like chicken.*

c) *What does it look like?*

d) *What's it like?*

e) *What do you like doing on holiday?*

Active grammar

1 **like** (v) = to enjoy something or think that it is nice

A: _____

B: *Visiting markets and shopping.*

2 **would like** (v) = want

A: _____

B: *I'd like to see the statue of Molly Malone.*

3 **look like** (v, conj) = seem (appearance)

A: _____

B: *Like other European cities.*

4 **be like** (prep) = describe or give your opinion of this person/thing

A: _____

B: *It is a lively and vibrant city.*

5 **like** (conj) = the same way as

A: *Is that food good?*

B: _____

---

see Reference page 87

9 Complete the dialogues using expressions with *like*.

1 A: I have never been to Paris. What _____ _____ _____ ?

B: Oh, it is a wonderful city.

2 A: What _____ _____ _____ _____ do today?

B: I don't mind. You decide.

3 A: Have you seen the new concert hall?

B: Yes, it _____ _____ an airport terminal!

4 A: What _____ _____ _____ most about Krakow?

B: I love the market square with all the cafés and restaurants.

5 A: I went to that new French restaurant last night.

B: Really? What _____ _____ _____?

A: It was great. The food was delicious.

6 A: I am not sure if I will recognise Mr Williams. What _____ he _____ _____?

B: He is tall, with dark hair.

7 A: Why didn't you like the food?

B: Because it was horrible! It _____ _____ rubber.

8 A: I _____ really _____ modern art.

B: Neither do I. The paintings often _____ _____ the work of children.

9 A: Have you seen the Sagrada Familia church in Barcelona?

B: Yes, I thought _____ _____ _____ an enormous cake!

Person to person

10 Write three questions (using the different expressions with *like*) to ask your partner.

Who do you look like in your family?

Writing

11 a In pairs, talk about the town where you were born or a city you know well.

1 What is it like?

2 What are the people like?

3 Why do you like/dislike it?

4 What do you like doing there?

5 What would you like to change about it?

6 Does it look like any other cities that you know?

b Write a Quick Guide to a city you know well, recommending things a visitor should do. Use expressions from the text as a model.

The first place to go is ...

One of the best places to visit is ...

You mustn't miss ...

If you enjoy X, make sure you include a trip to ...

Don't leave without seeing/trying/going to ...

Finally, why not try ...?

c Share your Quick Guide with other students and read theirs. Which city/places would you like to visit? Why?

81

Vocabulary | describing nature

1 **a** Label the photos with an adjective from box A and a noun from box B.

A (desert sandy mountain
green rocky tropical)

B (rainforest range valley
coastline island beach)

b In pairs, make a list of other types of natural places.

c Discuss.

1 Could any of the places in the photos be in your country?

2 Have you ever been to any of these types of place?

3 Which is your favourite for a holiday?

Reading and speaking

2 **a** Describe what is happening in the pictures. What strange events/coincidences do they show?

b Read the text to find out.

3 Read the text again and answer the questions.

1 What event happened recently that inspired this text?

2 Is the text very serious, semi-serious or not serious? How do you know?

3 In your opinion, which are the most amazing events/ coincidences in the text? Which are lucky? Which could have logical explanations?

4 Have you experienced a strange event/coincidence?

4 Work with a partner. Retell the stories from the text using the key words to help.

1 family/Australian coast/whale/boat

2 dog/India/Scotland/boat

3 Karen/beach/ring

4 Roger/drowning/saved/Alice/beach/husband

Strange things happen when you travel ...

A whale jumps out of the water and on to your boat. What are the chances of that? A billion to one? There are 217 million square kilometres of ocean and the boat was only 9 metres long. But it happened last week. A family from Coventry, UK, was sailing off the Australian coast when the whale jumped on to the boat. 'Amazing!' we all say. Yes, but unbelievable events happen to travellers every day. Read about some of them below.

Some of the most incredible travellers, it seems, are pets, who may return home after years away. These stories normally involve cats, though there is a famous story of a dog that travelled 4,800 kilometres from Calcutta, India to Inverkeithing, Scotland on a boat. After several months, the boat arrived and the dog ran all the way home!

What about the things people lose and find when they are travelling? Rings are top of the list. In Hawaii, Ken Da Vico, who is a diver, says he finds about 15 wedding rings a year in the sea. He returns many of them to their owners. Even if a fish eats the ring, there is still hope. There are many cases of rings being found years later inside the stomachs of sharks, mussels and other kinds of fish. Less common is when the loser finds the lost ring, as happened when Karen Goode went to a beach in the UK and found a ring she had lost ten years before.

But the best beach story involves Roger Lausier, aged four, who was saved from drowning by a woman called Alice Blaise. Nine years later, on the same beach, a man was drowning. Roger Lausier dived into the water and saved him. It was Alice Blaise's husband.

F

E

Grammar | articles

5 Look at the Active grammar box and match the rules (1–6) with the example phrases/sentences (a–f).

a) *Ken Da Vico, who is **a** diver, says ...*

b) *In Hawaii, ...*

c) *... **the** best beach story involves Roger Lausier ...*

d) *Rings are top of the list.*

e) ***A** whale jumps out of the water ...*

f) *... **the** dog ran all the way home!*

Active grammar

1 Use *a/an* when we don't know which one we are talking about or it's the first time it has been mentioned.

2 Use *a/an* with jobs.

3 Use *the* when we know which one we are talking about OR it is the only one.

4 Use *the* with superlatives.

5 Use no article (–) when we make generalisations with plural or uncountable nouns.

6 Use no article (–) with most names of people and places.

Use *the* in names with *States, Kingdom* and *Republic*: *the United States, the United Kingdom, the Republic of China*

Use *the* if the name is a plural: *the Netherlands, the Andes, the Falkland Islands*

We say *the south of Spain*, but *southern Spain* And *the north of Africa*, but *North Africa*

Use *the* with rivers, seas, oceans and deserts: *the Pacific Ocean, the River Thames*

---

see Reference page 87

6 Find and correct the mistakes with articles in the sentences below.

1 The travellers should always respect other people's culture.

2 The Europe is not most beautiful continent.

3 The good way to see a country is to go by train.

4 It'd be really relaxing to go on trip along a river, like River Nile, for example.

5 The delayed flights are one of greatest problems travellers face these days.

6 Before going abroad, you should learn a few words of a local language.

7 The travel is a bit boring for me.

8 I hate travelling in the aeroplanes.

7 Read the stories and write *a/an/the* or – (nothing) in the spaces.

Alvaro Cortez met his girlfriend, (1)___ musician called Pilar, at college in Madrid, and she showed him her favourite guitar. (2)___ guitar was (3)___ same instrument that Alvaro's grandfather had played fifty years earlier. It had been lost when (4)___ grandfather moved to (5)___ new house in (6)___ Valencia, Spain.

Michael and Tamara Weisch, went on (7)___ two-week holiday to Warsaw. One evening, in (8)___ restaurant of (9)___ small hotel where they were staying, they started talking to another couple, who, they soon realised, were also called Michael and Tamara Weisch, also from (10)___ New York City. But (11)___ best coincidence of all: both couples had been to (12)___ same hotel in Prague exactly a year before.

Person to person

8 Read the sentences in Ex. 6 again. Write Yes (Y) if you agree completely, No (N) if you disagree, or Don't Know (DK). Discuss your answers with other students.

I agree with sentence 1 because ...
What do you think?

Pronunciation

9 a **6.6** Listen to the dialogues and complete the sentences.

1 **A:** I read an amazing story about a family that was sailing.
   B: _____ you? What happened?
   A: A whale jumped onto their boat.
   B: _____? Where?
   A: Near Australia.

2 **A:** A dog went home alone from India to Scotland.
   B: Really? _____?
   A: It travelled by boat and, after months at sea, it ran home.
   B: That's _____!

3 **A:** This diver finds fifteen wedding rings a year.
   B: _____ he?
   A: And he returns most of them.
   B: That's _____ !

4 **A:** Karen Goode found a ring she'd lost ten years before.
   B: Did _____? How?
   A: It was on the same beach.
   B: _____ incredible!

b When we emphasise words, sometimes we make the vowel sounds very long. Which vowels do you think are long in these words/phrases?

1 Really?!
2 That's amazing!
3 Oh no!
4 How awful!

c **6.7** Listen to check.

d **6.6** Listen to the dialogues in Ex. 9a again and copy the intonation.

e Practise the dialogues with a partner. Concentrate on your intonation.

10 a How do the listeners in Ex. 9a show they are interested? Read the How to ... box to check your ideas.

HOW TO ...	**show interest and surprise**	
	Use echo questions	*Does he? Did she? Were you?*
	Use short expressions	*Really?! Oh no!*
	Use expressions with *that's*/*how* + adjective	*That's amazing! That's a shame/pity! How interesting! How awful!*
	Ask a follow-up question	*When? Where? How? Why? What was it like?*

b Work with a partner. One person reads a sentence below and the other shows interest and surprise.

1 I'm really hungry.
2 I've been swimming in the river.
3 They're not going to Mexico now.
4 We can stay in Paris for two nights.
5 They didn't talk to us at all.
6 The doctor is sick.
7 I grew up here.
8 She won't help you.
9 I'll be here tomorrow morning.
10 I love Shakespeare.

Speaking

11 Work in pairs. **Student A:** turn to page 146. **Student B:** turn to page 148. Read your sentences to each other. Express surprise and interest and ask a follow-up question.

A: *I've travelled a lot.*
B: *Have you?*
A: *Yes, I've been to over thirty countries.*
B: *Really? Which was your favourite?*

6 | Vocabulary

Expressions with *get*

1 Look at the word map and tick the expressions with *get* that you know. Can you add any more expressions to the map?

buy:

He went to **get** a newspaper. Shall we **get** some drinks for the journey?

travel/go/arrive:

Can you tell me how to **get** to the airport? What time did you **get** here?

get + past participle:

She only **got** married/divorced last week! I need to **get** dressed. I don't know how we **got** lost.

fetch/collect:

He's gone to **get** Janice from the station. Can you **get** a chair from the bedroom?

Get

receive/obtain:

She **got** a letter from the bank this morning. Did you **get** the email I sent you? I **got** a distinction in my exams and I **got** the job!

become:

(often used with the Present Continuous for describing changes): I'm **getting** hungry. It's **getting** dark. My English is **getting** worse.

phrasal verbs:

I **got on** the wrong bus. I'll call her as soon as I **get back**. We **get on** really well (with each other).

2 Complete the sentences below with the words/phrases in the box.

> hungry   is getting   back   train   getting
> got on   tickets   get   lost   some stamps

1 Is the post office still open? I must get _____ for these letters.
2 What's the time? It's _____ dark already.
3 Mario has gone to _____ the children from school.
4 I'm getting _____. Shall we have some lunch?
5 Did you manage to get _____ for the match?
6 I don't have enough time to study, so my English _____ worse!
7 I think we should buy a map. I don't want to get _____.
8 I'm afraid I will have to leave early. I am getting a _____ to Leeds this evening.
9 I never really _____ with Jeremy's sister.
10 Will you call me when you get _____ from Rome?

3 **a** Work in groups. Write a story using the phrases from the box, and other *get* phrases you know.

> get married   get to the airport late   get lost
> get on (with)   get directions   get cold
> get wet   get to the hotel   get back   get ill
> get bored   get home   get someone a drink
> get divorced   get a taxi

b Write your story for other students to read. Leave spaces where there is an expression with *get*. Can the other students guess which word/phrase is missing?

Jim was planning to get _____ but on the way to the church ...

1   Work in groups. When you visit another city, what do you enjoy/not enjoy doing? Tell your group.

2   You are going to plan a day trip for your group in London. Look at the 'What's on in London' leaflet below and find:

1   a tour which lasts for half a day.

2   a colourful market.

3   the time it takes to go round the London Eye.

4   which musical you could see.

5   where the piano concert is playing.

6   two museums you could visit.

7   an exclusive shop to buy souvenirs.

3   **6.8** Listen to three people planning a day trip. Write down three things they decide to do.

4   a   Plan your day, using the leaflet below. You can spend £100 each. Plan activities for the morning, the afternoon and the evening. Try to include activities for everyone in your group.

b   Tell the class about your plans.

What's on in LONDON

G General

Tour around London on a Big Red Bus. Enjoy the views from the top of this famous London bus, as you learn about the sights from one of our friendly guides. Half-day tour, £25 per person.

London walks – Experience London on foot with one of our specialised walking tours. £5 per two-hour walk.

Camden market – the perfect place to walk

around and visit shops, eat in a local café, buy some arts and crafts and just sit with a coffee and watch London go by. Colourful, fun and cheap – this is real London.

Buckingham Palace – Entrance ticket: £12 per person. Watch the Changing of the Guard outside Buckingham Palace at 2p.m. every afternoon.

The London Eye – the Giant Observation Wheel, became operational in January 2000. The Wheel is the largest of its kind ever to be built and visitors to London from abroad are delighted by this new way of seeing the city. Tickets £12.50, duration 30 minutes.

☺ Theatre

Les Misérables – Palace Theatre 020 7494 5555. 'This musical has been playing for 18 years, and it is still like going to a first night.' Eves 7.30, Mats Thu and Sat 2.30. Tickets from £40.

♫ Music

Philharmonic Orchestra Hear Rachmaninoff's first piano concerto (with Michael Pletnev) accompanied by the Philharmonic Orchestra. Free. The Royal Festival Hall.

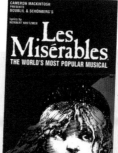

M Museums and Galleries

Madame Tussaud's – Visit the museum to see their world-famous wax models of famous stars, past and present. A very popular attraction, you might have to wait over an hour to get in. £24.50.

The British Museum – has outstanding collections that cover world cultures from prehistory to the present day. Free.

The National Gallery – The National Gallery, London, houses one of the greatest collections of European painting in the world, with over 2,300 paintings covering the period from about 1250 to 1900. Free.

🛍 Shopping

Shop at Harrods – the most famous department store in the world. Buy exclusive souvenirs for family and friends, and enjoy afternoon tea and wonderful views across London in our sky-view café.

Past Perfect Simple vs. Past Simple

Past Perfect Simple form: *had/hadn't* + past participle

Use

Use the **Past Simple** to talk about something that happened in the past, e.g. *I was ill.*
Use the **Past Perfect** to talk about what happened before that, e.g. *I had eaten something bad.*
We use it to make the order of events clear.
I was ill because I'd eaten something bad.

```
   I had eaten
   something bad      I was ill      now
───────x───────────────x──────────x────────▶
```

I went to Bali last year. I hadn't been there before.
Her shoes were dirty. She hadn't cleaned them.

! We don't use the Past Perfect when the sequence of events in the past is clear:
I came home and turned on my computer.

The Past Perfect uses many of the same expressions as the Present Perfect (*since, for, already*):
I had worked there since 1993.
She had been my teacher for eight years.
I had already studied Spanish before I started my Italian course.

We often use *by the time* + Past Simple + Past Perfect.
By the time I arrived the party had finished.

Uses of *like*

We can use *like* to talk about:
General descriptions
What is your new school like? I have never been to that area. What's it like?

Things being similar to other things or acting in a similar way to other things
It smells like chocolate. He eats like a horse.

Physical appearance
What does he look like? Sam looks like a popstar.

Personal preferences
I like fresh coffee. Harry doesn't like swimming.

A specific preference for the future
I would like a non-smoking seat, please.

Looks like also means 'seems'.
It looks like Rachel is going to be late again!

Articles

a/an
1 When it's the first time we've mentioned the subject.
   Last night I saw a ghost!
2 With jobs. *She's a doctor, he's a cook.*

the
1 When we already know which one we are talking about (it has been mentioned previously).
   What did the ghost look like?
2 The subject is unique (there's only one).
   The President of the USA.
3 With superlatives. *It's the best film.*

No article
When we make generalisations with:
a) plural nouns. **Trousers** are warmer than **skirts**.
b) uncountable nouns. **Progress** is possible.

Articles in place names
We use **no article** with:
1 Most place names. *Warsaw, Spain*
2 Names with South/East, etc. *South America*

We use **the** for:
1 Countries with the word State, Kingdom or Republic.
   the United States, the United Kingdom
2 Plural names. *the West Indies*
3 Rivers, seas, oceans, deserts. *the River Seine*
4 Describing where in a country. *the south of France, the west coast of Scotland*

Key vocabulary

Travel
adventure/package/beach/camping/sailing holiday
sightseeing tour   safari   (river) cruise   go abroad
new experiences and sensations   local culture
go sightseeing   famous landmarks   barren deserts
cultural and historical capitals   have fun and relax
independent travel   unforgettable journey

Places to visit in a city
castle/palace   museum/art gallery   pub/café
park/garden   lake/fountain   bookshop/library
shop/market

Places to visit (nature)
sandy beach   tropical rainforest   rocky coastline
desert island   mountain range   green valley

Expressions with *get*
get hungry/dark/worse/cold/wet/ill/bored
get a newspaper/a drink   get a letter/an email/
a distinction/a job/directions   get home/to the
airport   get someone from the station/a taxi
get on/get back/get on (with)
get married/dressed/lost

1 Choose the correct alternative.

When I got to the restaurant I realised that I *left/* ~~had left~~ her phone number at home.

1 By the time she was eighteen she *lived/had lived* in six cities.

2 On my birthday, when I *got/had got* home I found that my husband *had cooked/cooked* dinner.

3 That morning, she got up, had breakfast and *went/had gone* to work, as normal.

4 Tibet was incredible. I *never saw/had never seen* such a beautiful country before.

5 He called twice but no one answered. They *all went/had all gone* to bed.

6 When I arrived in France, my cousins *kissed/had kissed* me on the cheek.

7 When I returned a month later, I found that the weather *grew/had grown* cold and I *had/had had* to buy a new jacket.

8 It was Max! I *hadn't seen/didn't see* him for twenty-five years.

2 Put the words in order.

to you Would something eat like ?

Would you like something to eat?

1 is What like it ? been there haven't I before .

2 like I at prefer but films I watching going cinema to the home .

3 looks sister you like think Don't her Maria ?

4 to what see wait finished the house will look when like I it is can't .

5 early Tim up getting doesn't like .

6 Would have drink in like you come a to and ?

7 like your is job new What ?

8 my Do like hairstyle you new ?

9 a I walking in new I around am like when city .

10 tickets 'd like exhibition, two please for the I .

3 Do these use *the* or not?

the Black Sea

1 Canary Islands

2 Africa

3 Czech Republic

4 Andes mountains

5 River Nile

6 Canada

7 United Arab Emirates

8 northern Europe

9 Atlantic Ocean

10 Mount Kilimanjaro

11 Sahara Desert

12 Mediterranean Sea

4 Choose the correct alternative.

A: Why do you like this hotel so much?

B: It's *a hotel/* ~~the hotel~~ where I met Dave.

1 A: How was the restaurant?

B: *The food/Food* was wonderful.

2 A: Why don't you go to Australia for your holiday?

B: I don't like *the aeroplanes/aeroplanes*.

3 A: Who was Alexander Fleming?

B: He's *a/the* man who discovered penicillin.

4 A: Why didn't you buy a dog?

B: *The cats/Cats* are easier to look after.

5 A: What happened yesterday?

B: (a) *The/A* strange man knocked on our door and asked for water.

6 A: Why does Mariana always win prizes?

B: Because she is *the most/most* intelligent person in the class.

5 Complete the advertisement by choosing the correct word (a, b, c or d).

Would you like to (1) _go_ abroad? Would you like to (2) _____ the world? If you are only interested in (3) _____ a tan and lying on a (4) _____ beach with all the other tourists, then AMAZ Tours are not for you. We organise trips to the (5) _____ rainforest in Brazil. Here you will have a chance to learn (6) _____ new cultures and to experience something truly different. The Amazon is (7) _____ smaller and smaller. See it before it disappears. If you want to stay longer than a month we will even help you (8) _____ a job. We fly every Saturday. It takes fifteen hours to get (9) _____ and a whole lifetime to leave! (10) _____ your ticket before 12th July and we will give you a 15% discount!

1 (a) get (b) see (c) *go* (d) have

2 (a) visit (b) see (c) travelling (d) find

3 (a) get (b) have (c) being (d) getting

4 (a) sand (b) sandy (c) deep (d) heavy

5 (a) tropic (b) deep (c) whole (d) tropical

6 (a) about (b) in (c) over (d) at

7 (a) become (b) getting (c) now (d) grown

8 (a) getting (b) to (c) get (d) for

9 (a) over (b) us (c) arrive (d) there

10 (a) Have (b) Make (c) Get (d) Do

7 Education

Lead-in

1 Discuss.

Which of the learning situations in the photos have you experienced? When and where? Which are the most effective?

2 Make as many verb/noun collocations as possible using the nouns in the box and the verbs in the table below.

> a mistake   a degree   an exam   good marks   a course   progress
> some research   to lectures   to class   from university   notes
> a subject (History, Law, Architecture, etc.)

GET	TAKE	DO	PASS	FAIL	REVISE	GO	MAKE	GRADUATE
							a mistake	

3 **a** Complete the sentences with the verbs from Ex. 2.

1 Before exams do you usually _____ alone or with friends? Which is better?

2 Do you think that _____ mistakes is an important part of learning? Why/Why not?

3 What other courses have you _____/done in the past? What was good/bad about them?

4 If you _____ to a lecture, do you make lots of notes or just listen?

5 How can you _____ progress in English outside the classroom?

b Ask and answer the questions with a partner.

Grammar	subject and object questions
Can do	describe a learning experience

Listening

1 **a** What do you think the people are doing in the pictures?

b **7.1** Listen and write the number of the speaker next to the picture. Were you correct?

2 **a** Which picture do these phrases/sentences from the listening refer to?

a) ... nobody had time to show her.

b) ... my teacher told me to hold an orange in each hand as I played.

c) It was quite useful.

d) She wrote lists of verbs and tenses ...

e) He threw them in, pulled them up on the rope and then threw them in again ...

f) ... it was very difficult.

g) ... you had to keep the pencil on the paper all the time, so the picture was just one line.

h) 'I am practising,' she said. 'When I can do it standing still, then I will be ready to start moving forward.'

i) ... they are all good, strong swimmers now too!

j) He told us to sit opposite a partner, and draw their face without looking.

b **7.1** Listen again to check.

Vocabulary | education

3 Complete the phrases and expressions with the words and phrases from the box.

> steep   by doing   heart   fast   perfect
> strict   deep   up   bring

People

1) a _____ learner

2) a _____ teacher

Expressions

3) Practice makes _____.

4) It's a _____ learning curve.

Ways of learning

5) learn by _____

6) learn _____

7) pick (something) _____

Ways of teaching

8) throw someone in at the _____ end

9) _____ someone up to (do something)

A

B

C

D

E

4 Discuss.

1 Which pictures in Ex. 1 could the phrases relate to? One phrase may relate to more than one picture.

2 Do you think the techniques mentioned are good or bad ways of learning? Why/Why not?

3 Have you experienced any of these ways of learning/teaching?

5 a Think about a good (or bad) learning experience you have had. Make questions from the prompts below.

1 What/learning? Why?
2 Why/experience/good/bad?
3 How/you/learn?
4 Learn/in a group/on your own?
5 Easy/difficult to learn?
6 How/you/make progress?
7 You/learn/useful techniques?

b Answer the questions. Make notes.

c Tell a partner about your experience. Use the How to ... box and give as much detail as possible.

HOW TO ...	describe a learning experience	
	What you had to do/learn	*(My teacher) told me to ...* *You had to practise.*
	How you felt about it	*It was useful ...* *It was very difficult/easy.*
	How successful it was	*It worked in the end.* *It didn't really work.*

Reading

6 What do you think is the connection between light bulbs, crisps, bread and post-it notes? Read the text to find out.

Mistakes that work ...

People who don't make mistakes are unlikely to learn anything. The best way to learn something is to make mistakes first. Thomas Edison, who invented the light bulb, told his colleagues: 'Of the 200 light bulbs that didn't work, every failure told me something I was able to incorporate into the next attempt.' Benjamin Franklin, the US statesman and scientist once said: 'I haven't failed, I have had 10,000 ideas that didn't work.'

Both these people understood that failures and false starts are the condition of success. In fact a surprising number of everyday objects had their beginnings in a mistake or a misunderstanding. Post-it notes, packets of crisps and even bread are all unexpected inventions. In 2600 B.C., a tired Egyptian slave invented bread when the dough rose during his sleep. And crisps were first cooked by a chef in the USA when a customer complained that his fried potatoes were not thin enough.

Successful businesspeople have often made big, expensive mistakes in their past. When an employee of IBM made a mistake that cost the company $600,000, Thomas Watson, the chairman, was asked if he would fire the man. 'Of course not,' he replied. 'I have just spent $600,000 training him. I am not going to let another company benefit from his experience.'

The important thing to remember is that you need to learn from your mistakes. If you don't, then there is no sense in making them.

7 a Cover the text and try to complete the sentences. Compare your answers with a partner.

1 According to the article, the best way to learn something is to _____ mistakes first.
2 Thomas Edison invented the _____, but first he made a lot of _____.
3 Post-it notes, bread and packets of crisps were all unexpected _____.
4 An Egyptian slave invented bread by going to _____.
5 Crisps were invented by an American chef because a _____ complained that his fried potatoes were not _____ enough.
6 An employee at IBM made a mistake which _____ the company $600,000. However, his boss decided _____ to fire him because he now had lots of _____.
7 The important thing to remember is to _____ from your mistakes.

b Read the text again to check your answers.

8 Discuss.

1 Do you agree with what the text says about mistakes?
2 Give an example of a time when you did/didn't learn from your mistakes.

Lifelong learning

Learn from your mistakes!

Making mistakes can help you to improve your English. If you don't make mistakes, you probably use only very simple expressions. Be adventurous! Experiment with new grammar and vocabulary. Sometimes you need to get it wrong before you can get it right.

Grammar | subject/object questions

9 Look at the Active grammar box and complete the rules by choosing the correct alternatives.

Active grammar

Object questions

*Thomas Edison invented the **light bulb**.*
***What** did Thomas Edison invent?*

The light bulb is the <u>subject</u> /<u>object</u> of the question.

When the *Wh-* question word refers to the object of the question, we use:

Question word + auxiliary + subject + verb

***What did** Benjamin Franklin say?*

Subject questions

***Thomas Edison** invented the light bulb.*
***Who** invented the light bulb?*

Thomas Edison is the <u>subject</u> /<u>object</u> of the question.

When a *Wh-* word refers to the subject in a question we do not use the auxiliary verb. The word order is the same as the affirmative.

Subject + verb + object

***Who wrote** The Lord of the Rings?*

---

see Reference page 101

10 a Work in pairs (A + B). Write questions for the statements in Quiz A and Quiz B.

b Student A: look at the answers to Quiz A on page 146. **Student B:** look at the answers to Quiz B on page 149. Ask each other your quiz questions. Give 1 point for each correct answer.

11 In pairs, write your own quiz questions. Ask and answer the questions in groups.

Quiz A

1 A famous artist painted *Guernica* in 1937. (Who?)
2 Mozart started composing music. (When?)
3 A scientist discovered penicillin in 1928. (Who?)
4 One of the world's greatest scientists lived from 1879–1955. (Which?)
5 A famous city is nicknamed The Big Apple. (Which?)
6 Guglielmo Marconi is responsible for an invention. (What invention?)
7 This is the largest desert in the world. (Which?)
8 This man earned $34 million per day during the 1990s. (Who?)
9 This country is the oldest surviving republic in the world. (Which?)
10 Boris Becker became the youngest man ever to win the men's singles at Wimbledon. (When?)

Quiz B

1 Christopher Columbus discovered these islands in 1492, before he discovered America. (Which?)
2 An Italian artist painted the Sistine Chapel. (Who?)
3 This book made Umberto Eco famous. (What?)
4 This country has the smallest area of all European countries. (Which?)
5 David Beckham joined this team in 1993. (Which?)
6 A famous Beatle wrote the song *Imagine* in 1971. (Who?)
7 John Logie Baird invented something. (What?)
8 This is the world's longest river. (Which?)
9 One of the world's most famous writers lived from 1564–1616. (Which?)
10 Hong Kong became part of China again. (When?)

Reading and speaking

1. What can you remember about your first day at school? How did you feel? What did you do? What did you think of the teachers?

2. **a** Look at the picture below. What do you think this teacher is like?

b Now read the extract from *Matilda* by Roald Dahl. Were you right about Miss Trunchbull?

3. Mark the statements true (T) or false (F).

   1. Miss Honey reads the names of all the children.
   2. The school provides pencils for the children.
   3. All the children are new to the school.
   4. They will stay at the school for eleven years.
   5. Miss Trunchbull is the class teacher.
   6. Miss Honey tells the children how to behave in front of the headmistress.
   7. Miss Honey advises the children not to argue with each other.
   8. The children are happy about being at school.

4. Look at the words/phrases from the text and <u>underline</u> the correct definition.

   1. strict discipline (line 13): making people *obey rules/have fun*
   2. take my advice (line 14): *do what I suggest/ give me a suggestion*
   3. behave yourselves (line 14): *act like a good/ bad child*
   4. argue (line 15): *agree/disagree with someone by talking or shouting*
   5. answer back (line 16): *reply politely/rudely* (especially for children)
   6. deals severely with (line 20): *punishes/rewards*
   7. gets out of line (line 21): behaves in the *correct/incorrect* way

1   After the usual business of going through all the names of the children, Miss Honey handed out a brand-new exercise-book to each pupil.
   'You have all brought your own pencils, I hope,' she said.
5   'Yes, Miss Honey,' they chanted.
   'Good. Now this is the very first day of school for each one of you. It is the beginning of at least eleven long years of schooling that all of you are going to have to go through. And six of those years will be spent right
10   here at Crunchem Hall, where, as you know, your headmistress is Miss Trunchbull. Let me for your own good tell you something about Miss Trunchbull. She insists upon strict discipline throughout the school, and if you take my advice you will do your very best to behave
15   yourselves in her presence. Never argue with her. Never answer her back. Always do as she says. If you get on the wrong side of Miss Trunchbull she can liquidize you like a carrot in a kitchen blender. It's nothing to laugh about, Lavender. Take that grin off your face. All of
20   you will be wise to remember that Miss Trunchbull deals very severely with anyone who gets out of line in this school. Have you got the message?'
   'Yes, Miss Honey,' chirruped eighteen eager little voices.

From *Matilda* by Roald Dahl

5. **a** Complete the sentences using some of the words/phrases in Ex. 4.

   1. I didn't _____ myself when I was at school.
   2. I believe that _____ _____ is important when you are bringing up children.
   3. I think you should _____ your father's _____ . He is usually right.
   4. My brother and I _____ a lot, but we still get on well.
   5. My teacher _____ _____ with anyone who arrives late at school.

   b Change a few of the sentences so that they are true for you. Compare with a partner.

Vocabulary | teachers

6 Check you understand the meaning of the words/phrases in the box. Are they the qualities of a good or a bad teacher?

Things a teacher does	Things a teacher is
loses his/her temper	patient
shouts	boring
smiles	knowledgeable
talks slowly	understanding
asks difficult questions	inspiring
punishes students who behave badly	frightening
gives clear answers to your questions	open-minded

7 Choose the correct alternative.

1 Her classes were so *open-minded/boring/inspiring* that everyone fell asleep.

2 Our teacher is very calm. She never *talks slowly/behaves badly/loses her temper*.

3 My teacher is very *patient/knowledgeable/frightening*. He explains things many times.

4 The students know everything about the topic. They are extremely *patient/knowledgeable/open-minded*.

5 If we do stupid things, our teacher *shouts/smiles at/punishes* us.

6 When students have problems, our teacher helps them. He is very *boring/understanding/open-minded*.

7 Our teacher gets angry if we *shout/do our homework/arrive on time*.

8 My French teacher was really *inspiring/boring/frightening*. All the students wanted to speak French fluently.

Listening

8 〔7.2〕 Listen to two people discussing their teachers. Complete the information in the table.

	Subject	Good/bad qualities	Other information
Mr Halsworth			
Miss Matthews			
Madame Bouchier			
Mr Ford			

9 〔7.2〕 Listen again to check. Which expressions from Ex. 6 do they use?

Grammar | *used to* and *would*

10 a Complete the sentences (a–d) in the Active grammar box by looking at the tapescript on page 173. Then choose the correct alternatives to complete rules (1–3).

Active grammar

1 Use *used to* + verb and *would* + verb to talk about <u>single actions</u>/<u>repeated actions</u> in the past which don't happen now.
  a) *We _____ throw paper at him.* (action)
  b) *She _____ play us Mozart.* (action)

2 Only use <u>*used to* + verb</u>/<u>*would* + verb</u> to talk about states in the past.
  c) *We _____ like her lessons at all.* (state)
  NOT: ~~We wouldn't like her lessons at all.~~

3 <u>*Used to*</u>/<u>*would*</u> is usually contracted to 'd in spoken English.
  d) *We' _____ learn about the stars.*

see Reference page 101

b <u>Underline</u> other examples of *used to* and *would* in the tapescript on page 173.

11 Read the text and circle the correct form.

Going to school

I didn't (1) *used to/use to/did* like the journey to school. I (2) *wouldn't/would to/would* go by bus, but I was afraid of the other children. They were bigger than me, and they (3) *used to/wouldn't to/would to* shout at me. I always sat at the back of the bus, even though it (4) *would be/used to be/used be* the hottest place, and I (5) *wouldn't/didn't use to/would* hope that no-one could see me. It's funny to think that those boys were probably only eight years old, but I (6) *would be/used to be/used be* so frightened.

12 a Complete the sentences using *use(d) to* and a suitable verb from the box.

> live not watch be like not behave do
> not go eat

1 Did your life _____ very different when you were a child? How?
2 I _____ playing outside with my friends.
3 I _____ TV in the evenings.
4 We _____ in the countryside, but now I live in Vienna.
5 My family _____ to the seaside at the weekend.
6 Did you _____ ice cream every day?
7 My best friend at school was called Sam. We always _____ our homework together.
8 I _____ very well at school.

b Change the sentences so that they are true for you and answer the questions.

c Compare your answers with a partner.

Pronunciation

13 **7.3** Listen to the sentences. How are *used to* and *didn't use to* pronounced? Which letters are silent? Repeat the sentences.

Speaking

14 a Think about a good (or bad) teacher from your past. Use the questions to help you write a few notes.

1 What did he/she look like? What clothes did he/she use to wear?
2 What subject did he/she use to teach?
3 What did he/she use to do that was so special/bad?
4 Did all the students particularly like/dislike this teacher? Why?
5 How did this teacher treat you personally? Was he/she very different from the other teachers you had?
6 Would you like to meet him/her again? What would you say to him/her now?

b Tell other students about your teacher.

Writing

15 Look at the Writing bank on page 163 and complete the exercises.

16 Write an entry for the website below about a favourite teacher from your past.

GREAT**TEACHERS**

| Log-in | News | Events |

The College of Education is compiling stories of great teachers and the qualities that made them memorable. You can help by submitting a memory of your special teacher below.

- Your favourite teacher's name:
- What is the first characteristic that you think of when you remember this teacher?
- Describe a specific memory of this teacher:
- Describe how this teacher treated you as a student:

Grammar	modals of ability, past and present
Can do	talk about abilities in the past and present

Vocabulary | old age

1 Match the words in **bold** in sentences (1–4) to the definitions (a–f) below.

1 At what age do people **retire** in your country?

2 Do **senior citizens** get a **pension**?

3 Is it common for **elderly** people to live in **nursing homes** in your country?

4 Do young people generally **respect** the old in your country?

a) a place where old people go to live and be looked after (n)

b) old people (n)

c) old (used to describe people) (adj)

d) money you receive (from the government or your employer) after you stop working (n)

e) stop working because of your age (v)

f) treat them like important people (listen to them and appreciate them, etc.) (v)

Listening

2 [7.4] Listen to three people discussing three of the questions in Ex. 1. Which questions do they talk about?

Part 1: _____

Part 2: _____

Part 3: _____

3 [7.4] Listen to the conversations again and circle the correct phrase.

1 In Ghana, old people *are involved in family decisions /often ask their children for help*.

2 In England, old people *can do some things for free /have to pay the same as young people*.

3 When people get old in Ghana, they *live in nursing homes /live with extended family*.

4 Nursing homes in England *can be very good/ are usually very bad*.

5 In Africa, old people usually *retire at 65 /don't retire*.

4 In groups, discuss the questions in Ex. 1.

Reading

5 **a** Read the texts about some remarkable people. Work in pairs. **Student A:** read the texts below. **Student B:** turn to page 150. As you read, make notes about the following:

> Name   age   activity/achievement
> personal philosophy/attitude to being old

b Tell your partner about the three people.

It's never too late ...

Ella Scotchmer, 104

Ella took up solo travelling at the age of 96, touring the USA for three months on a Greyhound bus. She enjoys dancing, and has recently taken up tai chi.

'I don't think I look my age, so people don't believe I'm 104. Up until a couple of years ago, I was still bowling and swimming and doing all manner of things. I can't remember how many cruises I've been on since I turned 100. I've done the Norwegian fjords, the Canaries, the Caribbean. In the future, I'd still like to go to Mexico, and I haven't been to Malta or Gibraltar yet. I'll just have to wait and see what happens.'

'I don't think I look my age, so people don't believe I'm 104.'

Elizabeth Collins, 94

Elizabeth Collins is the wife of the famous British artist Cecil Collins, but she is also an artist herself. In her nineties, she was able to sell some work to the Tate Gallery, London.

'When my husband died eight years ago it made work easier – although in some ways much harder. Alone, you can easily get into a negative hole. But I think my painting now is wiser, more understanding about life, and innocent. It's not about being old; you paint when you have time or possibility. I have that possibility now. I've thought of dying quite a lot. I like the idea. But it's got to be the right time. I walk into the traffic all the time without looking. I could get hit but I don't. Obviously, it's not the right time for me yet.'

6 Discuss.

1 At what age is someone 'old'?

2 Do you know any very active elderly people?

3 Are you inspired by them or by the people in the texts?

4 What would you like to be doing when you are old?

7 Complete the sentences below with the phrases from the box.

> (a) managed to run   (b) could swim
> (c) was able to continue   (d) could sing
> (e) wasn't able to finish her studies
> (f) couldn't write seriously

1 Ella Scotchmer _____ and do many other activities until recently.

2 When Louisa May was younger she _____ at the Royal Academy because her father died.

3 Elizabeth Collins _____ painting after her husband died.

4 Before the age of 70 Mary Wesley _____ because she was looking after her family.

5 Max Jones _____ a 54-mile Ultra-Marathon in South Africa.

6 Kyra Vane _____ beautifully when she was younger.

Max Jones, 71

Aged 71, Max Jones managed to finish the Comrades Ultra-Marathon of 54 miles in South Africa in 10 hours 39 minutes. He ran his 100th marathon In April 1999.

'I train for half an hour every day – that's about 2,000 miles a year. I don't consider it old to be 71. I don't know if I could live without running. Every time I come to grief in a marathon, my family beg me not to continue with it but I say there are two kinds of serious runner – the injured and the severely injured. You have to get your priorities right. Now I'm retired, they are the family, the dog, then running.'

Grammar | modals of ability

8 Read the sentences in Ex. 7 and complete the Active grammar box with the words/phrases from the box.

> could   were able to   couldn't   can't
> weren't able to   didn't manage to

Active grammar

To describe general ability in the present, we say :

➕ : *I **can** swim.*

➖ : *She _____ play the violin.*

To describe general ability in the past, we say:

When I was/we were young ...

➕ : *We _____ climb trees.*
: *I **was able to** dance for hours.*

➖ : *I **couldn't** drive.*
: *We _____ speak French.*

To describe something that happened at a particular moment in the past, we say:

Yesterday ...

➕ : *They _____ finish their work.*
: *I **managed to** book the holiday.*

➖ : *She **wasn't able to** go to the meeting.*
: *They _____ find a hotel.*
: *He _____ visit his friends.*

see Reference page 101

9 Rewrite the sentences using the words in brackets. Write 2–4 words.

1 In 1994 John Parr finally climbed Mount Everest after eight attempts. (managed)
John Parr finally _____ Mount Everest in 1994.

2 When he was a child Orgosky was already a composer. (able)
Orgosky _____ write music when he was a child.

3 We didn't go. The weather was bad. (weren't)
We _____ because of the bad weather.

4 He wasn't able to meet his friends. (couldn't)
He _____ his friends.

5 I wasn't able to buy the cards because the shop was closed. (manage)
I _____ the cards because the shop was closed.

10 Correct the sentences.

1 I didn't manage finish my homework.

2 We couldn't to eat out because we had no money.

3 Were you able to sleeping last night?

4 Did you managed to speak to Shen Yung last night?

5 When he was younger he could spoke four languages.

6 I was ability to call for help on my mobile phone.

7 How was you manage to work with all that noise yesterday?

8 Was she able pay her bills last month?

Pronunciation

11 **7·5** Listen to the recording and tick (✓) the sentence you hear.

1 a) I could do it. ☐
  b) I couldn't do it. ☐

2 a) He was able to stop. ☐
  b) He wasn't able to stop. ☐

3 a) I could run fast. ☐
  b) I couldn't run fast. ☐

4 a) They were able to play. ☐
  b) They weren't able to play. ☐

5 a) We could see it. ☐
  b) We couldn't see it. ☐

6 a) Were you able to go? ☐
  b) Weren't you able to go? ☐

Person to person

12 Discuss.

1 What can you do now that you couldn't do ten years ago? *I can speak English.*

2 What important or difficult things were you able to do last week/last month/last year? *I was able to ...*

3 What important or difficult things didn't you manage to do last week (or last month/ last year)? *I didn't manage to ...*

Speaking

13 Ask a partner about his/her abilities. Tick (✓) the appropriate columns in the table and note any extra information.

'Can you run five kilometres?' 'I can't now, but I could a few years ago.'

	CAN DO NOW	COULD IN THE PAST BUT CAN'T NOW	WAS ABLE TO/ MANAGED TO ONCE	EXTRA INFORMATION (WHEN/WHAT/ WHERE, ETC.)
Run five kilometres				
Make a cake				
Swim for one hour				
Play a musical instrument				
Ride a horse				
Stay up all night				
Sing three songs in English				
Touch your toes (not bending your knees!)				
Throw with your 'wrong' hand				

7 | Vocabulary

Idioms about learning

1 a Which subjects do you associate with the sentences below?

1 I read five novels a week. I'm a complete **bookworm**. *Literature*

2 **I haven't got a clue** about Algebra. _____

3 I **picked up** a lot of new words when I visited Poland last summer. _____

4 The question about bacteria was so difficult. I just **made a wild guess**. _____

5 I had to **learn** the dates of Kings and Queens **by heart**. _____

6 I **know** Puccini's operas **inside out**. _____

7 I need to **brush up on** the theories of Nietzsche and Sartre. _____

8 Simon always gets good grades for his paintings. He's **the teacher's pet**. _____

9 My teacher **gave me a hand** with my essay about African deserts. _____

b Match the words in **bold** in Ex. 1a to the definitions below.

a) helped someone ☐

b) memorise ☐

c) don't know anything about ☐

d) study something again to try and remember it ☐

e) the teacher's favourite student ☐

f) know a subject or topic very well ☐

g) a person who reads a lot of books ☐

h) gave an answer without thinking about it (the answer may be completely wrong) ☐

i) learned something without trying ☐

2 Which idioms do the pictures illustrate?

3 Choose the best alternative.

1 She didn't study this, so she *hasn't got a clue/ knows it inside out*.

2 I know how to say the Portuguese alphabet because I've *made a wild guess/learned it by heart*.

3 He'd never played baseball but he *picked up/ brushed up* a lot of tips by watching it on TV.

4 She read all the works of Shakespeare in one month. What a *teacher's pet/bookworm*!

4 Correct the sentences.

1 This is too difficult for me. Can you give a hand?

2 I have to brush on up my German before I go to Austria.

3 We learned all the Maths formulas to heart.

4 She asked him a difficult question so he did a wild guess.

5 I picked up on some Chinese when I was in Beijing last year.

6 She knows inside the poems of Sylvia Plath out.

7 I understand the question but I haven't got the clue how to answer it.

8 He always brings presents for the teacher. He's the pet's teacher.

9 You read all the time! I've never met such a booksworm.

5 Choose five of the sentences to complete so that they are true for you.

1 I know _____ inside out.

2 I haven't got a clue about _____.

3 I picked up some _____.

4 I sometimes make a wild guess if _____.

5 I've learned _____ by heart.

6 I know a bookworm called _____. He/ She reads _____.

7 I need to brush up on _____.

8 The teacher's pet in my _____ class was _____.

9 The last time I gave someone a hand was _____.

6 Compare your sentences with other students. Ask at least one follow-up question for every sentence you hear.

1   **a** **7.6** Listen to a childhood story. Which photo illustrates the story?

b Read the questions below. Answer as many as possible. Tell a partner.

1   How old was the speaker?
2   What was the background to the story (what happened before it)?
3   Who was involved?
4   Where did the story happen?
5   How was the scene described (weather, time of day)?
6   What happened?
7   How did the speaker feel?
8   What happened afterwards?
9   Did the speaker learn anything from it?

c Listen again to check.

d Look at the tapescript on page 174. Find words/expressions that we use to:

1   show the moment when the story starts _____ _____
2   return to the main story (after making a comment) _____
3   say something happened quickly and unexpectedly _____ _____ _____ _____
4   say something happened after a long time _____
5   say it's something (she) will always remember _____ _____ _____ _____

2   Follow the instructions below.

1   Think of two stories from your schooldays, or when you were young. Look at the questions in Ex. 1b and make notes.
2   Now invent another story about your schooldays which is NOT true. Think about the questions in Ex. 1b and make notes.
3   Prepare to speak about your stories.
4   Tell another student your stories. Answer their questions. Can they guess which story is not true?
5   Listen to another student's stories. Ask questions to find out which story is not true.

Subject/object questions

Object questions

When a *Wh-* question word is the object of the question, we use the normal question word order:

Form: question word + auxiliary + subject + verb

Who did you shout at?

What did you buy?

Most questions that we ask are object questions.

Subject questions

When a *Wh-* question word is the subject of the question, the word order is the same as an affirmative sentence (there is no 'inversion' and we don't use an auxiliary verb).

Form: question word + verb + object

Who shouted at you? (NOT: ~~Who did shout at you?~~)

What happened? (NOT: ~~What did happen?~~)

Used to/would

*I **used to** live in Rome.*

*She **didn't use to** like olives.*

*She **wouldn't** return my phone calls.*

***Did** you **use to** live in Italy? Yes, I did./No, I didn't.*

***Would** your parents tell you off for shouting?*

! There is no 'd' in the spelling of *use to* in negatives and questions.

*We didn't **use to** like our teacher.*

*Did you **use to** study art?*

Use *used to* to talk about past habits and states which are no longer true. Use *would* to talk about past habits only.

*They **used to/would** meet every day.* (past habit)

*I **used to** love him.* NOT: ~~I would love him.~~ (past state)

Use the Past Simple, not *used to*, to describe how long something lasted.

I worked in Italy for five years. NOT: ~~I used to work in Italy for five years.~~

Use the Past Simple, not *used to/would*, to talk about a single event in the past.

I broke my leg skiing. NOT: ~~I used to break my leg skiing.~~

Use the Present Simple, not *used to*, to talk about habits which are true now.

I usually play football three times a week.

Modals of ability

Use *can* + verb to describe general ability in the present.

*I **can** swim but I **can't** dive.*

Use *could* + verb to describe general ability in the past.

*I **could** speak French but I **couldn't** speak German when I was at school.*

Use *was able to* to talk about general ability in the past or a particular situation in the past.

*I **was able to** swim twenty kilometres when I was younger.*

*I **was able to** save up and buy the car that I wanted.*

If we want to emphasise that the action is difficult, we can use *manage to* in the present or past.

*I usually **manage to** visit forty countries every year.*

*I **managed to** finish the book but it was very boring.*

In the negative we can use *couldn't, wasn't able to*, and *didn't manage to* for one particular moment.

*I **couldn't** book the tickets.*

*I **wasn't able to** book the tickets.*

*I **didn't manage to** book the tickets.*

Key vocabulary

Learning

get good marks/a degree   take an exam/a course/notes/a subject   do a degree/an exam/a course/some research/a subject   pass an exam/a subject   fail an exam/subject   revise notes/a subject   go to lectures/to class   graduate from university   make a mistake/progress/notes   a fast learner   learn by doing   throw someone in at the deep end   a strict teacher   practice makes perfect   learn by heart   a steep learning curve   pick (something) up   bring someone up to (do something)

Teachers

lose one's temper   shout   smile   talk slowly   ask difficult questions   punish students who behave badly   give clear answers to your questions   patient   boring   knowledgeable   understanding   inspiring   frightening   open-minded

Old age

retire   senior citizens   elderly   pension   nursing home   respect

Learning words/idioms

know (something) inside out   haven't got a clue   make a wild guess   learn (something) by heart   give (someone) a hand   brush up on   bookworm   the teacher's pet

1 Make questions using the words in brackets.

Something went wrong. (what?)

What went wrong?

1 Somebody phoned me last night. (who?)
2 He gets the train at 18.00. (when?)
3 Maria taught her to play the piano. (who?)
4 He failed the exam. (why?)
5 Something fell on the floor. (what?)
6 An old man lives in that house. (who?)
7 She ran into one of the offices. (which?)
8 They met at a party. (how?)

2 Complete the sentences with *used to* and a suitable verb from the box.

> dream ~~wake up~~ stay study have spend read go out love stay get

When I was a child, I used to <u>wake up</u> at 5.30 in the morning, and want to get up. My mother (1)_____ very angry if we went into her bedroom before it was light. So we (2)_____ in bed and sing songs until she came to get us. We didn't (3)_____ much for breakfast, just a piece of toast and glass of milk.

I (4)_____ going to school, and playing with all my friends. We didn't (5)_____ very much, and our exam results were never very good.

At weekends, I (6)_____ a lot of time at home. We didn't (7)_____ much, instead we (8)_____ at home and help my mother. My father (9)_____ the newspaper, and watch the sport on television. I (10)_____ of being a famous footballer.

3 Correct the mistakes in six of the sentences

Alice used read books to her sister.

Alice used to read books ...

1 Sam use to smoke but now he has given up.
2 He didn't use to go to the gym, but now he has started going every week.
3 Tomas would to go to the market every day with his father.
4 Emil used love riding horses on the beach.
5 They'd leave the keys in the door so I could open it.
6 Tom didn't use have a girlfriend, but now he has lots!
7 Myra used to being a dancer when she was younger.
8 She would dance for me one time when I came to visit.

4 Choose the correct alternatives.

We *could/managed not to/weren't able to* meet. I was too busy.

1 When he was ten, he *could/manage to/was able* answer difficult Mathematics questions.
2 I lost my passport but luckily I *managed to/could/can* find it before my holiday.
3 He *was able to/wasn't able to/didn't manage* get the job because he failed the exam.
4 I *can't/could/manage to* ski well before I broke my leg last year.
5 It wasn't easy to pass my driving test but eventually I *could/managed to/am able to*.
6 Unfortunately, we *could/aren't able to/managed to* give refunds for broken items.
7 I *manage to/was able to/can't* speak German because when I left Germany I was a baby.
8 He *didn't manage to/could/couldn't* draw when he was young, but now he's an artist.

5 Complete the school reports by choosing the correct word (a, b, c or d).

Megan Bradman   **Form: 7BI**

Megan worked hard in History this term. She did very well in the final exam, and she knows the key events (1) <u>inside out</u>. She just needs to (2)_____ up on her dates. Megan reads a lot – she is a real (3)_____! – and this has helped her pick (4)_____ a lot of information about the subject. An excellent term!

Dorothy Miller   **Form: 7TG**

Dorothy got 5% in her final exam, and she clearly hasn't got a (5)_____ about Geography. In the exam, she made several (6)_____ guesses about fairly easy questions. Some of the facts are easy to (7)_____ by heart, and she needs to do this quickly. Myself and the other students can (8)_____ her a hand, but Dorothy must work.

---

1 (a) perfect (b) *inside out* (c) inside (d) up and down
2 (a) push (b) work (c) study (d) brush
3 (a) bookie (b) bookkeeper (c) bookworm (d) book reader
4 (a) up (b) on (c) to (d) over
5 (a) idea (b) hope (c) knowledge (d) clue
6 (a) errors (b) mad (c) wild (d) crazy
7 (a) study (b) memorise (c) know (d) learn
8 (a) give (b) take (c) help (d) get

8 | Change

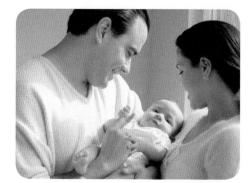

Lead-in

1 Discuss.

1 What life changes can you see in the photos?

2 What are the most/least dramatic changes in your opinion?

2 <u>Underline</u> the words and phrases which go with the verb *change*.

> an arrangement   time   your mind   your head   your clothes
> your hairstyle   your happiness   career   some money
> your password   talking   the subject

3 **a** Read the dialogues.

1 **A:** The sun is shining! **B:** That **makes a change**.

2 **A:** Let's go to a different restaurant. **B:** Yes, **it's time for a change**.

3 **A:** Why did you cancel your wedding? **B:** I **had a change of heart**.

4 **A:** Shall we take the car? **B:** No. Let's walk **for a change**.

b Complete the sentences so they are true for you.

It was time for a change, so I ...

I was planning to ... but I had a change of heart.

Last week/month/year I ... . It made a nice change.

This weekend I think I'll ... for a change.

c Read your sentences in groups. Tell the class about the most interesting changes.

Speaking

1 Discuss.

1 Why is New York City famous? Think about the people, the lifestyle, how New York City appears in films, etc.

2 What was New York City like a few years ago/a hundred years ago? How do you think it has changed?

3 Have you ever been to New York City? Would you like to go/go back? Why/Why not?

4 Do you know any other names for New York City?

Reading

2 Read about some changes in New York City. Which of your ideas from question 2 above are mentioned?

3 Read the text again. Mark the statements true (T) or false (F)?

1 Some activities have recently become illegal in New York. ☐

2 It is now illegal to smoke or drink alcohol anywhere in New York. ☐

3 Eating sandwiches in the park is illegal. ☐

4 The police like the new laws. ☐

5 It is illegal to sleep on the subway. ☐

6 Elle and Serge Schroitman were fined because they parked in the wrong place. ☐

7 The editor of *Vanity Fair* magazine thinks some of the new laws are stupid. ☐

8 Some people like the new laws. ☐

9 New York is now clean and safe compared to in the past. ☐

The Forbidden Apple

New York used to be the city that never sleeps. These days it's the city that never smokes, drinks or does anything naughty (at least, not in public). The Big Apple is quickly turning into the Forbidden Apple.

If you wanted a glass of wine with your picnic in Central Park, could you have one? No chance. Drinking alcohol in public isn't allowed. If you decided to feed the birds with the last crumbs of your sandwich, you could be arrested. It's illegal. If you went to a bar for a drink and a cigarette, that would be OK, wouldn't it? Er ... no. You can't smoke in public in New York City.

What's going on? Why is the city that used to be so open-minded becoming like this? The mayor of New York is behind it all. He has brought in a whole lot of new laws to stop citizens from doing what they want, when they want.

The press are scandalised[1]. Even the New York police have joined the argument. They recently spent $100,000 on a 'Don't blame the cop[2]' campaign. One New York police officer said, 'We raise money for the city by giving people fines for breaking some very stupid laws. It's all about money.'

The result is a lot of fines for minor offences. Yoav Kashida, an Israeli tourist, fell asleep on the subway. When he woke up, two police officers fined him because he had fallen asleep on two seats (you mustn't use two seats in the subway). Elle and Serge Schroitman were fined for blocking a driveway with their car. It was their own driveway.

The angry editor of *Vanity Fair* magazine, Graydon Carter, says, 'Under New York City law it is acceptable to keep a gun in your place of work, but not an empty ashtray.' He should know. The police came to his office and took away his ashtray.

But not all of New York's inhabitants are complaining. Marcia Dugarry, 72, said, 'The city has changed for the better. If more cities had these laws, America would be a better place to live.' Nixon Patotkis, 38, a barman, said, 'I like the new laws. If people smoked in here, we'd go home smelling of cigarettes.'

Recent figures show that New York now has fewer crimes per 100,000 people than 193 other US cities. And it's true – it's safer, cleaner and more healthy than before. But let's be honest – who goes to New York for its clean streets?

> **Glossary**
> [1] *scandalised (adj)* = shocked/angry
> [2] *cop (noun)* = police officer (US English)

4 Discuss.

1 What is the writer's attitude to the new laws in New York, and to the mayor? Is the article 100% serious? How do you know?

2 Do you think the laws in the article are 'stupid'?

3 Would these laws be popular in your country?

4 Should smoking be banned in all public places?

5 Which is more important – individual freedom, or health and safety for everyone?

Grammar | Second Conditional

5 Read the Active grammar box and choose the correct alternatives.

Active grammar

*If more cities **had** these laws, America **would** be a better place to live.*

*If people **smoked** in here, we'**d** go home smelling of cigarettes.*

1 Use the Second Conditional to describe an imaginary situation /a real situation in the present or future and its result.

2 In the *if* clause, use the Present Simple / the Past Simple.

3 In the result clause, *would* (or *'d*) is used because the situation is in the past / imaginary (hypothetical).

4 It is possible to use a modal verb such as *could* or *might* instead of *would*, if you are certain /not sure of the result.

First and Second Conditional:

In a real situation use the First Conditional / Second Conditional.

In a hypothetical situation use the First Conditional /Second Conditional.

The First Conditional /Second Conditional uses the Present Simple + *will*.

The First Conditional /Second Conditional uses the Past Simple + *would*.

see Reference page 115

6 Make Second Conditional sentences using the verbs in brackets.

1 If you _____ (be) a New York police officer, _____ (arrest) someone for feeding birds?

2 I _____ (not like) the new laws if I _____ (live) in New York.

3 Where _____ (go) if you _____ (want) a cigarette at work?

4 If the laws _____ (not make) money, they _____ (not exist).

5 I _____ (not be) very happy if I _____ (have to) pay a fine for using two subway seats.

6 If New York _____ (not have) these laws, tourists _____ (find) it dangerous and dirty.

7 If these laws _____ (exist) in your country, _____ (be) popular?

8 There _____ (be) less crime if the police _____ (have) more power in my country.

7 Talk to a partner. Are the situations in the box real/possible situations in your life or imaginary? In what circumstances *would/ will* you:

lie to a police officer   miss my English lesson
live in another country   go away next weekend
stay in bed until 12.00p.m.   take a taxi
make a long distance phone call
write to the government   sing in public
run a marathon/five km

I would lie to a police officer if I was a criminal!
I will miss my English lesson if I have too much to do at work.

Pronunciation

8 **a** 8.1 Underline the word you hear.

1 A: Where *would/will* you go with all that money?
B: To Hawaii.

2 A: She's got four brothers, hasn't she?
B: I *didn't/wouldn't* know that. I don't know her very well.

3 A: So who wants to do the shopping?
B: *I'll/I'd* do it, but I have to do my homework.

4 A: Is it possible to get some help? The job *wouldn't/won't* take very long with three of us.
B: You're asking for help? That makes a change!

b Practise the dialogues with a partner.

Speaking and listening

9 a Work in groups. If you could propose five new laws for your town, what would they be?

b Tell the class about your laws/proposals and together, choose the five best.

'If we could propose one new law, we'd stop cars from entering the city centre.'

10 a ▶8.2 Listen to four speakers talking about things they would like to change about their city. Match the speaker to a subject: a) noise, b) buildings, c) pollution or d) disabled facilities.

1 Gabriel (Mexico City) _____
2 Luciana (São Paulo) _____
3 Clive (Manchester) _____
4 Olivia (Naples) _____

b Listen again. Complete the extracts below.

1 Mexico City has too many cars, _____ it's really polluted. So, if I could change one thing, I'd have a law against all the traffic. I'd stop cars from going into the city centre.

2 I'd improve the facilities for disabled people. People in wheelchairs have real problems _____ _____ the roads and pavements. Even in public buildings sometimes there are no elevators _____ they can't use the rooms on the higher floors.

3 There's no peace and quiet here. All the noise and mess is _____ _____ these students. They scream and shout every night. _____ I would make some new laws against all the noise so we could get some sleep!

4 _____ _____ the stupid laws here, everybody builds these terrible buildings. They are really ugly, _____ _____ the city isn't so beautiful these days. If I was mayor, I would pass a law to stop these buildings.

c Check with the tapescript on page 174.

11 a Read the How to ... box. Put the formal expressions below in the correct place.

1 *Therefore, ...*
2 *This leads to* (+ noun or gerund) *...*
3 *As a result of* (+ noun) *...*
4 *As a result, ...*

b In written English which words or expressions can start a sentence? Which words/expressions can join two clauses?

c Complete the sentences.

1 Tourists love Venice, so ...
2 London is very expensive, which means ...
3 Many travellers like Brazil because of ...
4 Parts of Africa are very hot. Therefore, ...
5 As a result of ..., Saudi Arabia is a rich country.
6 Many tourists don't understand the culture of the countries they visit. This leads to ...
7 English is the language of tourism. As a result, ...
8 The pollution in many cities is caused by ...

Writing

12 a Read the article in the Writing bank on page 164 and do the exercises.

b Choose one of the laws you proposed in Ex. 9. Write an article for a newspaper about the issue you'd like to change.

Grammar	adverbs
Can do	talk about change/lack of change

Vocabulary | global issues

1 1 What can you see in the photo?
   2 Do you think this is an effective way to initiate change?
   3 Can you think of other ways?

2 Put the words and phrases in the box in pairs. They may be opposites or have similar meanings.

problems – solutions

> developed countries   lifestyle   famine
> security   war   disease   ~~problems~~
> crime   the environment   peace   pollution
> standard of living   developing countries
> ~~solutions~~   starvation   cure

3 **a** Use the words and phrases to fill the gaps.
   1 A lot of _____ is caused by factories and cars. This damages _____ _____. What should be done about it?
   2 Many African countries suffer from _____ when it doesn't rain for a long time. This causes _____. How can we help?
   3 Do you think scientists will find the _____ for many _____, such as cancer?
   4 _____ _____, like the G8 nations, give millions of dollars every year to _____ _____. Is this enough?
   5 Is it right for children to fight when their country is at _____. Would you protest and demand _____?

   b Discuss the questions in pairs.

Lifelong learning

Put them in pairs!

When you record new vocabulary, try writing words in pairs. It may help you to remember them.

Use **opposites** (e.g. problem/solution), **similar meanings** (lifestyle/standard of living), **collocations** (terrorist attack, solve problems).

Listening and speaking

4 **8.3** Listen to two people discussing how the world has changed since they were children. Which issues in Ex. 2 do they talk about?

5 **8.3** Listen again and tick the phrases you hear from the How to ... box.

HOW TO ...	talk about change/lack of change	
	Talk about change	It has got better/worse. The situation (in ...) has deteriorated/improved. (Laws) have become more/ less ...
	Talk about lack of change	... is/are still ... ... is/are the same ... The situation ... hasn't changed.
	Express your attitude towards the change	Luckily, ... Unfortunately, ... (Not) surprisingly, ... Interestingly, ...

6 **a** Work in groups. Group 1: write five things that have made the world better in the last 25 years. Group 2: write five things that have made the world worse in the last 25 years

Group 1 (optimists): *The standard of living has improved in most countries.*

Group 2 (pessimists): *There are new diseases which don't have cures.*

b Read your sentences to the other group. Respond with a more optimistic or pessimistic point of view!

Reading

7 **a** Describe the photos and write down the following:

  1 three things you know about the Live 8/Live Aid concerts.

  2 three things you would like to know about the Live 8/Live Aid concerts (write questions).

  b Read the text to find out/check your information. Compare your information with a partner.

3 July 2005

'Are you ready to start a revolution? Are you ready to change history?' ...

These were the words of Madonna as she walked onto the stage of the London Live 8 concert. On 3rd July 2005, Live 8 concerts were held in ten cities around the globe. The idea was to highlight the problem of poverty in Africa. Hundreds of millions of people around the world watched the concerts on their televisions. But how did this all start?

The day that rock and roll really changed the world was twenty years earlier, on 13 July 1985, and all because of one man, Bob Geldof. On that day more than a billion and a half people around the world united together to watch the biggest rock concert ever held – Live Aid.

30 million people were suffering in a terrible famine in sub-Saharan Africa. It was an event so completely shocking – happening on our television screens, with children dying in front of our eyes – that it moved everyone who saw it. The concert raised £140 million.

Live Aid was a miracle – technologically, emotionally and politically. It is difficult now to understand what an amazing achievement it was to broadcast the first live,

all-day, multi-artist concert to the whole world. In 1985 there were no mobile phones and hardly any fax machines. In many countries international phone calls usually had to be booked, sometimes hours in advance. Computers were outside the experience of most ordinary people. Email was a future dream.

Yet surprisingly, simultaneous concerts on two continents were co-ordinated. Global television schedules were cleared. Concorde was put on stand-by. Even the Space Shuttle astronauts lined up to make a contribution. Live Aid started new ways of thinking and behaving – in broadcasting, in putting political pressure on governments and in raising money. Nowadays, these have become normal as more and more charities regularly use music as an instrument for change.

Bob Geldof, the organiser of Live Aid and Live 8, saw an opportunity. He wanted to make governments and people do something important to change the terrible situation. He used what he says is 'the lingua franca of the planet – not English but rock 'n' roll', and it was a fantastic success.

Live Aid was one of the first indications that we now lived in a globalised world. Interestingly, its language was music, and the message it delivered so loudly and clearly was of the need for change.

8 What is the significance of the following words/phrases/numbers. Tell a partner.

> one and a half billion people   famine
> £140 million   a miracle   mobile phones/
> computers   ten   the lingua franca
> new ways of thinking   the need for change
> simultaneous concerts   put on stand-by

9 Answer the questions with a partner.

  1 Do you think Live Aid and Live 8 were successful?

  2 Have you heard of or been to other charity events or concerts? What did you think of them?

  3 If you organised a concert like this, what would you raise the money for? Why?

  4 Do you agree that 'music is an instrument for change'?

Grammar | adverbs

10 a Read the Active grammar box and match the example sentences (1–4) to the rules (a–d).
b Choose the correct <u>underlined</u> alternative to complete the rules.

1 *International phone calls usually had to be booked.*
2 *Surprisingly, simultaneous concerts on two continents were co-ordinated.*
3 *... the message it delivered so loudly and clearly ...*
4 *It was an event so completely shocking ...*

Active grammar

To make an adverb we usually add *-ly* to the adjective. *quiet – quietly clear – clearly*

a) Adverbs of manner modify verbs. They describe the way in which something happens.
*She talked **quietly**. Drive **carefully**!*
Sentence: ____
These adverbs usually come <u>before</u> / <u>after</u> the verb.

b) Adverbs of frequency/probability describe how often something happens or how probable it is.
*She **usually** comes to my house on Fridays. She will **probably** arrive at six o'clock.*
Sentence: ____
These usually come <u>before</u> / <u>after</u> the main verb.

c) Adverbs of degree make a verb weaker or stronger. They may be used for emphasis.
*I **really** want to leave now. I'm **completely** confused.*
Sentence: ____
These usually come <u>before</u> / <u>after</u> the main verb.

d) Adverbs may also be used as discourse markers to **describe your attitude**.
***Interestingly**, she didn't phone back. **Surprisingly**, he waited until the bus had left.*
Sentence: ____
These often come at the <u>beginning</u> / <u>end</u> of the sentence.

see Reference page 115

11 a Match the adverbs in the box to their uses.

> (un)fortunately basically obviously hopefully actually (not) surprisingly definitely personally

1 ____ when something good or lucky happens
2 ____ when something is not as you would expect
3 ____ what you hope will happen
4 ____ in my opinion
5 ____ when talking about the real situation
6 ____ when describing something simply
7 ____ without any doubt
8 ____ when describing something you can understand easily

b Delete the adverb which **cannot** be used in the sentences below.

1 I will *hopefully/surprisingly/definitely* contact you as soon as we have any news.
2 *Personally/Actually/Definitely*, I am not sure that is the best plan.
3 *Hopefully/Personally/Fortunately*, Xavier will meet us at the stadium.
4 I understand the problems, but *actually/hopefully/unfortunately* I can't help.
5 The office is in a terrible mess. They *obviously/definitely/hopefully* left in a hurry.
6 The school has very few books, so *not surprisingly/fortunately/obviously* the exam results are poor.
7 *Personally/Hopefully/Actually*, I would like to thank you for all your hard work.
8 I would love to go to Africa, but *actually/personally/unfortunately* my boyfriend hates travelling.

Person to person

12 a Discuss in groups.
1 Which continent has the most people?
2 What percentage of the world's people don't have enough food to eat?
3 What percentage live in houses without running water and electricity?
4 What percentage of people can read/have been to university/own a computer?

b Check the answers to the questions on page 150. Did you find any of the facts surprising/interesting/shocking? Discuss in pairs.

Personally, I was most surprised by ...

Vocabulary and speaking

1 Read the problem and discuss the solutions with a partner.

Your life,
your decisions ...

This week's problem

Linda is in her mid-thirties. She has worked in a big city bank for 12 years but isn't happy in her work. She doesn't like the people she works with, or the long hours she has to work. She feels that she doesn't spend enough time with her three young children, and her elderly mother. She has always wanted to have her own business and she is very interested in fashion. Her husband earns enough money for the whole family. What do you think Linda should do?

A Leave her job and spend more time at home looking after her children and her mother.

B Leave her job and try to start her own fashion business.

C Keep her job but try to find more time to spend with her family.

D Ask if she can work part-time.

Or do you have a better idea? Write to us with your suggestions. The best answers will be published in next week's edition.

2 Discuss.

1 Are you good or bad at making decisions?

2 If you have an important decision to make, do you talk to anyone about it? Who?

3 Have you made any of the following decisions in your life? Choose three or four and make some notes in the table. Then, tell your partner about what happened. Listen to your partner's decisions and make notes in the table.

DECISION	YOU When/where? Why?	YOUR PARTNER Easy/difficult?
1 choose subjects to study at school		
2 leave school/your home/country		
3 go to university		
4 buy or sell a house/flat		
5 have a baby or start a family		
6 start or change your career		
7 start your own business		
8 leave a job		
9 take up or give up a hobby/sport		
10 retire or give up work		

Listening

3 **a** [8.4] Listen to these people talking about important decisions they have taken. Write the name of the speaker (Tunde, Sarah or Roger) under their photo. Which decisions from Ex. 2 do they talk about?

A

_____

B

_____

C

_____

b Listen again. Who says these phrases? Write the letter R (Roger), T (Tunde) or S (Sarah).

1 'I stopped work a year ago ...'

2 'My family wanted me to work in the family business ...'

3 'All I thought about was making money for my family.'

4 'We ... sold our house, left our jobs, and said good-bye to our friends.'

5 'I had always dreamed of going to study in another country ...'

6 '... it changed our world completely.'

7 '... we just fell in love with the house the moment we saw it.'

8 '... maybe I'll change career and start my own business.'

9 'I met my fiancée, Nancy, here, and we are planning to get married ...'

c Check your answers in the tapescript on page 174.

d Which speaker do you think had the most difficult decision to make? Why? Tell a partner.

Grammar | Third Conditional

4 **a** Read the sentences and answer the questions.

If I had stayed at work, I wouldn't have spent time with Jack when he really needed me.

1 Did Roger stay at work?

2 Did he spend time with Jack?

I wouldn't have met Nancy if I hadn't come to France!

3 Did Tunde come to France?

4 Did he meet Nancy?

b Look at the Active grammar box and choose the correct alternative to complete the rule.

Active grammar

Use the Third Conditional to talk about a real /hypothetical situation in the present/past.

Form the Third Conditional with:

If + subject + past perfect + *would(n't) have/could(n't) have* + past participle.

If I had stayed at work, I wouldn't have spent time with Jack.
Past condition   Past result (hypothetical)

or

I would've cooked dinner, if I'd known you were coming.
Past result (hypothetical)   Past condition

In spoken English, *have* and *had* are usually contracted to *'ve* and *'d* (see example above).

see Reference page 115

5 **a** Match the sentence beginnings (1–8) with the endings (a–h).

1 If I had known the test was today,

2 I wouldn't have missed the last train

3 If I'd known it was you on the phone,

4 If you'd asked me out to dinner,

5 I wouldn't have felt so tired this morning

6 If I hadn't gone on holiday to Greece,

7 I would have organised a party for you

8 I wouldn't have spent so much time with my children

a) if I'd gone to bed earlier.

b) I'd have said 'yes'.

c) I would have done some revision.

d) if I'd known you were coming.

e) I would've answered it.

f) if I hadn't stopped work.

g) if I had left home earlier.

h) I wouldn't have met my husband.

b 【8.5】 Listen and check.

6 Write Third Conditional sentences using the prompts.

I didn't know Mary was ill.
I didn't send her any flowers.

If I had known Mary was ill, I would have sent her flowers.

1 Taxis were very expensive. We didn't take one.
2 They didn't ask anyone for directions. They got lost.
3 The weather wasn't very good. We didn't enjoy the holiday very much.
4 It was raining. They crashed the car.
5 I didn't see you when you passed me in the street. I didn't say 'hello'.
6 I wasn't hungry. I didn't eat lunch.
7 I didn't know that Eva had to get up early. I didn't wake her.
8 I didn't like my History teacher. I gave up History.

Pronunciation

7 **a** **8.6** Listen to this sentence. Which words are contracted?

If I had left home earlier, I wouldn' t have missed the train.

b Listen to the rhythm of the sentence. Do the stressed words fall with a regular beat in the sentence?

8 **a** **8.7** Underline the stressed words in these sentences.

1 If I'd known the test was today, I would've done some revision.
2 If I'd gone to bed earlier, I wouldn't've felt so tired.
3 If you'd asked me out to dinner, I'd've said 'yes'.

b Listen and check. Practise saying the sentences using the same rhythm.

Speaking

9 **a** Draw two large circles in your notebook and label one of them 'Now' and the other 'Ten years ago'. Read the questions and write short answers in the 'Now' circle.

1 Where are you living?
2 Who is your closest friend?
3 What do you do?
4 How do you spend your time?
5 Do you spend much time with your family?
6 Are you studying?
7 Do you play any sports?
8 What music do you enjoy?
9 What are your dreams/ambitions?

b Change the questions in Ex. 9a to make questions in the past. Write short answers for these questions anywhere in the 'Ten years ago' circle.

10 Show your circles to a partner. Tell them about how much your life has changed in the past ten years. Ask questions to find out as much information as possible.

11 Discuss.

1 What have been the important turning points (important moments or events which have changed things) in your life?
2 How might your life have changed if these turning points had been different?
3 Do you think you have always made the right decisions?

Writing

12 Write a paragraph describing an important turning point in your life and the effect this had. Think about what happened before/after the event, and how things might have been different.

get married?

back to college?

change job?

move house?

1 Add some examples of prefixes to the table below.

PREFIX	MEANING	EXAMPLE	YOUR EXAMPLES
over-	too much	**over**cook	
under-	not enough/below	**under**developed	
dis-	not/separate	**dis**honest	
in-/im-	not	**in**human	

2 Complete the text using prefixes.

Life CHANGE

Many people _dislike_ their job. Maybe they are (1) _____ worked or (2)_____ paid. Maybe they feel (3)_____ valued in the company or they (4)_____ agree with the company's methods. If you are one of these people, why not change things? LifeCHANGE workshops show you how to be (5)_____ dependent. You will see (6)_____ credible differences in your life as your problems (7)_____ appear. Change is never (8)_____ possible, but you have to make the first move.

Call us on **0879 997 5543** for an (9)_____ formal chat.

3 Add some examples of suffixes to the table below.

SUFFIX	EXAMPLE	RULES	YOUR EXAMPLES
-tion/-ation	crea**tion**, civili**sation**	If the verb ends in -e, cut the -e. If the verb ends in -se, the suffix is usually -isation.	
-ence/-ance	intellig**ence**, ignor**ance**	There are no clear rules about which words end in -ence or -ance. You have to learn them!	
-ment	move**ment**	Add -ment to the verb.	
-ness	dark**ness**	If the word ends in -y, change the -y to -i. happy → happ**iness**	

4 Complete the text by adding suffixes to the words in bold.

Vote for the Perfect Party.

1 Our priority is **educate**.
2 We will increase **employ**.
3 We promise to give free **accommodate** to people over 65.
4 There will be free hospital **treat** for everyone.
5 We promise proper **punish** for criminals.
6 We believe in the **important** of free speech.
7 Giving you, the voter, your **independent**.
8 A **govern** for the 21st century.
9 Taking the country in a new **direct**.
10 Your vote can make a **different**.

5 **a** Choose one of the topics below and make some notes on it.

an inspiration

new forms of entertainment

globalisation

a great achievement /my greatest achievement

what happiness means to me

cultural difference

my development

b Work with two or three other students. Speak for about a minute on your topic using your notes to help you.

c Change groups. EITHER speak about the same topic more fluently, OR choose a new topic. What new things did you learn about your classmates?

8 Communication

Time for a change?

1 If you could change one thing in your life, what would you like to change? Tell a partner.

I'd like to have a bigger flat so that I could invite my friends to stay.

2 **a** Work in pairs.
Student A: Add one or two more questions to the questionnaire below. Ask your partner the questions. Ask for more information with questions like: *Where? Which programmes?*
Student B: Add one or two more questions to the questionnaire on page 148. Ask your partner the questions. Ask for more information with questions like: *Why? Which hobbies?*

Circle the answers your partner gives you.

Are you ready FOR CHANGE?

1 Do you like to go to new places, and meet new people? Yes/No

2 Do you regularly watch the same television programmes every week? Yes/No

3 Do you go to the same place on holiday every year? Yes/No

4 Do you hope to have the same job for your whole life? Yes/No

5 Do you usually go out with the same group of people? Yes/No

6 Can you imagine living in many different places? Yes/No

b Did your partner answer 'yes' to more than half the questions? Does your partner like change?

3 **a** Read the questions below.

1 Do you think you like change?

2 Is it important for people to change their routine?

3 Does your job/lifestyle give you new, interesting experiences?

4 Has anything in your life changed for the better recently? Think about your friends/family/town/country.

5 What changes do you think you might make in the future?

b **8.8** Look at the people in the photos and listen to them talking about change. Write the number of the question they answer from Ex. 3a next to each photo.

c What do they say? Discuss in pairs. Listen again to check.

d Discuss the questions in groups.

Second Conditional

To talk about an unreal/imaginary/hypothetical situation and its consequences, use:

If + Past Simple + *would('d)/wouldn't*

*If I **had** a car, I **would** drive to work.*

*I'd live in Jamaica if I **could** live anywhere.*

The '*if* clause' can come first or second in the sentence. If it is first, there is a comma before the result clause.

We can use *would, could* or *might* in the result clause.

*If he **had** a change of heart, I **might** forgive him.*

When the subject is *I* and the verb is *to be*, we can say *If I was* or *If I were*.

*If I **were** you, I **wouldn't** wear that dress again!*

! Use the First Conditional to talk about possible/real situations (*if* + Present Simple + *will('ll)/won't*).

*If I **go** to France, I **will** visit the Louvre.*

Adverbs

We usually make an adverb by adding *-ly* to the adjective.

interesting – interestingly   *quick – quickly*

Some adverbs are irregular.

good (adj) – well (adv)   *hard (adj) – hard (adv)*

*Do you feel **well**?*   *Natasha works **hard**.*

1) **Adverbs of manner** describe how something happens – they modify the verb. They usually come after the verb.

*The news spread **quickly** around the office.*

*He held her **gently**.*

2) **Adverbs of frequency/probability** describe how often something happens or how probable it is. They usually come before the main verb.

*Newspapers **rarely** report on these important issues.*

*We could **possibly** catch the last train.*

3) **Adverbs of degree** modify an adjective or a verb. They make it weaker or stronger.

*It was **totally** unexpected. He's **quite** late.*

*She **absolutely** loves her job.*

4) **Adverbs which describe the speaker's attitude** towards the information in the clause.

***Luckily**, the money was still there when I returned.*

***Sadly**, we missed the end of the film.*

! Some adjectives look like adverbs because they end in *-ly*, but they are not. (e.g. *silly, lovely, lively*)

Third Conditional (for unreal past situations)

Use this form to talk hypothetically about past situations, and imagine different consequences.

*If there **hadn't been** so much traffic on the motorway, I **would have got** to the meeting on time.*

Form: *If* + past perfect + *would have* + past participle

To indicate possibility, rather than certainty, we can use *might have/could have* instead of *would have*.

*If she **had studied** harder, she **might have passed** her exams.*

These unreal past situations have unreal past results.

*If I **had studied** Art I **would have been** happier.*

*If she **hadn't left** work early she **might have finished** the report.*

***Would** you **have been** happier if you **had stayed** in England?*

Sometimes the hypothetical past situation has a present result.

*If I **had finished** my university degree, I **would be** an architect now. (If + Past Perfect + would + verb).*

Key vocabulary

Expressions with change

change (your) mind/clothes/hairstyle/career/ password   change an arrangement/some money/ the subject   it's time for a change   makes a change have a change of heart   (do something) for a change

Global issues

developed/developing countries   security/crime lifestyle/standard of living   famine/starvation war/peace   disease/cure   problems/solutions the environment/pollution

Life decisions

choose subjects   leave school/home/your country go to university   buy/sell a house/flat have a baby/start a family   start/change your career start your own business   retire/give up work take up/give up a hobby/sport   leave a job

Prefixes and suffixes

overcook   **under**developed   **dis**honest   **in**human crea**tion**   civili**sation**   intellig**ence**   ignor**ance** move**ment**   dark**ness**   educa**tion**   employ**ment** accommod**ation**   treat**ment**   punish**ment** import**ance**   independ**ence**   govern**ment** direc**tion**   differ**ence**

1 Rewrite the following using *if* sentences with *would*:

I am too old. I can't learn to play rugby. (If)

If I was/were younger, I would learn to play rugby.

1 She doesn't have Dave's number. She wants to call him. (If)
2 I can't go out. I have an exam tomorrow. (I'd)
3 We want to buy a new car. We don't have enough money at the moment. (If)
4 There isn't time. They can't see the show. (They'd)
5 I don't have a choice. I want to live in the city. (If)
6 We want to go swimming. The sea is polluted. (We'd)

2 Make questions to complete the dialogues using the verbs in brackets. Use the correct conditional (first or second).

What (do) *would you do if you lost your passport*?
Lost my passport? I'd go to the Embassy.

1 How (feel) ...?
   Got the job? I'd be extremely happy!
2 Which (buy) ...?
   If I had the choice? I'd buy the house on the hill.
3 What (do) ... ?
   A train strike? I'll take a taxi.
4 Where (go) ... ?
   Fully booked? We'll find a different hotel.
5 How (celebrate) ... ?
   Passed all my exams? I'd have a big party.
6 What (wear) ... ?
   If I'm invited to the film premiere? My best suit.

3 Make adverbs from the words in brackets. Write the adverb in the correct space to complete the sentences.

_____ we will see _____ them at the party. (hopeful)

Hopefully we will see them at the party.

1 I _____ go _____ to the supermarket on Saturdays. (usual)
2 Susana is so _____ busy that I _____ ever see her anymore. (hard)
3 Steve _____ drives when we _____ go on long journeys. (normal)
4 I exercise _____ in _____ the gym. (regular)
5 We _____ don't _____ want to damage the relationship. (certain)
6 _____ I can't see _____ how we can do it any other way. (personal)

4 Complete the following sentences with the phrases in the box.

> hadn't listened to the radio   had decided
> hadn't gone   ~~wouldn't have woken up~~
> wouldn't have gone   wouldn't have worked in
> ~~had gone dancing~~   wouldn't have met
> had known   wouldn't have heard

If I *had gone dancing* all night, I wouldn't have woken up this morning.

1 If I _____ to university, I _____ Sam.
2 If I _____ that England was so cold in the summer, I _____ there.
3 If I _____ to study medicine, I _____ an office all my life.
4 If I _____ this morning, I _____ the news.

5 Put the verbs into the correct form to make Third Conditional sentences.

If she *had asked* (ask) me to help her, we *would have finished* (finish) the job yesterday.

1 If I _____ (know) you were coming, I _____ (cook) some more supper.
2 If Ken _____ (leave) five minutes earlier this morning, he _____ (miss) the train.
3 If you _____ (tell) me you needed to get up early, I _____ (wake) you.
4 If she _____ (see) the mess, she _____ (be) angry.
5 If I _____ (not drink) that coffee, I _____ (fall asleep) during the film.
6 If I _____ (not lose) my camera last week, I _____ (take) some photographs of the children.

6 Complete the sentences with the correct words/phrases from the box.

> forbidden give up cure pollution standard
> environment ~~mind~~ lifestyle subject

I planned to study Art, but I changed my *mind* and studied French.

1 He didn't want to talk about politics so he changed the _____.
2 Smoking in the office is _____.
3 All the traffic in the city causes _____.
4 Waste from industries is bad for the _____.
5 We haven't found a _____ for AIDS yet.
6 It's very difficult to _____ smoking.
7 Most African countries have a very low _____ of living.
8 We don't have a TV or a car because we like a simple _____.

9 | Jobs

Lead-in

1 Discuss.

1 Describe the working environments in the photos.

2 What are the pros and cons of working in each place?

3 What would be your ideal working environment? Why?

2 **a** Read the questions and check the meaning of the words in **bold**.

1 Are there many **unemployed** people in your country?

2 Would you like to be **self-employed**? What are the advantages/disadvantages?

3 What **qualifications** do you have for your job/future job? How **experienced** are you?

4 When you **apply for** a job, do you normally **send a CV**? Do you need to include **references**?

5 How do you hear about **job vacancies** in your (future) profession?

6 Do you do a **9–5 job**? Would you like to **work flexitime**?

7 Do you **work long hours**? How often do you **work overtime**?

8 What are the **perks** of your job/being a student?

9 Is your work or subject **rewarding**? What do you like about it?

10 What are the biggest **challenges** in your job/studies?

11 How often do you expect to **get a pay rise** in your job/future job? Is it easy to **get promoted**?

12 Would you like to **work on commission?** Why/Why not?

b Work in pairs. Ask and answer the questions.

Speaking

1 a Read the quotes. Write A (agree), D (disagree), or M (maybe).

'People who work sitting down get paid more than people who work standing up.' (Ogden Nash) ☐

'The longer the title, the less important the job.' (George McGovern) ☐

'Most workplaces have too many rules. Employees aren't children, and the office isn't a junior school.' (Araba Green) ☐

'Most managers spend their time making it difficult for workers to work.' (Paul Shorter) ☐

b Compare your ideas with other students.

Reading

2 Which workers normally do these things? Write answers, then compare with a partner.

> wear uniforms   meet guests in reception
> decide start/finish times/working hours
> set salaries   fix equipment
> do the photocopying   type letters

type letters – *secretaries*

3 a Read the introduction to the text. Who is Ricardo Semler? What problem did he have?

At 21, Ricardo Semler became boss of his father's business in Brazil, Semco, which sold parts for ships. Knowing his son was still young, Semler senior told him, 'Better make your mistakes while I'm still alive.'

Semler junior worked like a madman, from 7.30a.m. until midnight every day. One afternoon, while touring a factory in New York, he collapsed. The doctor who treated him said, 'There's nothing wrong with you. Yet. But if you continue like this, you'll find a new home in our hospital.' Semler got the message. He changed the way he worked. In fact, he changed the way his employees worked too.

b What changes do you think Semler made? Discuss with other students and write a list. Read the rest of the text to find out.

Semco

❛ Everyone at Semco, even top managers, meets guests in reception, does the photocopying, sends faxes, types letters and dials the phone. ❜

He let his workers take more responsibility so that they would be the ones worrying when things went wrong. He allowed them to set their own salaries, and he cut all the jobs he thought were unnecessary, like receptionists and secretaries. This saved money and brought more equality to the company. 'Everyone at Semco, even top managers, meets guests in reception, does the photocopying, sends faxes, types letters and dials the phone.'

He completely reorganised the office: instead of walls, they have plants at Semco, so bosses can't shut themselves away from everyone else. And the workers are free to decorate their workspace as they want. As for uniforms, some people wear suits and others wear T-shirts.

Semler says, 'We have a sales manager named Rubin Agater who sits there reading the newspaper hour after hour. He doesn't even pretend to be busy. But when a Semco pump on the other side of the world fails and millions of gallons of oil are about to spill into the sea, Rubin springs into action. He knows everything there is to know about our pumps and how to fix them. That's when he earns his salary. No one cares if he doesn't look busy the rest of the time.'

Semco has flexible working hours; the employees decide when they need to arrive at work. The employees also evaluate their bosses twice a year. Also, Semco lets its workers use the company's machines for their own projects, and makes them take holidays for at least thirty days a year.

It sounds perfect, but does it work? The answer is in the numbers: in the last six years, Semco's revenues have gone from $35 million to $212 million. The company has grown from eight hundred employees to 3,000. Why?

Semler says it's because of 'peer pressure'. Peer pressure makes everyone work hard for everyone else. If someone isn't doing his job well, the other workers will not allow the situation to continue. In other words, Ricardo Semler treats his workers like adults and expects them to act like adults. And they do.

4 Answer the questions in pairs.

1 What do employees at Semco do that they probably wouldn't do in other companies? Look at the list in Ex. 2.

2 How does Semco and its staff look different from other companies?

3 Who is Rubin Agater and why is he important at Semco?

4 How does Semco show that it trusts its workers?

5 Do Semco's methods work? How do we know?

6 What is 'peer pressure' and why is it important at Semco?

5 Discuss.

1 What do you think of Semco's policies?

2 Would you like to work in a company with these policies?

3 Would any of the 'rules' at Semco be possible where you work/in your country? Why/Why not?

Grammar | make, let, allow

6 **a** Read the example sentences (a–c) and complete the Active grammar box with *make*, *let* or *allow*.

Active grammar

a) *Semco **lets** its workers use the company's machines*

b) *Semco **makes** the workers take holidays.*

c) *Semler **allowed** the workers to set their own salaries.*

Meaning

__ and __ mean give permission to do something.

__ means force to do something.

Form

__ + person + verb (force to do)

__ + person + verb (give permission to do)

__ + person + *to* + verb (give permission to do)

Use

Don't use ___ in the passive.

---

b Find other examples of *make*, *let* and *allow* in the text.

see Reference page 129

7 Correct the sentences. Use the same verb.

My company lets us to take a month's holiday.
*My company **lets us take** a month's holiday.*

1 We don't allowed to smoke here.

2 Did you let her using my pen?

3 I made her to do the washing-up.

4 He isn't allow to leave the building.

5 My dad doesn't to let me use his car.

6 The Customs Officer made take off my shoes.

7 You're allowed keep pets in these flats.

8 Did your teacher make you done the exam?

8 Complete the sentences with the correct form of *make, let* or *(not) allow(ed)*.

1 Our boss was very relaxed. She _____ us take long breaks.

2 The employees have great holidays. They're _____ to take one month off at Christmas.

3 He was wearing dirty clothes in the office. So the boss _____ him get changed.

4 He was really strict with the workers. He _____ them work at weekends.

5 It's my favourite airline. They _____ young children to fly for free.

6 I don't like going to that company. They _____ you wait ages before the manager sees you.

7 Don't go near the computer! You're _____ to touch the office equipment!

8 My last employers were really easygoing. They _____ us go home early on Fridays.

Person to person

9 Do you agree with the following statements? Why/Why not? Discuss in pairs.

1 Companies should allow people to work flexitime.

2 Businesses shouldn't let people smoke in the workplace.

3 Businesses should allow workers to set their own salaries.

4 Companies shouldn't make workers retire at sixty-five.

Listening and speaking

10 a **9.1** Listen to a speaker giving a talk about a new business and answer the questions.

1. What type of business is it?
2. What is special about this business?
3. What will chefs be allowed to do?
4. How many people will they employ?
5. What perk will employees get?
6. What is the name of the business?

b Listen again and make a note of the phrases the speaker uses to start/finish her talk.

11 Read the How to ... box and put the phrases/ sentences below in the correct place.

To sum up, ...
Are there any questions?
Good afternoon.
The most important thing for us is ...

HOW TO ...

present ideas to a group

Welcome	*Hello everyone.* *1) _____*
Introducing the topic	*I'd like to tell you about ...* *Firstly, I'm going to talk about* *... Secondly, I'll talk about ...*
Emphasising	*Our main idea is ...* *2) _____*
Conclusion	*In conclusion, ...* *3) _____*
Final comments	*Thank you for listening.* *4) _____*

12 a You are going to set up a new company. Work in groups and decide:

1. what your company does.
2. the company's name.
3. how big it is.
4. where it is based.

b Think about how you will treat your employees. Will you:

1. let them work flexitime?
2. make them work long hours/overtime?
3. allow them perks? Give examples.
4. let them take lots of responsibility? How? make them wear uniforms? etc.

13 a Make notes in the Company Profile.

COMPANY PROFILE

Name:

Address: _____

Contact: _____

Type of business: _____
_____

Client profile: _____

Future plans: _____
_____
_____

Number of employees: _____

Notes for employees: _____
_____
_____
_____
_____

Holidays: _____
_____

---

b Present your ideas to the rest of the class (future employees). Other students make notes and ask questions. Which company would you want to work for? Why?

Lifelong learning

Prepare to succeed!

Before speaking, spend some time thinking about exactly what you will say. Take notes if necessary. Try and predict what the listener will ask you. Which words and expressions will you need?

Listening and speaking

1   **a** Look at the cartoon. What kind of boss do you think this is? Have you ever known a boss like this?

b Write down three things a good boss does and three things a bad boss does. Compare your ideas with other students.

2   **a** [9.2] Listen to people talking about their managers and make notes in the table.

	Are they happy with their boss?	Why/Why not?
Speaker 1		
Speaker 2		
Speaker 3		
Speaker 4		

b Compare with a partner.

3   **a** Listen again and choose the correct words/phrases to complete the sentences.

1   Speaker 1's boss makes her feel a) organised b) angry. She says, 'I find her really *annoying/ annoyed.*'

2   Speaker 2's boss a) listens and understands his feelings b) goes to hospital a lot. He says, 'She is a great boss, and very *understand/ understanding.*'

3   Speaker 3's boss makes her feel a) scared b) angry. She says 'It can be very *frightened/ frightening.*'

4   Speaker 4 describes working with his boss as very a) boring b) interesting and fun. He says, 'It's very *excited/exciting* to work with Michael.'

b Check your answers in the tapescript on page 175.

Vocabulary | *-ing/-ed* adjectives

4   Look at the examples and complete the rules.

I am frightened.

It is frightening.

1   We use *-ed* adjectives to talk about feelings/ the situations that cause the feelings.

2   We use *-ing* adjectives to talk about feelings/ the situations that cause the feelings.

5   Choose the correct adjective.

1   I'm going to watch the World Cup final tonight. I'm so _____! (excited/exciting)

2   I'm _____. I've just been for a long run. (exhausted/exhausting)

3   Can we stop talking about politics? It's very _____. (bored/boring)

4   I'm not watching that horror film. It's too _____. (frightened/frightening)

5   I hate getting up early every day. It's so _____.(tired/tiring)

6   I don't watch the news on television, because I find it too _____. (depressed/depressing)

7   I don't walk on my own at night. I'm too _____. (frightened/frightening)

8   I love sitting in a café and reading the newspaper in the morning. I find it very _____. (relaxed/relaxing)

9   I find English grammar a bit _____. (confused/ confusing)

6   Think about these questions and then discuss them with another student. Ask follow-up questions like 'Why?'

1   What do you find confusing?

2   What makes you annoyed?

3   What do you do when you are bored?

4   What do you find depressing?

5   What do you find relaxing?

Reading

7 **a** The words and phrases in the box are from a story. What do you think it is about?

> promise   lost   hot air balloon   come down
> problem   engineer   manager

b Read the story to see if you were right.

c Discuss.

Do you agree with what the story says about managers? And technicians/engineers?

The Engineer and the Manager

A man flying in a hot air balloon realised he was lost. He started to come down until he could see a man on the ground who might hear him. 'Excuse me,' he shouted. 'Can you help me? I promised my friend I would meet him a half hour ago, but I don't know where I am, or where I am going.'

The man below responded: 'Yes. You are in a hot air balloon, approximately 30 feet above this field. You are between 40 and 42 degrees North Latitude, and between 58 and 60 degrees West Longitude.'

'You must be an engineer,' responded the balloonist. 'I am,' the man replied. 'How did you know?' 'Well,' said the balloonist, 'everything you have told me is technically correct, but I have no idea what to do with this information, and the fact is I am still lost.'

Whereupon the man on the ground responded, 'You must be a manager.' 'I am,' replied the balloonist, 'but how did you know?' 'Well,' said the man, 'you don't know where you are, or where you're going. You've made a promise which you can't keep, and you expect me to solve your problem. The fact is you are in the exact same position you were before we met, but now it's my fault.'

Grammar | reported speech

8 Match the sentences (1–3) to what the people actually said (a–c).

1 *The manager asked if the engineer could help him.*

2 *The manager said (that) he didn't know where he was going.*

3 *The manager told the engineer (that) he was still lost.*

a) 'I am still lost.'

b) 'Can you help me?'

c) 'I don't know where I am going.'

9 Read and complete the Active grammar box.

> ### Active grammar
>
> With reported speech we usually use *say* or *tell*. Use a pronoun after *tell*.
>
> He **said** (that)/**told me** (that) he was lost.
>
> When you report speech, you usually change the tense one step back.
>
> | Direct speech | Reported speech |
> | --- | --- |
> | *will/can*
 '*I'll help you.*' | *would/could*
 He said he _____ help me. |
> | **Present Simple**
 '*Carly is in a meeting.*' | **Past Simple**
 She told me Carly _____ in a meeting. |
> | **Present Continuous**
 '*I am going to meet Marc.*' | **Past Continuous**
 He said he _____ going to meet Marc. |
> | **Present Perfect/ Past Simple**
 '*Tom has been late every day.*' | **Past Perfect**
 He told me Tom _____ been late every day. |
> | '*He didn't buy it yesterday.*' | *She told me he _____ bought it the day before.* |

see Reference page 129

10 Complete the sentences with the correct form of *say* or *tell*.

1 Please _____ Jenny I'll call tomorrow.

2 Excuse me. Can you _____ me the time?

3 The guide _____ that the museum was closed.

4 I _____ you that we'd be late.

5 I didn't hear you. Can you _____ that again?

6 _____ me what the interviewer _____.

7 She _____ that we should wait here.

8 They _____ me not to go to Moscow.

11 Report the following dialogues.

1 'I'm the new technician.' He said …

2 'I'll be back tomorrow.' Mum said …

3 'I've been stuck in traffic.' Mara told us …

4 'He won't be away for long.' She said …

5 'I'll carry your bag for you.' He said …

6 'We're going on holiday next week.' He told me …

7 'I went shopping yesterday.' He told us …

8 'I'm feeling better.' She told him …

Listening

12 a **9.3** Listen to the interview and choose the correct option.

1 He says that a) he has a lot of problems b) he likes talking about his problems c) people like talking to him about their problems.

2 He tells her that he a) works hard b) hardly works c) doesn't like work.

3 He says that a) he is organised b) he is disorganised c) he likes organising things.

4 He tells her that a) he doesn't panic b) he often panics c) he doesn't have a calm character.

5 He says that a) he finds working on his own difficult b) he likes working with people c) he doesn't like to work from home.

b Put the words in the correct order to make questions from the interview.

1 good people are listening at you to ?

2 usually solutions find difficult you can to problems ?

3 weaknesses do what and you think your strengths are ?

4 work you do pressure well under ?

5 working own on do like you your ?

c Match the questions (1–5) above to the reported questions (a–e) below. Complete the sentences.

a) She asked him whether he liked working on his _____.

b) She asked him what his _____ and _____ were.

c) She asked if he could usually find _____ to _____.

d) She asked him whether he was good at _____.

e) She asked him if he worked well under _____.

d Listen again. What did Mr Wilkins reply to each question?

13 Read and complete the Active grammar box.

Active grammar

We use the verb *ask* to report questions.

We use *if* or *whether* to report <u>*Yes/No*</u> questions / <u>*Wh-* questions</u>.

Direct question	Reported question
'_____ you like working in an office?'	*I **asked** her **if**/ **whether** she liked working in an office.*
'_____ is your name?'	*I **asked** her what her name was.*

see Reference page 129

14 Write questions 1–6 in reported speech. Start with 'She asked me …'.

1 Are you good at organising people?

2 Do you enjoy working in a team?

3 What do you do when your ideas don't work?

4 Do you listen to other people's advice/ suggestions?

5 What do you do when you have too much work?

6 What time do you normally start work?

15 There are mistakes in some of the sentences below. Find the mistakes and correct them.

1 Anna said me that she would be back by five o'clock.

2 Mara told me to switch the computer off.

3 My brother asked to wait for him at the station.

4 The driver told he was feeling sick.

5 The shopkeeper asked if we needed help.

6 Her husband said her that she could use his credit card.

Person to person

16 a Write five questions to ask your partner to find out if he/she would make a good manager.

Do you like …? Are you good at …? What …? Can you …? Do you …?

b Interview your partner. Would he/she make a good manager? Why/Why not? Report what your partner said back to the class.

I asked Maria if she prefers working on her own or in a team, and she told me she likes …

Reading and speaking

1 Discuss.

1 What do you think are the best and worst things about being famous?

2 Would you like to be famous? What for?

2 Read the text and answer the questions.

1 What was Jane and Denise's dream?

2 How did they achieve it?

3 What problems did they have?

Operatunity

(a) _____

Operatunity is a TV talent show for amateur opera singers. The winners get the chance to sing with the English National Opera. When two housewives, Denise Leigh and Jane Gilchrist won in 2002, their lives changed forever. As they sang Verdi's *Rigoletto* at the Coliseum in Rome, they were transformed from working mothers into opera celebrities.

(b) _____

'I live in the village I was born in,' says Denise, who is blind. 'Lots of my neighbours are family, and my life revolved around my three children.' Jane, who worked as a cleaner and a shop assistant, was in a similar situation. She says, 'All I had to look forward to was seeing my four children grow up, and I love that, but ... you think "there must be more to life". Winning *Operatunity* has opened up avenues I never knew existed.'

(c) _____

'This last year has been amazing,' Denise continues. 'Last month was Paris, before that we were recording at Abbey Road, in London, and recently we had our album launch at the Royal Opera House.' 'We've been treated like princesses,' laughs Jane. '... champagne, chocolates, five-star hotels ...'

(d) _____

But it wasn't all so easy. For Denise, the worst part was waiting at the beginning. 'After I'd sent in my application form I worried for a month. Then I had to wait ten days after my first audition. That was awful.' Even when they won the competition they were allowed to tell their close family but they weren't allowed to tell anyone else until later. Denise and Jane also found the travelling difficult. They couldn't take their children with them while they were away singing so they had to organise childcare. However, there's been no problem with the physical side of singing: 'We didn't have to worry about that as we've had lots of help and wonderful voice training,' says Jane. They also had to learn to deal with the media. 'The kids loved the fact that they could stay up and watch us on TV, but I just couldn't understand why some newspapers were more interested in the fact I divorced at 21, rather than the fact I had just sung at the Coliseum,' says Denise.

(e) _____

When asked if they'd recommend the experience, Denise says, 'It's been the most fantastic thing I've ever done. I wake up in the morning and think I must be the luckiest person in the world. My profession is something I used to do as a hobby.' And their advice to other hopeful singers out there? 'Live your dream,' says Jane. Denise agrees: 'If you think you can do it, then try it. No one else is going to do it for you.'

3 **a** Match the headings below to the paragraphs (a–e). <u>Underline</u> the phrases in the text that helped you.

> **The difficult parts**
>
> **Living the new life**
>
> **The competition**
>
> **Their lives before**
>
> **Advice**

b Summarise each paragraph in just one sentence.

4 Correct the eight mistakes in the summary.

Jane and Denise won a pop singing competition on the radio, even though Denise is blind. The competition gave them the opportunity to sing a famous Beatles' song at Wembley Stadium, and it changed their lives forever. Although they are both housewives with families – Denise has three children, and Jane has two – they now get the chance to travel and see the world, singing. Their new lives have not been very exciting, and they have been treated very well. They found the travelling easy because their children were at home. They would recommend the experience to other singers, and say that if your dream is to sing, you should keep it as a hobby.

5 Discuss.

Would you ever enter/consider entering a competition like *Operatunity*? Why/Why not?

Grammar | past obligation/permission

6 **a** Look at the example sentences in the Active grammar box and complete the rules (1–4).

Active grammar

necessary (in the past)
*They **had to** organise childcare.*

not necessary (in the past)
*We **didn't have to** worry about that.*

OK/permitted (in the past)
*They **were allowed to** tell their close family.*
*They **could** stay up to watch me on TV.*

not OK/not permitted (in the past)
*They **weren't allowed to** tell anyone else.*
*They **couldn't** take their children with them.*

1 The past of *must* is <u>had to</u> / <u>was/were allowed to</u>.

2 The past of *mustn't* is <u>didn't have to</u> / <u>wasn't/weren't allowed to</u>.

3 *Could/couldn't* are followed by the infinitive <u>with</u> / <u>without</u> *to*.

4 *Had to/didn't have to* and *was(n't)/were(n't) allowed to* are followed by the <u>gerund</u> / <u>the infinitive without *to*</u>.

---

b [9.4] Listen to the pronunciation of the example sentences from the Active grammar box. Practise saying the sentences, paying attention to the pronunciation of the modal verbs (the words in **bold**).

see Reference page 129

c What is the difference in meaning, if any, between these sentences?

1 a) We were allowed to sing.
  b) We had to sing.
  c) We could sing.

2 a) We could watch TV.
  b) We had to watch TV.
  c) We weren't allowed to watch TV.

3 a) I wasn't allowed to study.
  b) I didn't have to study.
  c) I had to study.

7 Complete the sentences with modal verbs from the Active grammar box. There may be more than one answer.

1 Martin wasn't in the office, so I _____ phone him on his mobile. (It was necessary.)

2 When I was at school, we _____ run inside the building. (It was not permitted.)

3 In my last job, we _____ work from home for two days a week. (It was permitted.)

4 Luckily, we had our passports with us, so we _____ go back to the hotel. (It wasn't necessary.)

5 We _____ smoke in the restaurant, so we _____ go outside. (It was not permitted/it was necessary.)

6 I stayed up all night, because I _____ finish my assignment by today. (It was necessary.)

7 As a young child, I was _____ travel alone on buses. (It was permitted.)

8 The flight was delayed, but we _____ wait very long before take off. (It wasn't necessary.)

8 **a** Correct the mistakes in the following sentences.

1 I wasn't be allowed to stay out late.

2 We could to eat chocolate all day long.

3 Did you were allowed to buy new clothes?

4 We didn't allowed to watch television.

5 I couldn't to use the telephone, because it was too expensive.

6 We always did have to finish our food.

7 We didn't had to help with the housework.

8 We had to practising very hard.

b Are the sentences true for you when you were a child? Tell a partner.

Person to person

9 Discuss in groups.

1 Are there more rules for children now, or when you were a child? Give examples.

2 Do schools and universities give students more or less freedom than in the past? Give examples.

Vocabulary | job requirements

10 a Match the definitions (1–6) to an expression from the box.

> **You (don't) have to be good at:**
> dealing with people
> solving problems
> listening to people
> organising
> persuading people
> languages
> delegating
> prioritising
> making decisions

1 planning or arranging events or activities
2 giving jobs to others to do
3 deciding which jobs are more/less important
4 getting people to do things they don't want to do
5 working with others
6 finding answers to problems

b Complete the sentences below using words/phrases from the box.

> **You (don't) have to be able to:**
> work accurately
> work irregular hours
> work under pressure
> speak more than one language
> work quickly
> type fast
> give good presentations
> remember a lot of information
> drive well
> use a range of computer software

1 In an international company it is useful to be able to _____.
2 Our company is very hi-tech so you need to be able to _____.
3 A good salesperson can _____.
4 I have to _____because mistakes are very expensive.
5 People get stressed when they continually _____.
6 People _____ in my company – some start early and some finish late.

c **9.5** Listen and check your answers.

A

B

C

D

Listening

11 a Look at the photos and answer the questions.

1 What types of things do they do in their jobs?
2 What personal/professional abilities do they need?

b **9.6** Listen to the people talking about their jobs. Match the speakers (1–4) with the photos (A–D).

1 Do they still do this job now or did they do it in the past?
2 What do they say about their job?

12 **9.6** Listen again. Write the number of the speaker (1–4) next to each expression (in Ex. 10) as you hear it said.

13 a Find someone in the class who you think:

is good at delegating   is good at persuading people
works well under pressure   is good at solving problems
is good at organising   can remember a lot of information
can type fast   can use a range of computer software
works irregular hours

b Ask them questions to see if you were right.

Magda, are you good at solving problems?

Yes, my friends often ask me for advice.

Speaking

14 a Choose one of the following.

EITHER Imagine you are leaving your job. A friend is interested in your job. Prepare to describe the job.
OR Prepare to describe a job you would like to do in the future. Make notes on the following:

> What is the job?   Where do you work?   Main tasks
> Abilities/requirements   Good and bad things about the job

b When you are ready, describe the job to a partner.

9 Vocabulary

UK and US English

1 Do you know what the things in the photos are called in US English?

2 Match the words in **bold** in the sentences below with their US equivalent in the box.

> restroom   mall   subway   gas   high school
> round trip   fries   soccer   check   cell phone
> freeway   mail   movie   apartment   vacation

1 Can I use your **mobile phone**? _____
2 Can we have the **bill,** please? _____
3 Do you want **chips** or a baked potato? _____
4 Was there any **post** today? _____
5 We need to stop for **petrol**. _____
6 Turn left to get onto the **motorway**. _____
7 See you in the **shopping centre** at 4.30. _____
8 When did you buy your **flat**?
9 Next year she's going to **secondary school**.

_____

10 How much is a **return ticket**? _____
11 The **underground** is so expensive. _____
12 We like watching **football**.* _____
13 Let's see a **film**. _____
14 I'm on **holiday**! _____
15 Where's the **toilet**? _____

* in US English, *football* means *American football*, a game played mainly in the USA.

3 **a** Is the speaker using UK or US English? Use a word from Ex. 2 to complete the sentences.

1 She first learned soccer from her teacher at _____.
2 We went to a restaurant near the shopping centre. As usual, I paid the _____.
3 For my holiday I bought a _____ to Paris.
4 There's a place on the _____ where we can stop and buy gas.
5 If you want to use the toilet, we can go to my _____. I live close to here.
6 I never get any mail, only stupid text messages on my _____.
7 Let's get some burgers and fries and go watch a _____.
8 A: How are you getting to the mall? B: On the _____.
9 Excuse me. I'd like the check, and could you show me where the _____ is, please?
10 There's a restaurant by the underground station which sells great fish and _____.

b 〔9·7〕 Listen to check your answers.

4 **a** There are some differences between UK and US spelling. Look at the table.

UK	US	Explanation
centre	center	UK words ending in -*tre* are usually spelled -*ter* in US English.
organise	organize	Where UK English uses -*ise* at the end of some verbs, US English generally uses -*ize*. There are exceptions: e.g. *advertise* uses -*ise* even in US English.
colour	color	UK nouns (with two syllables) ending in -*our* often lose the -*u* in US English.

b Write these words in US English.

> neighbour   criticise   humour   summarised
> theatre   prioritise   flavour   realised   metre

5 **a** Work in groups of three or four. Write a paragraph using one of the following titles:
- The restaurant
- My last big trip
- The best things in life

Group As: use as many US words from Exs. 1 and 3 as possible. **Group Bs:** use as many UK words from Exs. 1 and 3 as possible.

b Exchange paragraphs.

Group As: find all the UK words and spellings. Write them in US English. **Group Bs:** find all the US words and spellings. Write them in UK English.

9 | Communication

Job advertisements

1 Choose the job you would most like to apply for. Work with a partner who chose the same job. Write a list of questions you would expect to be asked in an interview.

2 Prepare your answers to the questions.

Wanted

FISHES Restaurant & Bar. Part-time exp. bar & restaurant service staff required. Top rates of pay/conditions. Must be vibrant, confident & smart.

FISHES Restaurant & Bar

GRAPHIC DESIGNER

ATG GROUP is a fast-growing import company. We are currently looking for a GRAPHIC DESIGNER for a busy design department. We require a dynamic, highly motivated individual with at least 2 years' experience. You must have knowledge of a range of software applications and digital media, including photography. You need to be able to work under pressure, be a good communicator and have a flexible approach to work.

Tour Guide

Fun & Sun ... Looking for a new start? Working abroad? Aged 19 to 55? Time for a change?

- We have immediate vacancies in: Portugal, Malta & the Canary Islands.
- Average working day: 9.15 to 17.30, 5 days per week. No experience required, as full training will be given. Travel & work in a team dealing with the public. Fantastic long term career & job prospects.

News editor

We are a leading international newspaper group. We are looking for new journalists to join our friendly team. If you're an experienced editor looking for a new challenge, or a journalist with previous experience, we would like to hear from you. Languages an advantage, as well as knowledge or experience of specific areas.

Marketing Manager

We are a supplier of educational products to primary and secondary schools. We produce consistently excellent results and show continued growth in profitability. The successful applicant needs experience in managing advertising and promotions campaigns, and reporting on the results. Ability to read data and manage people is vital.

3 Work with someone from another pair. You're going to interview them for their chosen job. Prepare some questions. Interview your partner. Your partner will interview you.

4 Report back to the class on how your interview went. What questions were you asked? Do you think you would get the job?

Reported speech

When we report what someone said, the verbs often 'shift' into the past, because what the person said is in the past.

Will → *Would*

'*I'll go tomorrow.*' *He said he **would** go the next day.*

Present Simple → Past Simple

'*I **live** in São Paolo.*' *She said she **lived** in São Paolo.*

Present Continuous → Past Continuous

'*I'm **working** for a fashion company.*'

*He said he **was working** for a fashion company.*

Present Perfect/Past Simple → Past Perfect

'*I'**ve been** here for three months.*'

*She told me she **had been** there for three months.*

Time references can also change in reported speech.

'*Call me later today or tomorrow.*'

*She told me to call her later **that day** or **the next day**.*

Pronouns can also change in reported speech.

'*I'll see you soon.*' *He said **he** would see **us** soon.*

If what the person said is still true, we can keep the present tense.

'*I still love you.*' *He said he still **loves** me.*

Look at the verb patterns for *say/tell/ask*.

Say cannot be followed by a person.

*She **said** (that) it was late.* NOT: ~~She said me ...~~

Tell must be followed by a person.

*He **told me** I was special.* NOT: ~~He told that ...~~

*He **told me** to lock the door.* NOT: ~~He told to me ...~~

In *Yes/No* questions, *ask* is followed by *if/whether*.

*She **asked** me **if/whether** I knew the way.*

Reported questions

'*What time is it?*' *He asked me what time it was.*

'*Do you understand Spanish?*' *She asked me if/whether I understood Spanish.*

In reported questions the word order is the same as in affirmative statements.

The auxiliary verb (*do/does/did*) is not used.

'*What do you do?*' *He asked me what I did/I do.*

NOT: ~~He asked me what do I do.~~

Yes/No questions use *if/whether*.

'*Do you live in Italy?*' *She asked if I lived in Italy.*

Tenses may shift back, as for reported statements.

'*What time is it?*' *She asked what time it was.*

Pronouns and time/place references may change.

'*Will you still be here tomorrow?*'

He asked if I would still be there the next day.

make, let and *allow*

Use *make* + object + verb (without to) to talk about obligation imposed by another person or set of rules.

*My father **makes me** clean my room.* (She doesn't want to clean the room, but she has to clean it.)

*She **didn't make/never made us** work very hard.*

Passive form: *be made to + verb.*

*We **were made to** clean the whole house.*

Use *let* + object + verb (without *to*) to talk about permission.

*Mum **lets/doesn't let me** drive.* (She says it's OK/not OK)

It is not possible to use *let* in the passive form.

Use *allow* + object + *to* + verb to talk about permission. The meaning is similar to *let*.

*My parents **allow me to** stay out late.*

Passive form: *be allowed to + verb.*

*They **weren't allowed to** borrow the money.*

Past obligation/permission

To talk about obligation in the past, use *had to* + verb.

*We **had to** be smart but we **didn't have to** wear suits.*

To talk about permission in the past, use:

allow (see above) and *could* + verb.

*We **could** watch TV but we **couldn't** stay up late.*

Key Vocabulary

Work

apply for   send a CV   references   get promoted
unemployed   self-employed   get a payrise
rewarding   do a 9–5 job   work long hours
flexitime   overtime   qualifications   perks
challenges   experienced   job vacancies
work on commission

Adjectives with -*ing*/-*ed*

tired/-ing   frightened/-ing   exhausted/-ing
excited/-ing   annoyed/-ing   bored/-ing
confused/-ing   depressed/-ing   relaxed/-ing

Job requirements

dealing with/listening to/persuading people
solving problems   delegating   organising/prioritising
making decisions   speak more than one language
type fast   work quickly/under pressure/accurately/
irregular hours   give good presentations
use a range of computer software

UK vs. US English

flat/apartment   football/soccer   holiday/vacation
toilet/restroom   petrol/gas   mobile phone/cell phone
bill/check   chips/fries   post/mail   film/movie
shopping centre/mall   secondary/high school
return ticket/round trip   underground/subway
motorway/freeway

1 Complete the text with the words in the box.

> let   lets   made   are   them   ~~allowed~~
> don't   make

Farmingham Summer camp

Farmingham

UK

Dear Ms Salvagnoni,

In reply to your questions, I can confirm that the children are not _allowed_ to leave the camp without an adult. This is for legal reasons. We (1)___ the children play in the gardens from 3.00p.m. to 5.00p.m., though we never (2)___ the children do any activity that they don't want to do. They (3)___ allowed to stay in their rooms in the afternoon. In the past we (4)___ the children clean their own rooms, but since 2003 we have employed a maid to do that. We (5)___ allow children to bring computer games to the camp, though the camp manager (6)___ students use the Internet. We also let (7)___ call home free of charge twice a week. I hope this answers your questions.

Yours sincerely,

Paula Cranston

2 Report what Jim said yesterday.

'We went to a fantastic concert last weekend.'

Jim told me that they had been to a fantastic concert the weekend before.

1 'I've just started at Manchester University.'
  Jim said he ...

2 'I'm studying Engineering.'
  Jim told me he ...

3 'I've made lots of new friends.'
  Jim told me he ...

4 'We're going to the Lake District at the weekend.'
  Jim told me that they ...

5 'I'll call you tomorrow.'
  Jim said he ...

6 'I went to a brilliant lecture this morning.'
  Jim said he ...

7 'I live in a flat with three other students.'
  Jim told me he ...

8 'We're having a party tonight.'
  Jim said they ...

3 Report the following questions.

'What's your name?' He asked me *what my name was*.

1 'Do you know where the post office is?'
  She asked ...

2 'Where can I change some money?' He asked ...

3 'Have you been here before?' She asked ...

4 'What time did the meeting finish this morning?'
  He asked me ...

5 'Will you look after the plants for me?'
  She asked ...

6 'Did you go to the cinema last night?'
  They asked if we ...

7 'What time did you arrive?' She asked ...

8 'Are you meeting anyone here?' He asked ...

4 Complete the sentences using *had to, didn't have to, could, couldn't, were allowed* and *weren't allowed.*

Working from home has changed my life. Before, I _had to_ be in my office by 9a.m., but now I work when I want to. And I can wear whatever I like. I (1)_____ wear pyjamas in the office! In fact, we (2)_____ wear a suit, which I hated. Another good thing is that I don't have to travel. Before, I didn't use to get home before 8.00 because we (3)_____ to leave the office before 6p.m. and I (4)_____ spend two hours a day travelling. Working at home is a bit lonely. In the past I used to talk to my colleagues in the office. Also, I have to pay for computer software. Before, I (5)_____ buy anything. And if my computer goes wrong, I have to fix it. Before, I (6)_____ ask the IT technician to do it. And the Internet is very expensive too. In the office I didn't pay anything and we (7)_____ to use the Internet as much as we wanted. Now I have to pay for every minute!

5 Choose the correct alternative.

We're good at *dealing/(solving)/organising* problems.

1 The workers are *confused/confusing/frightening* about the company's new rules.

2 The best thing about my job is that I *deal with/solve/delegate* people.

3 My job can be very *bored/tired/tiring*.

4 When I'm busy I always *prioritise/delegate/persuade* some of the work to my colleagues.

5 When you arrive, ask the *engineer/manager/receptionist* to call me in my office.

6 Eventually we *prioritised/persuaded/organised* the boss to give us a pay rise.

7 It was very *boring/annoyed/annoying* when my computer stopped working.

8 You need to work *accurate/irregular/quick* hours in this job.

10 Memories

Lead-in

1 **a** Choose the correct words/phrases to complete the sentences.

1 The Washington Monument was built so that we'd never <u>lose</u> /<u>forget</u> President Washington and his work.

2 People wear poppies each November to <u>remind us to</u> /<u>remind us of</u> the soldiers who died in the First World War.

3 This bench was placed here to <u>remember</u> /<u>remind</u> a local person.

4 The Taj Mahal was built by Emperor Shah Jahan between 1631 and 1653 <u>in memory of</u> /<u>to miss</u> his wife.

b Match the sentences to the photos.

c Are there any memorials in your country? Who built them and why?

2 **a** What's the difference between the following? Think about meaning and verb structure.

a) lose/forget

b) remind me to/remind me of

c) remember/remind

b Make sentences using these words/phrases.

3 Discuss.

1 What are you good at remembering?

2 What do you sometimes forget?

3 Do you use any special techniques to help you remember names, places, dates, appointments and meetings, English vocabulary or phone numbers?

Grammar	I wish / if only
Can do	talk about wishes

Reading and writing

1 Discuss.

1 Have you got a good memory?

2 How would your life be different if you had an amazingly good memory?

3 What things would be difficult if you lost your memory?

4 Is it possible to improve your memory? How?

2 a Look at the words and pictures (A–C) from three stories about memory. What do you think is happening in each story?

b Read the texts below and match the pictures to the stories.

A LOST, MEMORY, DOCUMENTS

C REMEMBER, FACTS, SECRET

B UNCONSCIOUS, FORGOTTEN, GIRLFRIEND

Story 1

Colin Brown, 29, fell unconscious after hitting his head in a cycling accident. When he regained consciousness in hospital two days later, he had forgotten four years of his life. Unfortunately, this included his three-year relationship with Lydia Davis, his girlfriend.

Lydia says Colin didn't even recognise her when she visited him in hospital. 'He would tell me to go away and would shout for the nurse to take me away,' she said.

But Lydia refused to give up. 'We went to the cinema, started eating out and talked about what we liked to do.'

Story 2

In 1999 a British man walked into a hospital in Sydney, Australia. He had lost all his documents and was suffering from a terrible headache. He'd also lost his memory. Despite police investigations and television appeals, no one was able to identify him.

He said, 'It is as though I don't exist. My life is senseless.'

Mr Nobody couldn't get a passport, and he spent his time at home watching videos or reading in the library. Mr Nobody was obviously an educated man. He played the piano, and spoke French and Italian. But what he really wanted was to find out who he was.

Story 3

S. was a journalist for a Moscow newspaper in the 1920s. He would never take notes, but his reports were always full of perfectly-remembered facts. He was so good that his editor sent him to a psychologist, a man called Luria. Luria discovered that S. could memorise, in a few minutes, long lists of numbers, and remember them for weeks. Nobody knew how he did it.

Thirty years after they first met, Luria tested S. and S. could still remember all the numbers perfectly. So Luria asked him how he managed to do it. Finally, he wanted to discover the secret of S's amazing memory.

3 Read again and mark the sentences true (T) or false (F).

1 Colin forgot everything about his life. ☐

2 Lydia tried to continue their relationship. ☐

3 Mr Nobody knew nothing about his identity. ☐

4 Mr Nobody was good at several things. ☐

5 S. went to see Luria to improve his memory. ☐

6 Luria tested S.'s memory every year for thirty years. ☐

4 Work together. Write titles and endings (three or four sentences) for the stories. Read them to other groups.

5 Turn to page 149 and read the real endings. Which story is the most interesting? Why?

Listening

6 **a** **10.1** Listen to Jack and Alice talking about things they remember or forget. What do they mention?

b Listen again and complete the sentences.

1 J: Have you got a good memory?
   A: I wish I _____!

2 I write them all down in my diary. I wish I _____ have to, but ...

3 I wish I _____ remember things like writers' names ...

4 I'd read an excellent novel and I wish I _____ _____ the name.

c Do they have good memories? Would they like to have good memories?

Grammar | *I wish/if only*

7 Read the Active grammar box and choose the correct alternatives.

Active grammar

Use *wish* + Past Simple to talk about imaginary things we would like in <u>the past</u> / <u>the present</u>.
***I wish I was** stronger.*
***He wishes** he **had** a sister.*

Use *wish* + Past Perfect to talk about imaginary things we'd like in <u>the past</u> / <u>the present</u>.
***I wish I had gone** to bed early yesterday.*

We use *wish* + *could* to talk about <u>ability</u> / <u>the past.</u>
***She wishes** she **could** drive.*

Use *wish* + *would* when you want someone or something to change.
***I wish** they **would** be quiet!*
***I wish** the bus **would** come.*
You can't say: ~~I wish I would~~ ...

We can also use *If only* instead of *I wish*. The meaning is a little bit stronger than *I wish*.
***If only I could** dance!*
***If only** you **hadn't left** your bag on the bus!*

---

see Reference page 143

8 Complete the sentences below using the words and phrases from the box.

> had   could sleep   hadn't arrived
> could swim   was here   hadn't done
> would be quiet   knew how

1 That water looks so warm! I wish I _____.
2 You're always talking! I wish you _____!
3 I miss my dog. I wish she _____.
4 You've broken it! I wish you _____ that.
5 I'm so tired. If only I _____!
6 We missed our flight. If only we _____ late.
7 I like those new phones. I wish I _____ one.
8 I love the mountains. I wish I _____ to ski.

9 Complete the sentences so that they mean the same. Use two or three words.

1 I'm hungry. I didn't eat earlier.
   I wish _____ earlier.
2 I'm bad at Maths. I want to be better.
   I wish _____ better at Maths.
3 You're late again.
   I wish _____ arrive on time!
4 We went to a boring museum.
   I wish _____ gone there.
5 I'd love to be a good dancer, but I can't do it.
   I wish _____ dance.
6 You always leave your dirty plate on the table!
   I wish _____ leave your dirty plate on the table!
7 I'm lonely. I'd like to have more friends.
   I wish _____ more friends.
8 I don't want to smoke any more, but I can't quit.
   I wish _____ give up smoking.

Speaking

10 In pairs, choose five skills from the box you wish you had. Explain which you chose and why.

> see in the dark   see the future
> learn languages perfectly in a week
> remember everything you read   change shape
> become invisible   be incredibly strong
> travel backwards and forwards in time
> read people's thoughts   fly like a bird
> run like a cheetah   swim like a fish

I wish I could fly like a bird because I would travel all over the world free!

Reading

11 a Look at the picture. What do you think the man and the horse are thinking?

b Does the picture remind you of a time or place in your life? Think for a few minutes, and then tell other students about it.

Stopping by Woods on a Snowy Evening

Whose woods these are I think I know,
His house is in the village though;
He will not see me stopping here
To watch his woods fill up with snow.

My little horse must think it queer[1]
To stop without a farmhouse near
Between the woods and frozen lake
The darkest evening of the year.

He gives his harness bells a shake
To ask if there is some mistake
The only other sound's the sweep
Of easy wind and downy[2] flake.

The woods are lovely, dark and deep,
But I have promises to keep,
And miles to go before I sleep,
And miles to go before I sleep.

Robert Frost

Glossary
[1] *strange*
[2] *soft*

12 Read the poem and answer the questions.

1. Where is the traveller?
2. Why does he stop?
3. Why does his horse think this is strange?
4. What does the traveller think of what he sees? Does he like the woods?
5. Why does the traveller continue on his journey?

Pronunciation

13 a **10.2** Listen to the poem and read it quietly at the same time. Concentrate on the rhythm.

b Mark the stresses (each line has four). Listen and read again at the same time.

14 Discuss.

1. Do you like the poem? Why/Why not?
2. What sights and sounds are described? How do they make you feel?

Lifelong learning

Make it rhyme!

When a word is difficult to pronounce, e.g. *though*, think of other words that have a similar pronunciation, e.g. *know/snow*. This will help you to remember. Find words which rhyme in the poem.

10.2 Famous women

Grammar	review of past tenses
Can do	say different types of numbers

A

B

C

D

E

Listening and speaking

1 Who are the women in the photos? Do you know anything about them? In what areas did they 'shape' the 20th century?

2 a **10.3** Listen and check. Why are the women famous?

b Listen again and complete the notes.

> 1 Mother Teresa helped the sick in India. Her charities are found in more than _____ countries.
> 2 Marie Curie worked with _____, and won the Nobel Prize in 1903 and _____.
> 3 Frida Kahlo was famous for her amazing and unusual _____.
> 4 Marilyn Monroe starred in _____ films.
> 5 Rosa Parks refused to give up her bus seat. She went to _____ because of this.

Vocabulary

3 a According to the listening texts, which of the women:

1 **encouraged** black people to fight for their rights? _____

2 was a very **brave** woman? _____

3 was a **talented** actress? _____

4 **dedicated her life** to helping the sick? _____

5 was **determined** to survive and made a remarkable recovery? _____

6 was a **brilliant** scientist? _____

7 was **involved in** a serious accident? _____

8 **inspired** many other people to start caring for others? _____

b Match the words in **bold** to the words/phrases in the box.

> had courage   was a great example to   never stopped trying
> excellent   played a part in   spent all her time
> very good at something   made people want to do something

4 Complete the sentences with a suitable word/phrase from Ex. 3a.

Frida Kahlo encouraged people to believe in themselves.

1 Rosa Parks' actions have _____ people all over the world to fight for equality between the races.

2 Mother Teresa was _____ _____ charity work in India and saved thousands of lives.

3 Marilyn Monroe was _____ to become a film star.

4 Marie Curie _____ _____ _____ to science.

5 Can you think of any other 'heroes' of the 20th century? Choose two people. What qualities did they have? Tell other students who you chose and why.

135

Reading

6 **a** Read about another famous woman of the 20th century. Stop at each question and, with a partner, guess the answer. Then follow the instruction.

b When you know who the famous person is, write her nickname in the gap in the title.

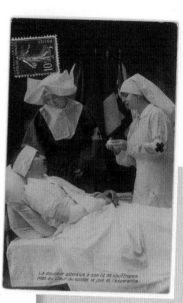

La douceur attentive à son lit de souffrance
Met du cœur au soldat la joie et l'espérance

7 She had worked for a short time as a nurse in World War I, but during World War II she went to Switzerland. She returned to France in 1953 and dressed many Hollywood stars such as Liz Taylor and Katharine Hepburn. What happened next?

a) She acted in a film about her life.

b) She died in the 1970s.

c) She moved to the West Indies.

Read 4 to find out ····}

1 She was born in a home for poor people in Saumur, France, on 19 August 1883, and christened Gabrielle. Her mother died when she was just six years old. This left her father with Gabrielle and four other young children. What happened next?

a) The father brought them up alone.

b) The children became film stars.

c) The father sent them away.

Read 5 to find out ····}

The Making of

4 She was still working up until her death on January 10, 1971, when her fashion empire brought in over $160 million a year. Before that, in 1969, Katharine Hepburn had starred in a Broadway musical about her life. She is considered one of the most influential fashion designers of the 20th century.

THE END

5 He sent them away to grow up with relatives. In her early twenties, while she was working as a singer in cafés, she met two wealthy men, one a soldier, the other an Englishman called Arthur Capel. What did the men do?

a) They shot each other because they loved her.

b) They helped her start a clothes business.

c) They paid for her to travel around the world.

Read 3 to find out ····}

3 With the men's money and contacts, she opened a hat shop in 1913. She soon expanded her business to include clothes, and opened a fashion shop at 31 rue Cambon, Paris. What happened next?

a) She married a politician.

b) She became a singer.

c) She designed clothes for women.

Read 6 to find out····}

6 She began to design clothes for women. She said, 'Most women dress for men and want to be admired. But they must also be able to move, to get into a car. Clothes must have a natural shape.' What was her other famous product?

a) Shoes.

b) Perfume.

c) Furniture.

Read 2 to find out ····}

2 In the early 1920s she introduced Chanel No. 5, which became one of the world's favourite perfumes. Throughout the 1920s and 30s her clothes were becoming more and more popular. But then, in 1939, World War II began. What happened to her?

a) She moved to Switzerland.

b) She designed uniforms for soldiers.

c) She worked as a nurse.

Read 7 to find out ····}

Listening

7 [10.4] Listen to a summary of the woman's life. The speaker gets three facts wrong. Which facts?

8 In pairs, retell the woman's life story using these numbers/dates.

> August 19, 1883   six years old   two men
> 1913   31 rue Cambon   No.5   1920s and 1930s
> 1939   1953   1969   January 10, 1971   20th
> century $160 million

Grammar | review of past tenses

9 a <u>Underline</u> the different tenses that are used in the text to describe the woman's life.

b Read the Active grammar box and complete the rules with the Past Perfect, Past Continuous and/or Past Simple.

Active grammar

1 Use the _____ to describe the main events of a story.

2 Use the _____ to describe things that happened before the main events in the past.

3 Use the _____ to describe actions that were already in progress when the main events happened.

4 We often use _____ and _____ together when one action was in progress and the other action happened suddenly.

   He **was sleeping** when the storm **began**.

5 We often use _____ and _____ together to make it clear which action happened before another action in the past.

   I **felt** ill because I **had eaten** bad food.

---

see Reference page 143

10 a Read about Gianni Versace. Put the verbs in brackets into the correct tense. There is one passive.

b Find three things he had in common with the woman in the text on page 136.

GIANNI VERSACE

Gianni Versace was born in Reggio Calabria, Italy, in 1946. His mother had a clothes shop, and it was while he (1)_____ (grow up) that he learned about making clothes. In 1972 he (2)_____ (move) to Milan to become a fashion designer, and in 1978 he (3)_____ (open) his first shop. In the same year, he (4)_____ (present) his first collection for women. He (5)_____ (already design) a leather collection for a company called Complice, but now, he worked for himself.

His designs (6)_____ (be) brightly coloured and sexy, and he used celebrities like Madonna, Tina Turner and Bon Jovi as models. In 1984 he (7)_____ (bring out) his own fragrance for men, 'Versace l'Homme'.

On July 16th 1997, while he (8)_____ (walk) outside his apartment in South Beach, Miami, he (9)_____ (shoot) dead by an unknown killer. During his life, his fashion empire (10)_____ (become) so successful that it was worth over $800 million.

Pronunciation

11 a Read the information in the How to ... box. Then look back at the numbers/dates in the box in Ex. 8 and say them aloud.

HOW TO ...

say numbers

	Written	Spoken
Dates	02/12/03	the second of December, two thousand and three
	1750s	the seventeen fifties
	C19th	the nineteenth century
Percentages	21.2%	twenty-one point two percent
Money	$78.32	seventy-eight dollars, thirty-two cents
Big numbers	1,265	one thousand two hundred and sixty-five
	1,000,000	a million/one million
Fractions	1½	one and a half
	¾	three-quarters

b Say the following:

a) 54½   b) 4,076   c) 9.3%   d) 2010
e) $4,375   f) 12/04/09   g) 1,300,000   h) 7¾
i) 21st May   j) 6.2%   k) 1920s

c **10.5** Listen and check. When do we use *and*? When do we use *the*?

12 Work in pairs.
Student A: look at page 147. **Student B:** look at page 150. You have some information missing. Ask and answer questions to complete your information.

Speaking

13 a Choose five numbers that are important to you. They could be dates, years, code numbers, prices, etc.

b Write down the numbers and give them to a partner.

c Ask questions to find out why each number is important. Then ask follow-up questions.

A: *Why did you write July 1992?*
B: *I graduated in July 1992.*
A: *What did you study?*
B: *I studied Law.*
A: *Where?*

10.3 Saying goodbye

Grammar	phrasal verbs
Can do	write a thank you letter

A

B

C

D

Listening

1   What types of goodbye are shown in the photos?

2   **a** `10.6` Listen to four goodbyes. What type of goodbyes do you hear? Number the situations below in the order you hear them.

   a) a father and daughter before she goes away __

   b) friends at the end of a party __

   c) a speaker at the end of a conference __

   d) two colleagues at the end of the day __

   b Listen again. In which recording:

   1   might some people meet again the following weekend? __

   2   will someone wait for an email? __

   3   is it probably Friday? __

   4   will someone wait for a phone call? __

   c Read the tapescript on page 176 to check.

Reading and speaking

3   Read the introduction to the text below and answer the questions.

> Paul Simon once sang 'There are fifty ways to leave your lover'. Here we tell you some of the worst. There are also plenty of ways to fire your staff but, as David Corey reports, there are nice ways and there are nasty ways.

   1   What is the text about? Do you think it is
        (a) very serious (b) a little bit funny (c) full of jokes?

   2   What two topics will the text talk about?

4   Work in pairs. **Student A:** read the text on the right. **Student B:** read the text on page 150. Answer the questions.

   1   What type of goodbye is described in your text?

   2   How did the companies/people say goodbye?

   3   What is the conclusion at the end of the text?

   4   What do you think of the behaviour described in the text?

   5   Is there a 'good' way to say goodbye in these situations?

5   Explain your text to your partner. Use your answers to Ex. 4 to help you. Quickly read your partner's text.

How not to fire your staff

One company text-messaged its employees, telling them to call a number. A recorded message informed the employees that 'all staff who are being retained will be contacted today. If you have not been spoken to, you have lost your job.' It's probably not the nicest way to **find out** that you are now unemployed. But it's maybe better than some.

Employees from a technology company **came back** from lunch and found that their security cards didn't work. 'What's **going on**?' they asked. The reply? They had been fired.

Another company invited its staff to a conference in Florida. When they **turned up** in the morning, some of the staff were told to go to Room A, others to Room B. The people in Room A listened to a presentation about the company's future. The people in Room B were told they were leaving the company.

It is impossible to **come up with** a 'nice' way to fire someone, but managers should at least do it in private and show respect for the employee. The problem is that bosses often panic. They are worried that the fired employees will steal important information. And they are sometimes right: in one company, the fired staff stole computers and other equipment and nearly destroyed the company's offices.

6 Now work together to find the phrasal verbs in **bold** in the texts that mean the following:

> continue   cancelled   returned   happening
> arrived   tolerate   think of/invent
> finished a relationship   discover
> experienced (something bad)

continue – *carry on*

Grammar | phrasal verbs

7 Read the Active grammar box and decide what type (1–4) the phrasal verbs from Ex. 6 are.

> **Active grammar**
>
> There are different types of phrasal verbs:
>
> 1 The verb takes no object (intransitive).
>   *I **turned up** late*
>
> 2 The verb takes an object (transitive) and the verb and particle can split.*
>   *I **called off** the wedding. I **called** the wedding **off**. I **called** it **off**.*
>   *When the object is a pronoun (*he*/*she*/ *it,* etc.) the verb and particle must split.
>   NOT: ~~I called off it.~~
>
> 3 The verb takes an object but the verb and particle cannot split (transitive, inseparable).
>   *He's **going through** a difficult time.*
>   NOT: ~~He's going a difficult time through.~~
>
> 4 The verb has two particles and doesn't split (transitive, inseparable).
>   *We **came up with** a new idea.*
>   NOT: ~~We came up a new idea with.~~

see Reference page 143

8 Put the words in order to make sentences.

1 girlfriend I up split my with .
2 We until out didn't later find .
3 back When you coming are ?
4 carry couldn't I tired because I was on .
5 always She late up turns .
6 with good they up Did any ideas come ?
7 going is here on What ?
8 match because rain The called off was of .
9 period is company going The a difficult through .
10 more I him up can't any with put .

9 Use words from Box 1 and Box 2 to complete the sentences below. Don't forget to change the verb tenses.

> Box 1   find   come (x2)   go (x2)   turn   split   carry   ~~call~~   put

> Box 2   up (x4)   on (x2)   with (x2)   ~~off~~   through   back   about   out

The concert was _called off_ because the singer was sick.

1 I will not _____ _____ _____ this noise! If it continues, I'll call the police!
2 If you want to _____ _____ _____ the history of science, you'll need to look in the library.
3 I don't need a break. I'm going to _____ _____ working.
4 It was a quiet party. There were only six of us, though more people _____ _____ later.
5 Can someone explain? I have no idea what's _____ _____ .
6 She _____ _____ a difficult period when she lost her job, but she's OK now.
7 Couples usually _____ _____ because of jealousy or boredom, or because they find other partners!
8 My best friend is _____ _____ from her holiday tomorrow, so I'm going to the airport to meet her.
9 You need to _____ _____ _____ a plan to improve your business, because you are losing money.

10 Which phrasal verbs do the pictures illustrate?

Listening

11 a Look at the photos. What do you think the song is about?

b [10.7] Cover the words. Listen to the song and write down any words you hear.

c Work with other students. What is the song about?

d Listen and read the words at the same time. Write one word in each space. Answer the questions.

1 What is the man going to do?

2 How does he feel?

3 Who is the song addressed to?

Leaving on a jet plane

All my bags are packed
I'm ready to (1)_____
I'm standing here outside your door
I hate to (2)_____ you up to say goodbye
But the dawn is breaking
It's early morn
The taxi's waiting
He's blowing his (3)_____
Already I'm so lonesome
I could cry

CHORUS
So kiss me and smile for me
Tell me that you'll (4)_____ for me
Hold me like you'll never let me go
I'm leaving on a jet plane
Don't know when I'll be (5)_____ again
Oh babe, I hate to go

There's so many times I've let you (6)_____
So many times I've (7)_____ around
I'll tell you now, they don't mean a thing
Every place I go, I'll think of you
Every song I sing, I'll sing for you
When I (8)_____ back, I'll wear your wedding ring

(CHORUS)

Now the time has come to (9)_____ you
One more time
Let me kiss you
Then close your eyes
I'll be on my (10)_____
Dream about the days to come
When I won't have to leave you alone
About the time I won't have to say

(CHORUS)

John Denver

12 Check together. Find phrasal verbs which mean:

1 what you do after sleeping (verse 1) _____

2 allow someone to leave (chorus) _____

3 done something wrong and disappointed someone (verse 2) _____

4 been unfaithful to a partner (verse 2) _____

5 return (verse 2) _____

Writing

13 a Read the thank you letters in the Writing bank on page 162 and do the exercises.

b Write a thank you letter to either (a) another student, (b) your teacher or (c) someone else at the school.

10 | Vocabulary

The senses

1 **a** Which senses – sight, sound, smell, touch or taste – do you associate with the photos?

b Which sense do you first associate with the words in the box?

> drums olives a cold wind petrol sunshine
> a mountain stream the sea fish red roses
> fresh bread a cotton shirt a stone floor

c Complete the phrases below with words/ phrases from the box.

1 The look/sight of ...
2 The sound of ...
3 The feel of ...
4 The smell of ...
5 The taste of ...

d In pairs, talk about things you like and dislike.
I love the taste of olive oil and fresh coffee.

2 **a** Look at the table and then do Ex. b

| It | looks/ feels/ sounds/ smells/ tastes | + adjective | It **looks** beautiful. It **tastes** delicious. |
| | | + like + noun phrase | It **sounds** like a mechanical problem. It **looks** like a nice day. |

b Match the sentences to make dialogues.

A	B
1 I love this dress.	a) Yes, he looked terrible.
2 A trip to the cinema?	b) Those roses smell beautiful.
3 I cooked the soup myself.	c) Yes, touch it. It feels very soft.
4 Can you hear the birds singing?	d) Yes, it looks great on you.
5 Miguel went home early.	e) That sounds like a great idea.
6 I've been working in the garden.	f) Yes, they sound lovely.
7 Are you sure this fish is fresh?	g) It tastes delicious.
8 Is the skirt made of silk?	h) No, it smells a bit strange.

c Cover the sentences in column B above, and practise the dialogues with a partner.

d **10.8** Listen to the tape. What do you think has just happened to each person?

1 A woman is cooking. She's just burned her hand!

3 **a** What is the difference between:
1 to see/to look at/to watch?
2 to listen to/to hear?
3 to touch/to hold?

b Write sentences using the different words.

4 Complete the sentences with the words/phrases from Ex. 3.
1 Can you _____ this bag for me? It's very heavy.
2 Have you _____ Jo's car? It's very fast.
3 Can you speak up, please? I can't _____ you.
4 Don't _____ that wire! It looks dangerous.
5 I was just _____ these beautiful photos.
6 Shall we _____ some music on the radio?
7 Did you _____ that TV programme last night?

5 **a** Read the poem below, and then write your own version using the model.
I love the look of ... *mountains with snow on top*,
I love the smell of ... *fresh coffee beans*,
I love the taste of ... *pasta with garlic*,
I love the sound of ... *a young boy singing*,
But most of all I love the feel of ... *a warm wind on my face*,
It reminds me of ... *walking by the sea.*

b Read your poem to other students.

1 a Spend a few minutes reading through the questions in the game below. Then read the instructions on how to play 'The Memory Game'.

b With your partners, play The Memory Game.

The memory game...

How to play...

1 Work in groups of three or more. Put your counters on the START box.
2 Roll the dice and move the correct number of squares.
3 Talk about the topic in the box.
4 The next student rolls the dice, moves, talks and so on.
5 The first person to reach the FINISH is the winner.

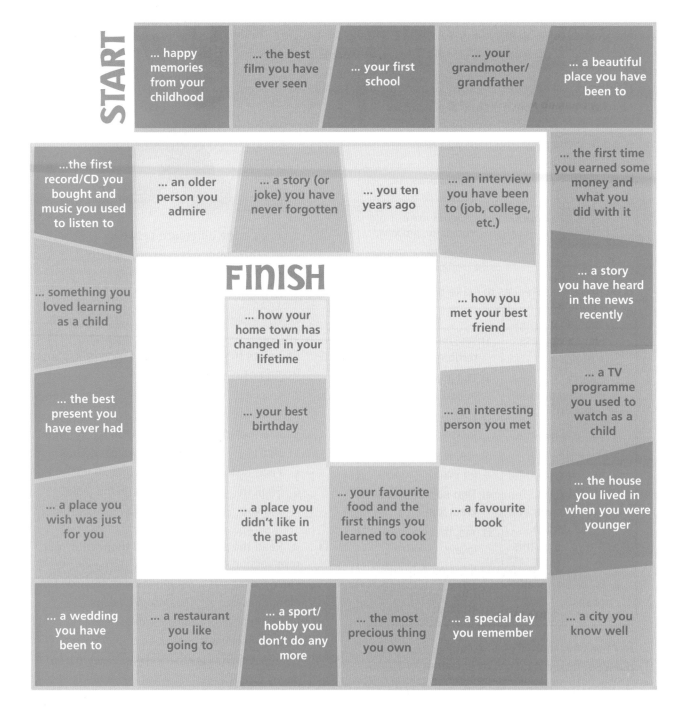

START

... happy memories from your childhood

... the best film you have ever seen

... your first school

... your grandmother/ grandfather

... a beautiful place you have been to

...the first record/CD you bought and music you used to listen to

... an older person you admire

... a story (or joke) you have never forgotten

... you ten years ago

... an interview you have been to (job, college, etc.)

... the first time you earned some money and what you did with it

... something you loved learning as a child

FINISH

... how your home town has changed in your lifetime

... how you met your best friend

... a story you have heard in the news recently

... the best present you have ever had

... your best birthday

... an interesting person you met

... a TV programme you used to watch as a child

... a place you wish was just for you

... a place you didn't like in the past

... your favourite food and the first things you learned to cook

... a favourite book

... the house you lived in when you were younger

... a wedding you have been to

... a restaurant you like going to

... a sport/ hobby you don't do any more

... the most precious thing you own

... a special day you remember

... a city you know well

I wish/if only

Use *wish* to say we would like something to be different from the reality.

To talk about a wish in the present, or a permanent wish, use **wish + Past Simple**. The most common verbs are *wish + was/were* and *wish + had*.

*She **wishes** she **was** taller.*

*I **wish** I **had** a pen.*

With the verb *to be* you can also say *I wish I were/ she wishes she were*.

To talk about a wish in the past, use **wish + had + past participle**.

*He **wishes** he **had gone** to the exhibition yesterday.*

*I **wish** I **hadn't eaten** that sandwich.*

Use **wish + object + would** to show you want something to change. We often use this structure to show anger or annoyance.

*I **wish** she **would** come on time.*

*I **wish** you **wouldn't** make that noise.*

! We can't say: ~~I wish I would.~~

Use **wish + could** to talk about an ability that you want but don't have.

*I **wish** I **could** play chess as well as you.*

*I **wish** I **could** fly.*

! We don't usually use *wish + couldn't*.

We can also use *if only* instead of *I wish*. The meaning is a little bit stronger than *I wish*.

If only we could go home!

If only they hadn't taken the money!

Past tenses review

We often use the Past Simple, Past Perfect and Past Continuous for narratives.

The Past Simple is used for the main completed events.

*I **took** the money and **ran**.*

The Past Perfect is used for an action that happened before another action.

*I **hadn't planned** to walk but **I'd left** my wallet at home.*

The Past Continuous is used for an action in progress over a period of time. It's often a background action in the narrative.

*When I got outside, it **was raining** hard.*

*I **was living** in Paris when I **married** Lily. I **had met** her in Austria.*

```
                        I was living in Paris
                       ┌──────────────────────┐
  I met Lily in Austria    I married Lily          now
  ───x────────────────────────x────────────────────x──────►
```

Phrasal verbs

There are four main types of phrasal verbs:

1 Intransitive

The verb has no object.

*I **grew up**.*

2 Transitive – separable

The verb has an object and the verb and particle can split.

*I **turned off** the light.*

*I **turned** the light **off**.*

*I **turned** it **off**.*

When the object is a pronoun (*he/she/it*, etc.) the verb must split.

NOT: ~~I turned off it.~~

3 Transitive – inseparable

The verb takes an object and the verb and particle cannot split.

*He **got on** the bus.*

NOT: ~~He got the bus on.~~

4 Three-part

The verb has two particles and doesn't split (transitive, inseparable)

*We're **looking forward to** seeing you..*

NOT: ~~We're looking forward seeing you to.~~

Key vocabulary

Memory

remember   remind   forget   lose   miss
remind us to   remind us of   in memory of

Describing great people

determined   talented   brave   brilliant
dedicate (one's life)   encourage   inspire
be involved in

Phrasal verbs

find out   come back   go on   turn up   call off
come up with   split up   carry on   go through
put up with   wake up   let (someone) go
let (someone) down   play around

The senses

it looks/feels/tastes/sounds/smells (like) ...

1 Complete the sentences using the verbs in brackets. You may need to add some extra words.

He has to wash all the dishes. He probably wishes he _____ (have) a dishwasher.

He has to wash all the dishes. He probably wishes he had a dishwasher.

1 I have to read so many books! I wish I _____ (be) such a slow reader.

2 She's so full she can't sleep. She probably wishes she _____ (eat) so much.

3 I loved Disneyland! I wish I _____ (go) there the last time I was in the US.

4 He hates taking trains. He wishes he _____ (have) a car.

5 There are some job vacancies in the Bahamas. Don't you wish you _____ (can work) there?

6 My favourite film was on TV yesterday, but at 1.00a.m. I wish they _____ (show) it earlier.

7 Those children have been inside all day. They probably wish they _____ (can play) outside.

8 It is such beautiful weather! Do you wish you _____ (be) on holiday?

2 Complete the dialogues using the correct form of the verbs in the box.

> do ~~answer~~ not hear listen

A: I knocked on the door last night but you *didn't answer*. What (1)_____?

B: Oh, sorry. I (2)_____ to music and I (3)_____ you.

> go stop have

A: (4)_____ a good weekend?

B: Yes, we (5)_____ for a picnic.

A: In the rain?

B: No! The rain (6)_____ by the time we got to the park.

> get back visit not go

A: Why (7)_____ to the New Year party? We missed you.

B: I was exhausted because I (8)_____ from Australia that morning.

A: Really? What were you doing there?

B I (9)_____ my cousins.

3 Write sentences from the words in brackets in the Past Perfect or Past Continuous.

We tried to call her. (She/switch off her phone)
She had switched off her phone.

1 I saw a friend after many years. She looked very different.
(She/change/a lot) _____

2 The book was completely new to me.
(I/never/read/before) _____

3 Tom was in the pool from 6.15a.m. to 6.45a.m.
(At 6.30 he/swim) _____

4 Javed didn't break the window at midnight.
(He/sleep/in his room/at midnight) _____

5 I couldn't cross the border into Mexico.
(I/lose/my passport) _____

6 Lola went to an interview every day.
(She/look for/a job) _____

4 Tick (✓) the two possible sentence endings.

They came up with (a) a great idea ✓ (b) a solution to the problem ✓ (c) brilliantly. ✗

1 We split up (a) *after many years* (b) *because we argued a lot* (c) *my husband.*

2 I went through (a) *a difficult time* (b) *hell* (c) *a nice month.*

3 They turned up (a) *on time* (b) *very well* (c) *to watch the match.*

4 We called off (a) *the party* (b) *my friends* (c) *our arrangement.*

5 I put up with (a) *the excellent service* (b) *the press* (c) *those stupid comments.*

6 He won't find out (a) *if we don't tell him* (b) *about the money* (c) *of the story.*

7 What's going on (a) *wrong?* (b) *here?* (c) *today?*

8 I'd like to carry on (a) *working* (b) *playing next year* (c) *to watch the film.*

5 Use the words/phrases in the box to complete the text.

> woods found out reminds dedicated
> horses ~~smell~~ encouraged turned up

The *smell* of dry grass always 1)_____ me of my grandmother. She lived in the countryside, and kept 2)_____. When I 3)_____ at weekends, she would take me out riding in the 4)_____. She loved children and 5)_____ her life to helping children who could not read or write. She started a special school, and 6)_____ parents to bring their children to her for help. When the local government 7)_____ what she was doing, they helped her to open schools in other towns. Many of them are still open today.

Communication activities

Lesson 2.1 | Ex. 1, page 20

The order in which they were invented is: newspapers, radio, TV, video, the Internet.

Lesson 2.2 | Ex. 13a, page 25

Group A

Complete the quiz questions with the correct relative pronoun.

Category: Sport

1 The football player _____ won the World Cup when he was seventeen years old was
(a) Pelé (b) Maradona (c) David Beckham (d) Ronaldo
(€100,000)

2 The boxer _____ went to prison for refusing to fight in the war against Vietnam was (a) Joe Frazier (b) Muhammad Ali
(c) George Foreman (d) Sugar Ray
(€100,000)

3 The USSR is the only country _____ team has beaten the US in the Olympic Games at (a) baseball (b) basketball (c) volleyball
(d) swimming (€100,000)
[answers: 1a, 2b, 3b]

Category: The Arts

1 A haiku is a type of poem _____ has
(a) 14 lines (b) a male hero (c) 3 lines (d) a description of an animal (€100,000)

2 Jackson Pollock was one of the artists _____ invented
(a) Cubism (b) Action Painting (c) Surrealism (d) Impressionism
(€100,000)

3 The place _____ Mozart, Haydn and Johann Strauss were born is
(a) Germany (b) Switzerland (c) Poland (d) Austria
(€150,000)
[answers: 1c, 2b, 3d]

Category: Geography

1 The name of the desert _____ extends across Mongolia and Northern China is
(a) The Sahara Desert (b) The Gobi Desert (c) The Kalahari Desert
(d) The Arabian Desert
(€100,000)

2 The name of the river _____ flows both north and south of the Equator is (a) The Congo (b) The Nile (c) The Mississippi
(d) The Amazon
(€100,000)

3 The canal _____ joins the Red Sea and the Mediterranean Sea is
(a) The Rhine Canal (b) The Panama Canal (c) The Suez Canal
(d) The Egyptian Canal (€150,000)
[answers: 1b, 2a, 3c]

Communication 2 | Ex. 1, page 30

Students A

You want to make money for your newspaper. You like celebrities on the front page. You don't like too many disasters or too much international news, because you don't think it sells well.

Now look at the list of stories in Ex. 2a on page 30.

Lesson 3.1 | Ex. 11, page 36

Student A

You want:

- a full refund of the €500 fee.
- more money because you had to buy sheets and towels.
- a written apology from *Yourhome-Myhome.com*.
- to take your home off the website.

Lesson 5.1 | Ex. 13a, page 64

Problems

1 Your hotel has been receiving complaints from the customers: the lifts are too slow. They are very old, expensive lifts with material on the walls. The cost of buying new lifts is extremely high, and the hotel doesn't have enough money. Think of a solution.

2 You work in a university hospital. You want to persuade the students to get an injection against tetanus. You have been sending brochures to the students for one year, but only 3% of the students have come for an injection. Another university hospital has been doing the same thing, but 28% of their students have had injections. They've been sending out one extra piece of paper with the brochure. What is on this piece of paper?

Communication activities

Lesson 4.3 | Ex. 3, page 54
Student B

How you are persuaded to spend more by ...

Supermarkets ...

We spend more time in them than we want to, we buy 75 per cent of our food from them and we buy a lot of products that we don't even need.

Supermarkets always have good marketing ideas. When shopping baskets were introduced in the 1950s stores, they were an immediate success. Now shoppers could walk around and pick up items they previously didn't even look at. Soon came trolleys, and the bigger the trolley, the more people will buy. Customers think 'If I buy lots now, I won't need to come back later.' Supermarkets help us enjoy shopping by making the environment pleasant. They play music to help us relax and blow air from the in-store bakery around the shop. Some stores have 'greeters' to welcome you. This gives the illusion of community – the notion that shopping in a giant store isn't so different from visiting a village shop.

Warning signs:

- Two for one deals: Supermarkets will usually offer these when a fruit or vegetable is in season, and so there is a lot of it, and it's cheap.
- Music: If the experience is relaxing, you will stay in the shop longer. The longer you stay, the more you buy.
- The influence of smell: As soon as you walk into the shop, you can smell the bread and coffee smells. Pleasant aromas can make you buy more.

Communication 2 | Ex. 1, page 30
Students B

You are responsible editors. You want a lot of news about developing countries. You think that major disasters and international news stories are very important. Now look at the list of stories in Ex. 2a on page 30.

Lesson 5.3 | Ex. 2b, page 68

Meal – a time when you eat food. For example, lunch.
Dish – food that is prepared in a special way. E.g. Roast beef.
Service – the help people give you in a hotel/restaurant. It may be included in the price.
Tip – extra money you leave if you think the service is good.
Dessert – a dish you eat it at the end of the meal, often sweet.
Side dish – a dish you eat with your main course, e.g vegetables.
Tablecloth – the large cloth which covers the table.
Napkin – a smaller cloth which you use to clean your mouth.

Lesson 7.1 | Ex. 10b, page 92
Quiz answers

Quiz A

1 Who painted Guernica in 1937? Picasso
2 When did Mozart start composing music? When he was 4 years old/1760
3 Who discovered penicillin in 1928? Sir Alexander Fleming
4 Which of the world's greatest scientists lived from 1879–1955? Albert Einstein
5 Which famous city is nicknamed The Big Apple? New York
6 What invention is Guglielmo Marconi responsible for? The radio
7 Which is the largest desert in the world? The Sahara
8 Who earned $34 million per day during the 1990s? Bill Gates
9 Which country is the oldest surviving republic in the world? San Marino
10 When did Boris Becker become the youngest man ever to win the men's singles at Wimbledon? 1985

Vocabulary 5 | Ex. 5, page 71
Student A

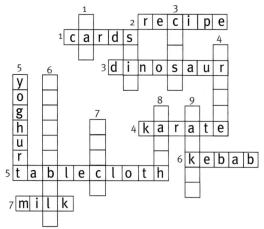

Lesson 6.3 | Ex. 11, page 84
Student A

Read these sentences to your partner and continue the conversation. (Invent a response!)

My cousin knows Harrison Ford!
My best friend has been married five times!
My partner is famous!
I eat pasta every single day!
I left home when I was fifteen!
I won the lottery last year!

Lesson 3.1 | Ex. 11, page 36

Student B

You will:

- NOT offer a refund of the €500 fee.
- offer some money because Miriam bought sheets and towels.
- offer a 75% discount on Miriam's next home swap, if she keeps her home on your website.
- explain that the cleaner was sick, so the house was a mess.
- explain that the heating and hot water were working, but they were switched off. Miriam needed to switch them on.

Lesson 6.2 | Ex. 5, page 79

Student B

Situation 1: In a train station:
You would like three return tickets to Cambridge (two adults and one child).
Find out:

1 how much they cost.
2 what time the next train leaves.
3 which platform to go to.

Situation 2: In a tourist office:
You work in the tourist office. Give directions to the Tate Gallery.

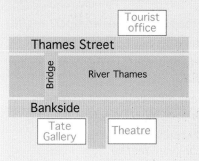

Opening times:
9.00a.m. – 5.00p.m. Monday – Thursday
9.00a.m. – 10.00p.m. Friday/Saturday
Closed Sundays

Tickets: adults £12.50, children – free

Lesson 10.2 | Ex. 12, page 137

Student A

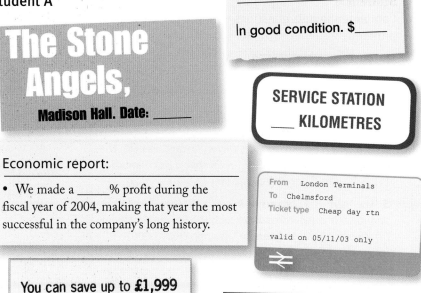

The Stone Angels,

Madison Hall. Date: _____

Economic report:

- We made a _____% profit during the fiscal year of 2004, making that year the most successful in the company's long history.

You can save up to £1,999 on household furnishings if you buy our **Millennium** package.

¾ of all accidents take place in the home.
BE CAREFUL!

Second-hand car.

In good condition. $_____

SERVICE STATION
_____ KILOMETRES

From London Terminals
To Chelmsford
Ticket type Cheap day rtn

valid on 05/11/03 only

As stated in legislation Section 1(d) of the Code of Amsterry Sports Club, 1962, the carrying of firearms is strictly forbidden on these premises.

Lesson 2.2 | Ex. 8b, page 24

Student B

THE MAN WHO NEVER LOST

MR. VAN DOREN

USA, 1958. The quiz show contestant was sweating. He nervously looked around the studio where he was being filmed. The television cameras focused on his face. He thought hard. Finally he gave the answer to the question, and the crowd cheered. Millions of Americans watching in their homes, were happy that their hero, Charles Van Doren, was again the winner of *Twenty-One*. It was only later that the truth came out. The man whose fame meant that he received 500 letters a day, who appeared on the cover of *Time* magazine and who had won more than $100,000 on the show, was also a cheat. TV quiz shows were very popular in the USA in the 1950s. And the idea that one person could keep on winning was especially popular. Audiences began to 'support' this winner, and wanted to see him win every week. The producer of *Twenty-One*, Dan Enright, decided that to keep his show popular, it was necessary to give Van Doren the answers before the show.
Herbie Stempel, the previous champion before Van Doren, was the person who revealed the truth. He told the public that contestants on the programme were given the answers and also taught what to do in front of the cameras: how to look nervous, how to pause and how to pretend to not know the answers. After an investigation which examined every moment of every *Twenty-One* show, Van Doren eventually admitted cheating. American TV had lost its innocence.

Communication activities

Lesson 2.2 | Ex. 13a, page 25

Group B

Complete the quiz questions with the correct relative pronoun.

Category: Cinema

1 Marilyn Monroe was the actress _____ original name was **(a)** Norma Jean Baker **(b)** Mary Monray **(c)** Grace Kelly **(d)** Jane Monroe Smith (€100,000)

2 The 1997 film _____ won eleven Oscars was **(a)** *The English Patient* **(b)** *Star Wars – Episode 1* **(c)** *Titanic* **(d)** *E.T.: The Extra-Terrestrial* (€100,000)

3 The man _____ directed *Reservoir Dogs*, *Pulp Fiction* and *Kill Bill* is **(a)** Alfred Hitchcock **(b)** Steven Spielberg **(c)** Woody Allen **(d)** Quentin Tarantino (€100,000)
[answers: 1a, 2c, 3d]

Category: Nature

1 The mammal _____ lives the longest is the **(a)** elephant **(b)** turtle **(c)** blue whale **(d)** lizard (€100,000)

2 An area of land _____ 2.75m of rain falls every year is **(a)** New York City **(b)** The Amazon Rainforest **(c)** The Alps **(d)** Europe (€100,000)

3 The camel is an animal _____ hump is made of **(a)** water **(b)** fat **(c)** muscle **(d)** hair (€150,000)
[answers 1c, 2b, 3b]

Category: Science and technology

1 The person _____ invented the telephone was **(a)** John Logie Baird **(b)** James Watt **(c)** Alexander Watt **(d)** Alexander Bell (€100,000)

2 The small piece of silicon _____ makes a computer work is called a **(a)** microchip **(b)** microphone **(c)** microsoft **(d)** microscope (€100,000)

3 Sir Alexander Fleming was the man _____ work in 1941 changed the state of medicine around the world. He discovered **(a)** AIDS **(b)** cancer **(c)** penicillin **(d)** x-rays (€150,000)
[answers: 1d, 2a, 3c]

Lesson 6.3 | Ex. 11, page 84

Student B

Read these sentences to your partner and continue the conversation. (Invent a response!)
My cousin has twenty brothers!
My best friend has climbed Mount Everest!
My partner works as a spy!
I play six instruments!
I learned Chinese, Japanese and French last year!
I lost my wallet yesterday!

Lesson 3.3 | Ex. 14, page 42

Student B

PHONE YOUR PARTNER.
1   Your partner works in an office (Smith and Co).
    Ask to speak to the manager (about a job).
2   Your partner works in a private bank (Jeeves Bank).
    Ask to speak to Mr Jones, your bank manager (about your bank account).
3   Your partner works at hotel reception (Hotel Paradiso).
    Ask to speak to Jill Orwell in Room 101.

ANSWER THE PHONE.
1   You work in a computer shop (Bust Computers). The engineer isn't in today.
2   You work in an office (Lula Incorporated). The line is engaged.
3   You work in a school (Cool School of English). The director is out shopping.

Vocabulary 5 | Ex. 5, page 71

Student B

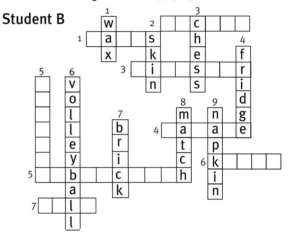

Communication 8 | Ex. 2a, page 114

Student B

Are you ready FOR CHANGE?

1   Do you always read the same newspaper? Yes/No
2   Do you like to take up new hobbies? Yes/No
3   Would you like to do a course to learn new skills for work? Yes/No
4   Do you have many different groups of friends who don't know each other? Yes/No
5   Do you like to experiment with new recipes when you are cooking? Yes/No
6   Do you always shop in the same place? Yes/No

Communication 2 | Ex. 1, page 30

Students C

You think that scientific developments are important for man's future. You also believe that there needs to be a balance between good news and bad news on the front page.
Now look at the list of stories in Ex. 2a on page 30.

Lesson 4.3 | Ex. 3, page 54

Student C

How you are persuaded to spend more by ...

Salespeople

If you really believe in a product, this will help you sell it. But the best professional salespeople can sell anything, to anybody, at any time. They do this by using very simple psychological techniques. It is human nature to prefer to speak rather than to listen, and good salespeople use this. They ask buyers what they want before showing how their product is the best.

Most salespeople will get to know their client by asking questions about hobbies, family and lifestyle. If customers think of the salesperson as a friend, they will probably keep coming back to the same man or woman.

Salespeople will try to behave like the buyer. If the buyer makes jokes, the salesperson will too. If the buyer wants detail, the seller provides it. The salesperson may even try to 'mirror' the body language of the buyer. Lastly, salespeople will use careful language. They will not say 'if you buy ...' , but 'when you buy', so that they cannot fail.

Warning signs:

- Body language: When the salesperson moves away from the desk, or towards the door, it gives the impression that the sale is complete.

- Appointment book open: It is hard to say 'no' when the salesperson is already making an appointment.

- Repetition: The salesperson repeats the last phrase you said. It gives the illusion of interest.

Lesson 6.1 | Ex. 13, page 78

Choose a photo. Imagine you were one of the people in this situation. Think about what you are going to say, then describe the photo to your partner.

Lesson 5.1 | Ex. 13c, page 64

Solutions

1 The hotel manager put mirrors in the lifts. The complaints stopped immediately. When people have something interesting to look at, they don't mind a delay!

2 The piece of paper contained a map of the university area showing exactly where the hospital was, and the times it was open for students to have their injection. The students knew the dangers of tetanus but wanted to know how to 'fit' the injections into their lives.

Lesson 7.1 | Ex. 10b, page 92

Quiz answers

Quiz B

1 Which islands did Christopher Columbus discover in 1492, before he discovered America? The Bahamas

2 Who painted the Sistine Chapel? Michelangelo

3 What book made Umberto Eco famous? *The Name of the Rose*

4 Which European country has the smallest area? Vatican City

5 Which team did David Beckham join in 1993? Manchester United

6 Who wrote the song *Imagine* in 1971? John Lennon

7 What did John Logie Baird invent? The television

8 Which is the world's longest river? The Nile

9 Which famous writer lived from 1564 –1616? William Shakespeare

10 When did Hong Kong become part of China again? 1997

Lesson 10.1 | Ex. 5, page 132

Story endings

1 When Colin left the hospital, his memory began to return. Lydia played him his favourite songs and took him to places they used to go to: his favourite restaurants and bars. Gradually, he and Lydia fell in love again. They got married and now live happily in Liverpool.

2 Mr Nobody's real name is David Rogers. Rogers is a sailor. He was hit on the head during a trip across the Pacific Ocean. At first he seemed OK. But when the ship stopped off in Australia he lost his memory. His real identity was discovered when his family back in England saw a photo of him in the newspaper. Today he doesn't remember all of his past, but he remembers family and friends and everything that happened to him before his last journey by boat.

3 The journalist, S, would imagine himself walking down a street, and in his mind he would see the objects on the street. His incredible memory was the result of what we now call visualisation technique. He also had synaesthesia – which means he associated one sense with another. For example, taste can be associated with colour. He once said to Luria, 'What a crumbly yellow voice you have.'

Communication activities

Lesson 7.3 | Ex. 5a, page 96

Student B

Louisa May, 88

Louisa May played the piano as a girl, and studied for two years at the Royal Academy of Music. She couldn't continue because her father died and she had to help with the family business, but 45 years later she started composing again. She has completed five major works, which can be found on two CDs. 'When I started composing again, life was in front of me; all my young hopes were coming through. I felt 30 years younger. Now I'm getting so very old. I may last 10 years but I may die tomorrow. That's all right now. My husband once said to me, 'Your music means more to you than I do.' I thought about that, then replied, 'Yes. And it means more to me than I do.'

Mary Wesley, 86

After many years writing, Mary Wesley finally published her first novel, *Jumping the Queue*, aged 70. Ten novels have followed. She has now sold more than 2.5 million books. 'I've written off and on all my life but I had a husband and children, so my writing was just a hobby. I was very surprised when this success came to me. It was a great help because it gave me some money. I don't feel 86. Age doesn't make any difference to me. The secret is to have friends who are much younger than you. When all your contemporaries have died, you have to look to younger people.'

Kyra Vane, 82

In 1995, the early recordings of this unrecognised soprano were sold on CD. The record was a surprise hit. A collection of new recordings was released in 1996. 'In my mid-seventies, I met somebody who listened to the tapes I had stored under my bed. He believed the world should hear my voice. If I had achieved this earlier in life, it might not have brought me happiness. One should keep one's brain alert and keep interested in things and people and the young. I mostly know people in their forties, fifties and sixties. I don't have many friends in my age group. The average woman in her eighties can be very dull, but I think people who have had children and grandchildren have achieved far more than me.'

Lesson 10.2 | Ex. 12, page 137

Student B

The Stone Angels,

Madison Hall. Date: 15th January 2005

Economic report:

• We made a 15.6% profit during the fiscal year of 2004, making that year the most successful in the company's long history.

You can save up to £_____ on household furnishings if you buy our **Millennium package.**

Second-hand car.

In good condition. $2,500

SERVICE STATION 1½ KILOMETRES

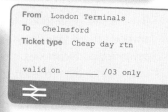

From   London Terminals
To   Chelmsford
Ticket type   Cheap day rtn

valid on _____ /03 only

As stated in legislation Section 1(d) of the Code of Amsterry Sports Club, 19 ____, the carrying of firearms is strictly forbidden on these premises.

_____ of all accidents take place in the home.
BE CAREFUL!

Lesson 10.3 | Ex. 4, page 138

Student B

How not to spilt up with your partner

OK, so the rich and famous always say 'It was an amicable break-up' or 'We **split up** because of work pressures'. Don't believe a word of it. They may **carry on** smiling for the cameras, but behind the smiles there are some angry people. Here are some examples of why.

One famous actress was expecting a baby when her long-term partner, and the father of the child, sent her a fax to inform her that he was leaving her. But maybe that's not as bad as actor Matt Damon. He split up with girlfriend Minnie Driver on the Oprah Winfrey chat show, live, in front of the US public. Billy Bob Thornton **called off** his relationship with Laura Dern by marrying Angelina Jolie. Dern said, 'I left our home to work on a movie and, while I was away, my boyfriend got married and I've never heard from him again.' But if you think they **went through** hell, times were even harder for women a few centuries ago. Take King Henry VIII's wives. Out of his six wives, he divorced two and he had another couple executed. When it's time to say the Big Goodbye, it seems that women have always had to **put up with** insensitive men.

Lesson 8.2 | Ex. 12b, page 109

1 Asia isn't the biggest continent but actually it has the most people.
2 Rich countries regularly throw away food but 50% of the world's people don't have enough.
3 Sadly, 80% don't have electricity or running water.
4 Unfortunately, only 30% of the world's population can read and only 1% of people in the world go to university. Surprisingly, only 1% of the world's population owns a computer.

1   Discuss.

  1   Do you enjoy watching comedy films? Do you have any favourites? What are they?

  2   Do you recognise any of the actors in the photos? Who are they? Do you know any of the films they appear in? What did you think of them?

2   You are going to watch two film extracts.

The first extract begins: 'We'd better get back to the hotel and get our things packed because the boat sails at 12 o'clock'. The second extract begins: 'I want my ball back'. What do you think happens in the extracts? Where are they?

3   Watch the film extracts and answer the questions.

  1   What is the relationship between the two men in each extract?

  2   Do you think they have a good or bad relationship? Why?

  3   Do you have any relationships like these? Who with? Is the relationship important to you? Why?

4   a   In which film extract (one or two) does someone ...

  1   have a secret? __

  2   have their picture painted? __

  3   get rescued by firemen? __

  4   receive a phonecall? __

  5   play a trick? __

  6   order a drink? __

  7   play football with some children? __

  8   send a letter to his girlfriend? __

  9   worry about losing his job? __

  10   climb onto the roof of a tall building? __

  b   Compare your answers with a partner.

5   Discuss.

  1   Do you like the film extracts? Do you find them funny? Why/Why not?

  2   Have you seen any other comedy films recently? Who starred in it/them? What happened? Why did you find it/them funny?

1 Discuss.

  1 What do you know about the people/places/objects in the photos? What big news stories/events are they associated with?

  2 When did the events take place? Who was involved? What happened?

2 Match the words/phrases in the box to the people/events in the photos.

> symbol   election   eclipse   division
> democratically elected   destroy the structure
> rays of light   temperature   the universe
> reconciliation   liberated territory

3 **a** The phrases below relate to the news stories in the photos. Complete each phrase to make a sentence.

  1 Berliners from both East and West ...

  2 It wasn't long before the first attempts ...

  3 I'm standing ...

  4 Some people have waited ...

  5 We had come to South Africa expecting ...

  6 They started dancing as soon as ...

  7 At 11.11p.m. on the 11th day of the month, ... the ... cameras show the moment when the last rays of light ...

  8 The light went very quickly and the temperature ...

  9 The people in Britain had a once-in-a-lifetime encounter with ...

  b Watch the film extracts and check your sentences. How much information can you remember about each news story?

4 Discuss.

  1 What are the biggest world news stories at the moment?

  2 Are they affecting you/your country? How?

  3 Are there any news stories/events from the past that you particularly remember? Why?

  4 Where were you when they happened? How did you feel about them?

1 Describe the properties in the photos and answer the questions.

1 Would you like to live in any of these places? Why/Why not?

2 What do you think are the advantages or disadvantages of living in each place?

2 Watch the film extracts. What do the speakers say about where they live? Make notes in the table below.

	Description of property/area	Good/bad things about where they live	Where they plan to live in the future
Speaker 1			
Speaker 2			
Speaker 3			
Speaker 4			

3 Discuss.

1 Do you agree with what the speakers say about living in the city/country?

2 Would you prefer to live in the city or the country? Why?

4 Tell your partner about where you live and what you like/dislike about it.

My Fair Lady

The Great Gatsby

Trading Places

The Count of Monte Christo

1 Discuss.

1 Have you seen any of the films in the photos?

2 What is the connection between them?

3 How did the people in the films become rich?

4 Do you know any other films with a 'rags to riches' theme?

2 **a** You are going to watch a film extract from *The Lavender Hill Mob*. Read the quotes from the extract below and check the meaning of any words you do not understand. Use a dictionary if necessary.

1 'It's your first visit to South America?' __

2 'Yes, I wish I could stay longer.' __

3 'Congratulations! A wonderful party! The President himself told my husband it was the occasion of the year.' __

4 'Thank you, señor. Always so generous.' __

5 'You rode a very good race.' __

6 'You run along and get yourself a little birthday present.' __

7 'You seem to have accomplished quite a lot in one year.' __

8 'For twenty years I've dreamed of a life like this.' __

9 'Most men who long to be rich know inwardly that they will never achieve their ambition.' __

10 'It was my job to supervise the deliveries of bullion from the gold refinery to the bank.' __

b Watch the film and match the quotes to the people below.

4 Put the events from the film extract into the correct order.

a He gives a jockey (someone who rides horses) some money. __

b He remembers when he was working hard in the city. __

c He donates money to 'Victims of the Revolution'. __

d He gives someone money for a birthday present. __

e He gives the waiter a tip. __

5 Discuss.

1 What type of film is *The Lavender Hill Mob*?

2 Who is the main character?

3 Where is he in the extract?

4 How do you know he is very wealthy?

5 How do you think he became rich?

6 Who is he telling his story to?

7 What do you think is going to happen to him now?

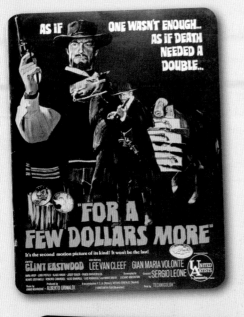

1 Discuss.
  1 Have you seen any of the films in the photos?
  2 Did you like them? Why/Why not?
  3 What sort of films are they (thriller, romance, horror, comedy, war film or western)?
  4 What sort of films do you like best? Why?

2 Watch the film extract and answer the questions.
  1 Where is it set? When?
  2 What type of film is it?
  3 Who stars in it?
  4 What are the most famous lines from the film?
  5 What film are the people talking about?
  6 What is the story about?
  7 What are the names of the main characters?

3 Watch the film extract again to check your answers.

4 What did you think of the film trailer? Did it make you want to see the film? What do you think is special about this film?

5 Tell your partner about your favourite film. Remember to mention what kind of film it is, who stars in it, where it is set, what happens and why you think it is a good film.

1 **Look at the photos and discuss.**

1 Which place looks (a) the most relaxing (b) the most interesting (c) the most enjoyable?

2 What other types of holiday can you think of?

3 What type of holiday do you like best?

2 **In which columns below would you put these holiday activities?**

> diving   hiking   visiting museums   reading long novels   sleeping a lot
> visiting historical sites   lazing in the sun   sailing   windsurfing
> going on day-trips   people-watching   skiing

LEARNING ABOUT THE WORLD	PRACTISING A SKILL	RELAXATION

3 **Watch the film extract and complete the table.**

	What does the speaker say about activities and things to do?	What does the speaker say about nature and animals?
The Maldives		
New Zealand		
Egypt		

4 **Discuss.**

1 Did you enjoy the film? Why/Why not?

2 Which holiday would you choose? Why?

3 Do you agree that 'many holidaymakers are active. They want to learn a skill, discover more about the world and make the most of the outdoors.'?

4 How did you spend your last holiday?

5 What is the best holiday you have ever had?

7 Cambridge

1 Look at the photos and discuss the questions.

1 What do you know about Cambridge?

2 What do you think you can see/do there?

3 What do you know about the university?

4 Do you think Cambridge is a good place for students to study/ live?

2 Complete the text about Cambridge using the words in the box.

> men   graduation   study   best   sports   colleges
> writer   career   river   style   famous   gowns

Cambridge University is one of the oldest and most (1) _____ universities in the UK. There are 31 (2) _____ within the university, many of them dating back to the 13th and 14th Century. One of the oldest colleges is Corpus Christi, which has been maintained in the original (3) _____. Christopher Marlowe, who was a (4) _____ at the same time as Shakespeare, studied here. Corpus Christi used to be for (5) _____ only. In 1660, however, they decided to allow women to (6) _____ here too.

Living in Cambridge is like stepping backwards in time. The students at Cambridge University, who wear (7) _____ for special occasions, like (8) _____ day, talk about why they chose Cambridge. Many believe it to be one of the (9) _____ universities in the country, so it offers good (10) _____ prospects. Also, it has an active social scene and there are lots of things to do in Cambridge, like go to clubs or bars, join in the (11) _____ activities, or hire a punt * and relax on the (12) _____.

* a boat which you move by pushing with a long stick

3 Watch the film and check your answers.

4 Discuss.

1 What did you think of the film?

2 What did the students say they enjoyed about being at Cambridge University?

3 Would you like to go to Cambridge University? Why/Why not?

4 Which cities do you think are good university cities? Why?

1 Discuss.

1 What changes generally take place between the ages of 0–5, 5–10, 10–20, 30–40 and 60–70 years old?

2 Have you changed much in the last year/five years/ten years? How? What do you do more/less of? What have you learned?

3 What does the phrase 'from cradle to grave' mean?

2 a Match the words and phrases in column A to the words and phrases in column B.

A	B
1 during	a) beats
2 achieve	b) fingernails
3 heart	c) incredible things
4 spend time	d) her lifetime
5 grow	e) in love
6 breathe	f) blood cells
7 produce red	g) of your life
8 fall	h) day
9 wedding	i) air
10 for the rest	j) on the telephone

b Which of these phrases describes (a) special moments (b) things we do all the time (c) a time period?

3 a Read the sentences below and circle the correct answers. In Britain, the average woman ...

1 spends 3½/5/10 years eating.

2 learns a new word every 20 minutes/2 hours/day for the first 10 years of her life.

3 spends 2/over 12/over 20 years watching TV.

4 spends 2½/5/10 years on the phone.

5 grows 9/95/950 kilometres of hair on her head during her lifetime.

6 works for over 2/8/20 years.

7 can name 200/2000/20,000 people (not famous people!).

8 has 15/150/500 friends.

9 falls in love once/twice/5 times.

10 spends £2,809/£6,809/£10,809 on her wedding.

11 has a 40 percent/60 percent/80 percent chance of staying married to the same person for the rest of her life.

12 has 1/2/3 children.

13 lives until the age of 70/79/83.

b Watch the film and check your answers.

4 Discuss.

1 Did you like the film? Why/Why not?

2 Do any of the figures surprise you?

3 Which figures do you think are different for men?

4 What is 'average'? In what ways do you think you are 'average'?

1   Look at the photos and answer the questions.

   1   Where do you think these people work? What do they have in common? What sort of jobs do you think they have?

   2   What is their daily routine like?

   3   What are the positive/negative aspects of working in an office?

   4   Do you/Would you like to work in an office? Why/Why not?

2   **a** Read the extract from an interview with Richard Semler below, and fill in the gaps with a word from the box.

> colour   away   process   suits   other   simple   choose   everything
> uniforms   time   trust   symbols

'It went into things like, you know, how could we possibly tell people that we (1) _____ them completely and then search them when they leave. So we started going from the very (2) _____ issues of, for example, getting people to choose what (3) _____ they wanted to use, if at all, and what (4) _____. We went from there, and I think we started with all the very small things, as (5) _____. But then people started saying, 'Well, but if we can (6) _____ our own this and that, why can't we choose what (7) _____ we work?' And slowly we started going through a (8) _____ which said that ... we applied a tool, it's a mental tool, to everything, which was really what we called the three 'why's, which was to ask three 'why's in a row about (9) _____. And almost nothing stands up after that. When you say, 'Why are we wearing (10) _____ and ties?' and people say, 'So we'll look more like each (11) _____' and so 'Why do we want to look more like each other?' and these things suddenly start going (12) _____.'

   b Watch the film and check your answers.

3   Discuss.

   1   Do you agree with what Semler says about treating people as adults?

   2   Do you think ideas like this would work in companies you know?

   3   In general, do you think traditional ideas or innovative ideas are more important in business? Give some examples.

   4   What is your idea of the 'ideal office' or working environment?

159

1 Discuss.

1 What do you know about the people in the pictures?

2 How did they become famous?

3 Why are they/have they been so influential?

4 Why are they regarded as 'icons'? Do you know any other 'icons' of the twentieth century?

2 **a** Match the words/phrases in A to the definitions in B.

A	B
1 crippled	a) the dividing of people (because of their colour)
2 self portrait	b) a place where children live, with a new family because of problems with their real family
3 bus boycott	c) when a big, organised group of people refuse to use something (the buses)
4 protest	d) political and social freedom for everyone
5 segregation	e) speak/act publicly against injustice
6 civil rights	f) a picture of the artist, by the artist
7 foster home	g) physically damaged, permanently

b You are going to watch a film about three other famous 'icons' – Frida Kahlo, Rosa Parks and Marilyn Monroe. Which of the words/phrases above do you associate with each woman?

3 Mark these sentences true (T) or false (F).

1 Frida Kahlo is the most famous woman artist of the twentieth century. ☐

2 She had a terrible accident when she was a teenager. ☐

3 She married Trotsky. ☐

4 Rosa Parks became famous because she refused to give up her bus seat to a white man. ☐

5 In her home town, African Americans refused to use the buses. ☐

6 Thirteen years later, segregation on buses was banned. ☐

7 Marilyn Monroe's real name was Norma Jeane Davies. ☐

8 Monroe was married to a famous sportsman and a famous writer. ☐

9 She died at the age of forty-six. ☐

4 Watch the film and check your answers.

5 Discuss.

1 Did you like the film? Why/Why not?

2 In what different ways did these women suffer?

3 Think of one other woman who is admired by millions of people. Explain why you chose her. What does she have in common with Frida Kahlo, Rosa Parks and Marilyn Monroe? Did she have to suffer? How will she be remembered in future?

Writing bank

Formal letter

Lesson 3.1 | Ex. 12a, page 36

1 Read the letter and tick the correct options. There may be more than one correct option.

1 The letter is a
A letter of complaint. ☐
B request for information. ☐
C thank you letter. ☐

2 Mrs Green would like to
A rent a house near Siena for two weeks. ☐
B stay in a hotel in Siena. ☐
C rent a house in Siena for a month in August. ☐

3 Mrs Green
A hasn't decided which house she would like to stay in. ☐
B would like a house without a swimming pool. ☐
C wants a house which sleeps up to ten people. ☐

4 Mrs Green would like to know
A if she can bring her dogs. ☐
B if the houses are safe for children. ☐
C if the company can give her some beds for the children. ☐
D about the other services the company offers. ☐

Use *Dear Sir/Madam* if you don't know the name of the person you are writing to. *Use Dear Mr Black/Mrs Green* if you know the name. Put a comma (,) after the name, not a colon (:).

Write the name, or title (e.g. *Director of Finance*), and address of the person you are writing to.

Write your address here. Don't write your name. Write the date here.

> 72 St. John's Rd
> London NW1
>
> Vacanze Italiane
> Via Cupramontana, 31
> 60100 Ancona
> Italy
>
> 30 May 2006
>
> Dear Sir/Madam,
>
> 1 I am writing in order to have some further information about your holiday villas in Italy. According to your website, you have villas located around all the important hill towns in Tuscany. I would like to rent a villa in that area this summer, and I am therefore interested in having some more information about a few of the houses.
>
> 2 I am looking for a large villa, which will sleep 8–10 people, and has a swimming pool. Ideally, the house would be a short drive from one of the major hill towns, such as Siena. We would like to rent the villa from 2–15 August.
>
> 3 I would be grateful if you could supply me with the following information:
>
> 4 Firstly, I would like to know if the houses 'Casa Mia' and 'Bella Vista' are available for this period.
>
> 5 Secondly, there are small children in our party. Could you tell me if these two houses are suitable for children, i.e. Are there barriers around the swimming pools? Do the houses have gates for the stairs? In addition to this, will it be necessary to bring beds for the children, or can you provide these?
>
> 6 Lastly, could you give me some more details about the services you offer, e.g. the cleaning service, car hire, etc.? I would like to know costs and conditions.
>
> 7 Thank you in advance. I look forward to hearing from you.
> Yours faithfully,
>
> *Sophie Green*

If you know the name of the person you are writing to, use *Yours sincerely.* Use *Yours faithfully, (Yours truly, (US))*, if you do not know the name. If you would like a reply, end the letter with *I look forward to hearing from you.*

Use formal language. Don't use contractions (*I would like* ... NOT: ~~I'd like~~).

Writing skill | paragraghs

2 Match the meanings below to the paragraphs in the letter above.
A general request ☐
B reason for writing ☐
C ask for a reply ☐
D specific details ☐

Useful phrases

First lines:	*I am writing (as I would like/in order) to ...* *I am writing in response to (your letter of 19 June) ...* *I am writing to ask (for information) about ...* *I am writing to complain about ...*
Last lines:	*I would be grateful if you could ...* *Could you please send me ...?* *I enclose (my CV/the application form/a cheque ...* *I look forward to hearing from you in the near future.* *Thank you in advance.*

Thank you letters

Lesson 10.3 | Ex. 13a, page 140

1 **Read the letters and answer the questions.**

  1 Why is Liliana writing?

  2 What did they do during Liliana's visit?

  3 Why is William Dabbitt writing?

  4 Did Ms Jenkins and her team do a good job? How do we know?

---

7 Waverley Close,
Bristol

Hi Andrea,

Thanks a lot for letting me stay with you this week. I had a wonderful time. It was great to visit the city and see so many things. I'm sure I'll be back next year. Enjoy the rest of the summer and I hope to see you soon. Keep in touch! Best wishes,

Liliana

Mygrave-Bapus and Associates
43 Blomfield Row
London EN2 7BT

Conference co-ordinator,
Cheadle Manor Hotel,
Cheadle Park,
Hertfordshire CM43 4ES

20 July 2006

Dear Ms Jenkins,

I am writing to thank you for hosting our conference this year. It was a great success. Your efforts were appreciated by all, and several participants commented on the excellent organisation. Please also pass on my thanks to your team. I look forward to working with you in future.

Kind regards,

William Dabbitt

William Dabbitt

Writing skill | formal/informal

2 **a Which letter is formal? How do you know? Are these features normally formal or informal? Write (F) or (I).**

  1 full verb forms (e.g We are) ___

  2 contractions (e.g I'm) ___

  3 the passive ___

  4 exclamation marks (!) ___

  5 abbreviations (e.g thanks) ___

b Underline examples of these features in the letters.

Useful phrases

Greeting	Informal: *Hi/Hello/Dear Enzo* Formal: *Dear Sir/Madam* or *Dear Mr Brown*
Opening line	Informal: *Thanks a lot for letting me stay.* Formal: *I am writing to thank you …*
Comment	Informal: *I had a great time.* Formal: *Your efforts were appreciated by all.*
Final message	Informal: *I hope to see you soon.* Formal: *I look forward to working with you …*
Goodbye	Informal: *Best wishes,/Love,/Lots of love,* Formal: *Kind regards,/Yours sincerely,*

Informal emails

Lesson 1.2 | Ex. 14, page 11

1 **Read the email and answer the questions.**

  1 Why hasn't Mark written recently?

  2 What are Fernando's hobbies?

  3 How does Mark know about Fabio's news?

  4 What is Felicity studying?

  5 What does Mark invite Fernando to do?

Informal greeting

Hi Fernando,

1 Thanks for your email. It's great to hear from you. I'm sorry I haven't been in touch for a while, but I've been very busy with work. I'm travelling a lot at the moment. I've been to Germany, Spain, Brazil, China and Japan in the last four months!

2 How are things with you? Are you still doing karate and running every day? Have you found a girlfriend yet? Do you remember Fabio? I saw him the other day and he's married now and has four children!

3 Anyway, life here is pretty good. Felicity is enjoying her course, and is very excited about becoming a teacher. We would love to see you sometime. Why don't you come and visit us next time you are in the UK?

4 Look forward to hearing from you again soon.

All the best,
Mark

Informal language for ending, e.g. *Love, Mark, Lots of love, Mark, All the best, Mark*

Writing skill | paragraphs

2 Match these descriptions to paragraphs 1–4 in the email.

  A Giving your news and making an invitation. ☐

  B Introduction and reason for writing/not writing. ☐

  C Finishing. ☐

  D Asking for news/talking about friends. ☐

Descriptions

Lesson 7.2 | Ex. 15, page 95

1 Read the descriptions about the teachers and do the exercises below.

2 Put the words/phrases in the box into the correct columns below.

> a great imagination   dressed conservatively   knowledgeable   calm and understanding   short, slightly chubby   very good-looking   have (her) hair tied back   a friendly face   enthusiastic   encouraging   kind and polite   organised, respectful and interesting

Physical	Clothing	Character
		a great imagination

3 Write any other useful expressions (from the texts/that you know) in the columns above.

4 Complete the sentences with words/phrases from the box.

  1 Rosa tells the most amazing stories. She has _____ _____ _____.

  2 He always wore a dark suit with a tie. He _____ _____.

  3 She listened carefully to my problems, and was able to help. She was _____ and _____.

  4 He's always keen to start a new job. He's very _____.

  5 The receptionist smiled, thanked us, and offered to find us a taxi. She was very _____ and _____.

My best teacher ever was my Geography teacher. He was a short, slightly chubby man, who was calm and understanding. He would always listen to you, and have some kind words to say, whatever your problem. He was knowledgeable too and always explained everything clearly. I will never forget some of the things he taught me.

Mrs Manley was of medium height, and had a very friendly face. She dressed conservatively, but she was very good-looking. She taught History and she was very enthusiastic about her subject. She taught it because she loved it, and she made us love it too. She was always encouraging, and she had a great imagination. The characters she described came to life and the dates of battles became unimportant even though we had to learn them by heart for exams. When she left the school to teach in Australia, I missed her terribly.

The best teacher I ever had was Miriam Starkey. She taught us Latin, and she was organised, respectful and interesting. She was a tall, skinny lady, who wore glasses and always had her hair tied back. She looked fierce, but she was always kind and polite.

5 Think about a teacher from your past and complete the text.

My best teacher ever was my _____ teacher. (S)He was a _____, _____ (wo)man, who was _____ and _____. (S)He would always _____, and _____. (S)He was _____ too and always _____. I will never forget _____.

Writing a summary

Lesson 5.3 | Ex. 13b, page 70

1 Read the description of the film *Babette's Feast* and mark the statements true (T) or false (F).

1 The sisters are from Paris.

2 The sisters are married.

3 Babette works for the sisters.

4 Babette saved a lot of money.

5 The sisters cook a fantastic meal for the village.

6 The meal is a great success.

Writing skill | summarising

2 **a** A summary gives important information in a few words. What type of information is cut out from a summary?

b Work with a partner. Look at the first paragraph of the description. Decide which words you can cut. e.g. *In Jutland, Denmark, two sisters live together and teach the Bible.*

Newspaper articles

Lesson 8.1 | Ex. 12a, page 106

1 Read the text and mark the statements true (T) or false (F).

1 Only smokers have problems.

2 Smoking poisons the air.

3 2,100 adults die every year in New Mexico because of second-hand smoking.

4 The writer wants new laws to stop people smoking in public.

Writing skill | paragraphs

2 Match these descriptions to paragraphs 1–4 in the article.

A Recommends future action to solve the problem. ☐

B Gives statistics to support the argument. ☐

C Gives scientific information to support the argument. ☐

D Introduces the topic. ☐

In a tiny village in Jutland, Denmark, two old sisters live together and teach the Bible, just as their father did before them. But a long time ago, Phillipa and Martina had been famed for their beauty. They both had chances to marry, one to a famous singer, the other to a handsome soldier. Instead, they chose a quiet life beside their father, a life of boiled fish, Bible study group and the villagers' constant arguing.

Many years later, a woman called Babette arrives from Paris. Her family is dead, and she will now spend her life helping the sisters. For fifteen years she serves them for free, working in the house while the sisters look after the very old villagers. Babette's only contact with her former life in France is a lottery ticket that a friend renews every year.

One day, news arrives that Babette has won the lottery. The sisters expect their helper to leave them. But Babette decides to cook a wonderful meal for the village. She imports the finest food from France and begins preparing the meal. At first, the villagers are worried; they know only the simplest of food. But after trying the first courses, the mood changes. The feast – so full of colour and delicious-looking that it seems to belong in a dream or a work of art – warms their cold hearts. The villagers stop arguing and remember why they love each other. The film ends with the villagers holding hands, together under a starry sky.

Useful phrases

Contrast	*Instead, they chose a quiet life ...* *But Babette decides to cook a wonderful meal ...*
Sequence words	*At first, the villagers are worried* *After trying the first courses,*
Setting the scene	*In a (tiny village) in (Jutland) ...* *Many years later, a woman called Babette arrives ...*
Ending	*The film ends with/In the end, the villagers ...*

---

1 Many of us choose not to smoke because of the effects smoking has on the body. But researchers have found that second-hand smoke leads to similar problems.

2 Every time someone lights a cigarette, poisons are released into the air. As a result, everyone inhales the smoke. Studies show that diseases such as lung cancer and heart disease are caused by second-hand smoke.

3 Every year in New Mexico, 2,100 adults die as a result of smoking. Between 230 and 390 of these deaths are caused by second-hand smoking, according to the Campaign for Tobacco Free Kids.

4 Therefore, we need more laws to protect us from second-hand smoke. It's time for a change, time to make more places safe for our health.

(Adapted from the Las Cruces Bulletin, Nov 5, 2004)

Useful phrases

Giving information to support your argument	*Researchers have found that ...* *Studies show that ...* *According to scientists ...*
Giving statistical information	*Every year, 2,100 adults die ...*
Concluding	*Therefore, we need more laws.* *In conclusion, we need a change.*

Irregular verbs

Verb	Past Simple	Past Participle
be	was/were	been
beat	beat	beaten
become	became	become
begin	began	begun
bend	bent	bent
bet	bet	bet
bite	bit	bitten
blow	blew	blown
break	broke	broken
bring	brought	brought
build	built	built
burn	burned/burnt	burned/burnt
burst	burst	burst
buy	bought	bought
can	could	been able
catch	caught	caught
choose	chose	chosen
come	came	come
cost	cost	cost
cut	cut	cut
deal	dealt	dealt
dig	dug	dug
do	did	done
draw	drew	drawn
dream	dreamed/dreamt	dreamed/dreamt
drink	drank	drunk
drive	drove	driven
eat	ate	eaten
fall	fell	fallen
feed	fed	fed
feel	felt	felt
fight	fought	fought
find	found	found
fly	flew	flown
forget	forgot	forgotten
forgive	forgave	forgiven
freeze	froze	frozen
get	got	got
give	gave	given
go	went	gone/been
grow	grew	grown
hang	hung	hanged/hung
have	had	had
hear	heard	heard
hide	hid	hidden
hit	hit	hit
hold	held	held
hurt	hurt	hurt
keep	kept	kept
kneel	knelt	knelt
know	knew	known
lay	laid	laid
lead	led	led
learn	learned/learnt	learned/learnt
leave	left	left
lend	lent	lent

Verb	Past Simple	Past Participle
let	let	let
lie	lay	lain
light	lit	lit
lose	lost	lost
make	made	made
mean	meant	meant
meet	met	met
must	had to	had to
pay	paid	paid
put	put	put
read /riːd/	read /red/	read /red/
ride	rode	ridden
ring	rang	rung
rise	rose	risen
run	ran	run
say	said	said
see	saw	seen
sell	sold	sold
send	sent	sent
set	set	set
shake	shook	shaken
shine	shone	shone
shoot	shot	shot
show	showed	shown
shrink	shrank	shrunk
shut	shut	shut
sing	sang	sung
sink	sank	sunk
sit	sat	sat
sleep	slept	slept
slide	slid	slid
smell	smelled/smelt	smelled/smelt
speak	spoke	spoken
spell	spelled/spelt	spelled/spelt
spend	spent	spent
spill	spilled/spilt	spilled/spilt
split	split	split
spoil	spoiled/spoilt	spoiled/spoilt
spread	spread	spread
stand	stood	stood
steal	stole	stolen
stick	stuck	stuck
swear	swore	sworn
swell	swelled	swollen/swelled
swim	swam	swum
take	took	taken
teach	taught	taught
tear	tore	torn
tell	told	told
think	thought	thought
throw	threw	thrown
understand	understood	understood
wake	woke	woken
wear	wore	worn
win	won	won
write	wrote	written

Pronunciation bank

Part 1 | English phonemes

Consonants

Symbol	Key word	Symbol	Key word
p	**p**an	s	**s**ell
b	**b**an	z	**z**ero
t	**t**ie	ʃ	fre**sh**
d	**d**ie	ʒ	mea**s**ure
k	**c**ap	h	**h**ot
g	**g**ap	m	**m**et
tʃ	**ch**urch	n	**n**et
dʒ	**j**udge	ŋ	ra**ng**
f	**f**ew	l	**l**ed
v	**v**iew	r	**r**ed
θ	**th**row	j	**y**et
ð	**th**ough	w	**w**et

Vowels

Symbol	Key word	Symbol	Key word
iː	f**ee**t	aɪ	**by**
ɪ	f**i**t	aʊ	br**ow**n
e	b**e**t	ɔɪ	b**oy**
æ	b**a**t	ɪə	h**ear**
ɑː	b**a**th	eə	h**air**
ɒ	b**o**ttle	ʊə	s**ure**
ɔː	b**ough**t	eɪə	pl**ayer**
ʊ	b**oo**k	əʊə	l**ower**
uː	b**oo**t	aɪə	t**ired**
ʌ	b**u**t	aʊə	fl**ower**
ɜː	b**ir**d	ɔɪə	empl**oyer**
ə	br**o**th**er**	i	happ**y**
eɪ	b**ay**	u	ann**u**al
əʊ	g**o**ld		

Part 2 | Sound-spelling correspondences

In English, we can spell the same sound in different ways, for example, the sound /iː/ can be 'ee', as in *green*, 'ea' as in *read* or 'ey' as in *key*. Students of English sometimes find English spelling difficult, but there are rules and knowing the rules can help you. The chart below gives you the more common spellings of the English sounds you have studied in this book.

Sound	Spelling	Examples
/ɪ/	i	this listen
	y	gym typical
	ui	build guitar
	e	pretty
/iː/	ee	green sleep
	ie	niece believe
	ea	read teacher
	e	these complete
	ey	key money
	ei	receipt receive
	i	police
/æ/	a	can pasta land
/ɑː/	a	can't dance*
	ar	scarf bargain
	al	half
	au	aunt laugh
	ea	heart
/ʌ/	u	fun sunny husband
	o	some mother month
	ou	cousin double young
/ɒ/	o	hot pocket top
	a	watch what want
/ɔː/	or	short sport store
	ou	your course bought
	au	daughter taught pause
	al	bald small always
	aw	draw jigsaw lawyer
	ar	warden warm
	oo	floor indoor
/aɪ/	i	like time island
	y	dry shy cycle
	ie	fries die tie
	igh	light high right
	ei	height
	ey	eyes
	uy	buy
/eɪ/	a	lake hate shave
	ai	wait train straight
	ay	play say stay
	ey	they grey obey
	ei	eight weight
	ea	break
/əʊ/	o	home phone open
	ow	show throw own
	oa	coat road coast
	ol	cold told

* In American English the sound in words like *can't* and *dance* is the /æ/ sound, like *can* and *man*.

Part 3 | Weak forms

In English, some words have two pronunciations – the strong form and the weak form. We usually use the weak form when the word is not stressed. Most of these words are 'grammar' words e.g. *a, an,* *than, have, been,* etc. Knowing weak forms helps you understand spoken English. The chart below shows some common weak forms.

Word	Strong form	Weak form	Examples of weak forms in sentences
the	/ðiː/	/ðə/	He's **the** person who cleans our office.
was	/wɒz/	/wəz/	He **was** an architect.
were	/wɜː/	/wə/	They **were** born in France.
been	/biːn/	/bɪn/	I've **been** to San Francisco.
do	/duː/	/də/	Where **do** you live?
does	/dʌz/	/dəz/	Where **does** he work?
have	/hæv/	/əv/	What **have** you got?
has	/hæz/	/əz/	Where **has** she been?
had	/hæd/	/həd/, /əd/	He **had** already gone. He'd already gone.
can	/kæn/	/kən/	She **can** sing very well.
to	/tuː/	/tə/ (before consonants)	I prefer **to** go home for lunch.
at	/æt/	/ət/	Let's meet **at** six o'clock.
of	/ɒv/	/əv/	There's a lot **of** food.
for	/fɔː/	/fə/	He's away **for** two months.
from	/frɒm/	/frəm/	She's **from** Brazil.
than	/ðæn/	/ðən/	She's taller **than** Juan.
could	/kʊd/	/kəd/	Where **could** I go?
would	/wʊd/	/wəd/əd/	What **would** you do?
should	/ʃʊd/	/ʃəd/ʃd/	What **should** I have done?

Part 4 | Silent consonants

Some letters appear in words where they are not pronounced.

Letter	Silent in:	Letter	Silent in:	Letter	Silent in:
b	dou**b**t clim**b**	h	**h**our w**h**at	p	**p**sychology recei**p**t
c	s**c**issors s**c**ene	k	**k**now **k**nee	s	i**s**land ai**s**le
d	We**d**nesday san**d**wich	l	ta**l**k ca**l**m	t	lis**t**en whis**t**le
g	ou**g**ht lon**g**	n	autum**n** colum**n**	w	**w**rite ans**w**er

Tapescripts

Unit 1 Recording 1
(See Unit 1 Recording 2)

Unit 1 Recording 2
Dialogue 1
M=Man W=Woman
M: What activities and hobbies are you good at?
W: I'm quite good at singing. I sing in a band with friends.
M: Do you make any money out of it?
W: No, we don't, no! No, we just play at birthday parties and that kind of thing.

Dialogue 2
M=Man W=Woman
W: What clubs do you belong to?
M: I don't belong to any, but my daughter is a member of a chess club.
W: Really? Is she good?
M: Yes, she is. She's very good, actually.
W: Does she play a lot?
M: Every day. She always beats me!

Dialogue 3
W=Woman T=Teenager
W: What types of exercise are you keen on?
T: I'm keen on running.
W: Do you do it regularly?
T: Er ... three or four times a week.
W: Where do you run?
T: In the park.

Dialogue 4
M=Man W=Woman
W: Apart from your own, are there any cultures that you're interested in?
M: I'm really interested in Mexican culture.
W: Have you been there?
M: Yes, I have. I went there on holiday a few years ago and just found it fascinating.
W: What particular aspects?
M: Well, it's full of old ruins, and I went to visit them, you know at Tulum, for example, and since then I've read a couple of books about Aztec and Inca culture.
W: Are you planning a return trip?
M: Yes, I am. Definitely.

Dialogue 5
M=Man W=Woman
M: How many languages are you fluent in?
W: Fluent? One: English. But I speak a bit of French and Spanish, and kind of beginner's Italian.
M: Did you study these or ...
W: Yes, I did. Well, I studied French and Spanish at school. I didn't study Italian, but I picked some up when I was travelling in Italy.

Unit 1 Recording 4
a 238
b €3,475
c 65.7
d 22%
e $423
f 98.2%
g 10,937
h €474
I 32.9%
j 6,292

Unit 1 Recording 5
Speaker 1
I met my best friend when I was at college studying. He lived in the room next door, and always played strange, very loud music. I was studying Chinese, which was really difficult, and I remember thinking, 'He is having a much better time than me!'. When we finished university we lost touch for a while, but when we met again we had so much to talk about.

Speaker 2
We actually met when I crashed into Anton's car when I was trying to park. Luckily, we've got the same sense of humour and we both started laughing about it. Then we went to have a coffee, and got to know each other. Soon we were really good friends.

Speaker 3
I met Juliet in her office. I was delivering a parcel and she was the receptionist. Juliet had a really big smile, and I thought 'She looks friendly', so I invited her to a party. We've been friends ever since, and I really enjoy her company. We still go to parties together!

Speaker 4
I've just met a new friend, Bulent, on the Internet. My job is really boring, so I spend a lot of time on the Internet, in chatrooms. Bulent is Turkish, like me, and we've found that we have a lot in common.

Speaker 5
It was a strange place to meet. We were both flying to Moscow, and the plane was delayed for four hours! We met in the coffee lounge at the airport, and we started talking. We found out we were flying to the same city, and staying in the same hotel! After that trip, we just kept in touch.

Unit 1 Recording 6
Speaker 1
My father has been a big influence on me. I really respect him. Um ... partly because of what he does – we do the same job – but I think also his character.
We're quite similar in many ways. Um ... he's sort of very calm. The only time he got angry was once, about twenty years ago when I was fifteen. I came home at five in the morning and I didn't call to say I'd be late. We had a big argument and didn't speak to each other for a week. But apart from that, I've never seen him angry and he has always been very kind to me.

Speaker 2
So, I want to speak about Romina. She was my best friend for about twelve years. Before meeting her most of my friends were boys and I didn't have many good girlfriends. We met at university and began studying together and going out in the evenings together, and we developed this method of studying before exams. We basically spent the whole night drinking coffee and testing each other. It was terrible for our health but good for our friendship. Unfortunately, we're not in touch any more. We had an argument over money while we were on holiday last year, and we haven't

seen each other since then. I miss her.

Speaker 3
I work in a supermarket and I've been there for about two years. When I started, I got on really well with all my colleagues. They were all really nice, except one. This one girl – I think her name was Sarah – she was always unfriendly to me. I don't know why. Then I found out that she was saying bad things about me. She said I was lazy and a bad worker, that kind of thing. So one day I asked her, 'What's the problem?' and she didn't say anything. Anyway, Sarah stopped working at the supermarket about a year ago. I don't know what she's doing now.

Unit 1 Recording 7
Dialogue 1
M=Man W=Woman
M: I've decided to stop smoking.
W: What a great idea! When did you decide this?
M: Last Monday. I haven't had a cigarette for three days.
W: Congratulations!
M: I had a cigar yesterday, though.
W: Oh.

Dialogue 2
M=Man W=Woman
W: Have you seen my handbag? I can't find it anywhere.
M: Yes, I saw it on the table a few minutes ago.
W: Ah, here it is. I've found it! Oh no. Where are the car keys? I've lost the car keys now.
M: They're on the table. I put them there for you before breakfast.
W: Oh. Thanks.

Unit 2 Recording 1
People: journalists, celebrities, editor
Things you find in a newspaper: main stories, the front page, headlines, sections, financial section, sports section, review section, reports, articles, interviews, advertisements
Other: the Sunday papers, the daily papers, online news

Unit 2 Recording 2
1 The story has been told many times.
2 Last week's article was written by our leading journalist.
3 The magazine is sold in twenty countries now.
4 The newspaper will be printed at 3.00a.m.
5 'This news report has been brought to you by Fox Cable News, USA.'
6 The World Wide Web was invented by Tim Berners-Lee.
7 These days, over 10,000 books are published every week.
8 The growth of television can't be stopped.

Unit 2 Recording 3
I=Interviewer J=Journalist (Alison)
I: Alison, I suppose the question most people ask is about the stories journalists write. What makes a good story?
J: All good stories need certain components, certain factors that make them interesting for the reader. And there are two main

types. Firstly, if something strange has happened that readers can relate to. Stories where you have ordinary people finding themselves in strange or funny situations, which we can all understand.

Unit 2 Recording 4

I=Interviewer J=Journalist (Alison)

I: Alison, I suppose the question most people ask is about the stories journalists write. What makes a good story?

J: All good stories need certain components, certain factors that make them interesting for the reader. And there are two main types. Firstly, if something strange has happened that readers can relate to. Stories where you have ordinary people finding themselves in strange or funny situations, which we can all understand.

I: And the other type?

J: The other type concerns celebrities: film stars, the royal family, sportspeople. I think people enjoy reading about celebrities who have done something wrong, because it shows their human side. Bill Clinton and his scandals, actors behaving badly. Even if you're rich and famous, you can still make mistakes.

I: There's been a lot of criticism of journalists for writing too much about people's private lives. What's your opinion? Is it right to invade someone's private life for a story?

J: In my opinion, it depends on who it is and what is being reported. Is it right to follow normal people on holiday and take photos of them and their family? No, I don't think it is. But if these people are famous or they are spending public money, politicians, for example, we should definitely check what they're doing.

I: So it depends on each individual case?

J: I think so, yes.

I: But what do you think of those newspapers who follow celebrities twenty-four hours a day and take pictures of them?

J: Well, there are different types of newspaper. Some are full of gossip and celebrity news. They don't contain serious news. They sell because the public wants to see famous people in their private moments.

I: Doesn't that seem wrong to you?

J: I'm not sure about that. I don't think so. If you become a film star or a TV celebrity you know what's going to happen to your life. And many celebrities need that publicity to keep them in the public eye. Celebrities need photographers and photographers need celebrities.

I: I'm sure the photographers would agree with you.

J: Definitely.

Unit 2 Recording 5

1 I think political news is boring.
2 In my opinion newspapers should be free.
3 I think there's too much sport on television.
4 I don't think the Internet has changed the world.
5 Journalists shouldn't write about people's private lives.

Unit 2 Recording 6

Speaker 1

Chat show producer: The worst thing is technical problems. Everyone is in the studio, and suddenly, it all goes black and people are running around trying to work out what the problem is, and to fix it. A major technical problem can be the microphone. Maybe it isn't working properly or you can't hear someone, because the microphone is in their jacket, and all you can hear is their clothes moving. Or people forget to take the microphone off when they finish. On one show I did we could hear this man being very rude about the producer. Obviously he didn't know that 30,000 people were listening to him, including me!

Speaker 2

News reader: Sometimes I have to read bad news, and that can be very difficult. And I hate it when there are difficult names that I can't pronounce. Names of places you've never heard of. And it's also hard trying to think of what to wear every day.

Speaker 3

Presenter: It's difficult when you are tired, and you keep making mistakes. I was interviewing a lady the other day, and I kept getting her name wrong. It was really embarrassing. Or sometimes the person you are interviewing gets nervous, and they don't say anything. You keep asking questions, but there is just silence. That's terrible. Or if they say something funny, and you start laughing, and then you can't stop.

Speaker 4

Soap opera actress: The worst thing is when you forget your words. Everything else is perfect, the lights, the sound, the other actors, but you can't remember what to say. That's very embarrassing. Or if the furniture falls down or breaks. I closed a door the other day, and the window fell off.

Unit 2 Recording 7

Dialogue 1

A: What's the matter?
B: The printer's broken, again.
A: Oh dear. Shall I call the engineers?

Dialogue 2

A: Oh no! My computer keeps freezing!
B: Try turning it off and on again.
A: Thanks.

Dialogue 3

A: What's the matter?
B: The photocopier isn't working. I think the paper's run out.
A: Don't worry. I'll deal with it.

Unit 2 Recording 9

1 The bank robbers escaped.
2 She saved the young boy.
3 They waited for her for an hour.
4 Who delivered this parcel?
5 She spent all the money she inherited.
6 We all helped them to do it.

Unit 3 Recording 1

The Dos Santos family

I=Interviewer M=Miriam C=Carlos

I: So how do you feel about the house swap?

M: Oh, I can't wait. I can hardly believe we're spending more than one month in London. We've never been there before.

I: I'm sure you'll love it.

M: Yes, I'm sure we will.

I: What are you going to do while you're there, Carlos?

C: We're going to see all the sights and the museums ...

M: And I'm going to do lots and lots of shopping.

I: Great. There are some wonderful shops in London. I'll give you the address of a great shoe shop.

M: I'm going to spend lots of money, and buy beautiful clothes and souvenirs for my family ...

C: And we're visiting some friends in Oxford on 3rd June.

M: I think they'll have nice shops there too and of course ...

The Armitage family

I=Interviewer J=Jeremy S=Sarah
G=Girl(s)

I: So, are you ready for Spain?

J: Yes, I think so. We've always wanted to visit Spain. It has such a rich culture. I want the girls to experience that while they are young, even though they're not very keen. We're going to see the cathedrals ...

G: Oh. Great.

S: And we love Spanish food, so we're going to try all the local dishes, and meet the men who do the cooking.

I: That won't be difficult. They love cooking!

J: That's right. So basically, Sarah and I will enjoy the Spanish culture. And the girls are going to sit outside and enjoy the sun.

G: Hooray.

J: I really hope this'll be the holiday of a lifetime for us all.

Unit 3 Recording 2

Miriam Dos Santos

I=Interviewer M=Miriam

I: Hi Miriam. So how was London?

M: Well London was fantastic, but the house was a disaster.

I: Oh dear. Why was that?

M: First of all, it was in the middle of nowhere. It was a long way from the centre, and very difficult to find. We got completely lost looking for it. In the end we had to ask a taxi-driver to take us there, which was very expensive. And when we went inside, my goodness, it was so old, and dark. I don't think they had changed anything in that house for thirty years. It was like something out of a film. Nothing worked properly. Even the heating didn't work, so there was no hot water, and the shower didn't work either. Anyway, I was really disappointed, and so we're going to complain to the company. We'll ask them about the central heating and why the information on the website was wrong and we'll also ask them ...

Tapescripts

Jeremy Armitage

I=Interviewer J=Jeremy

I: How was Spain?

J: I have to be honest with you. It wasn't good.

I: Oh dear. Why was that?

J: Well, the main problem was the flat. It was too small. The girls wanted to stay in the single room together, but it was more like a cupboard than a room. It was tiny! And it was the biggest room in the house! And it was so hot, and there was no fan, so we had big arguments. Also the mosquitoes were terrible, so it was very difficult to sleep at night. And downstairs there was a bar, which played loud music until four in the morning. I think the only reason the area was quiet during the day is because everyone was sleeping after being awake all night!

Anyway the girls refused to do the things I wanted to do. All they wanted to do was try and get a suntan. They don't care about culture, and didn't want to eat the delicious food. They just wanted chips!

At the end of the month, I was so pleased to get home. I am never going to do a home swap again!

Unit 3 Recording 4

J=John S=Simona

J: What do you think of the survey, Simona?

S: I think it's interesting, but you can't really compare small cities to other much bigger cities like Paris, so it's really not fair.

J: Yeah, I agree. It's much easier to organise things in a small city.

S: Definitely. And it's interesting – on the one hand people who live in cities always complain about the city, but on the other hand they always think their city is the best. Wherever you go, people say 'Yes, we have the best food, the biggest monuments, the most interesting culture'.

J: Do you agree with the rankings of those cities?

S: Not all of them. For example San Francisco should have a higher rating. It's bigger and more beautiful than a lot of the others. You know, there's the sea, the bay, Golden Gate Bridge ...

J: What about Tokyo and London?

S: Well, in my opinion London's not as expensive as Tokyo but Tokyo is more organised. Its transport is almost perfect, but maybe transport isn't the most important thing.

Unit 3 Recording 5

answer phone   washing machine   air conditioner   central heating   mobile phone   burglar alarm   DVD player   alarm clock

Unit 3 Recording 6

Call one

PA=Personal assistant   S=Mr Sharp

PA: Davies Electronics.

S: Hello, I'm calling from Washington DC. I'd like to speak to Mrs Davies, please.

PA: Yes. May I ask who's calling, please?

S: Sure, It's Mr Sharp.

PA: Thank you. I'm afraid she's not in the office at the moment, Mr Sharp. Can I take a message?

S: Yes. Could you ask her to call me back, please? It's about Friday's meeting.

PA: Yes, of course. Can I take your number?

S: It's 202 943 8226.

PA: That's 202 943 8226. I'll ask her to call you back this afternoon.

S: Thank you.

PA: Goodbye.

S: Goodbye.

Call two

PA=Personal assistant. G=Gabriella Jones

PA: Clanner Fabrics. Robert speaking.

G: Oh hello. This is Gabriella Jones from Accounts.

PA: Hello Mrs Jones.

G: Can I speak to Paul, please?

PA: I'll put you through. One moment ... His line's engaged, I'm afraid.

G: Oh OK. Can I leave a message?

PA: Yes, of course.

G: Can he call me, Gabriella Jones, on line 6. It's the Accounts Department.

PA: OK, no problem.

G: Thanks.

Call three

PA=Personal assistant   A=Andrea Jackson

PA: Good morning. Juarez and Son. How can I help you?

A: Good morning. Can you put me through to Ricardo Villas?

PA: Yes. May I ask who's calling?

A: It's Andrea Jackson.

PA: Anthea Jackson?

A: No, Andrea Jackson.

PA: Thank you. I'm afraid he's not at his desk at the moment. Would you like to leave a message?

A: Yes. Could you ask Mr Villas to fax me an invoice?

PA: Fax you an invoice. Does he have your fax number, Miss Jackson?

A: No, it's 682 3149.

PA: OK. I'll leave a message for him. The number's 682 3149. Is that right?

A: That's right. Thanks. Goodbye.

PA: Goodbye.

Unit 3 Recording 7

Speaker 1

I live in the suburbs of the city. I'd say I have quite a hectic lifestyle. I wear a suit every day. I work sixty hours a week. So I need a change, and I'd like to spend a year in this beautiful house in the country. What will I do? I'd like to stop working for a year and study nature. I'm going to learn the names of birds, trees and plants. I might also learn practical skills, like how to grow vegetables and how to make honey. The most important thing is to live without computers, alarm clocks, mobile phones and modern technology for a year. By the end of the year, I'll definitely be more relaxed and less stressed, so when I return to work, I'll be a better person. I think it's going to be the best year of my life.

Speaker 2

I'm from a very small town. It's the most boring place you can imagine. It's for people who want a quiet life. There's one school, one post office and only a few shops and that's all. So, I want to experience city life. I really like this apartment. It looks modern and spacious and I'm sure the area around it will be more interesting than where I live now. So, what am I going to do there? I'm planning to find a job, of course, because I know the city is expensive. In my free time, I'm going to meet people from different cultures, as many as I can. I might join a gym to meet people there. I'll definitely go clubbing a lot to try and meet people and make friends. I may do a course, learn another language. I might even stay in the city if I like it.

Unit 4 Recording 1

Narrator: Frank Abagnale, a good-looking English boy, pretended to be first a pilot, then a doctor and then a lawyer. For five years he travelled the world for free, stayed in expensive hotels and had relationships with beautiful women. Furthermore, by the age of twenty-one he had tricked and cheated his way to $250 million.

In the golden age of James Bond, Abagnale really was an international man of mystery. He was wanted by the FBI and Interpol (International Police) in twenty-six cities. Abagnale's charm was his most important tool. He dressed well and everybody believed everything he said. Leonardo DiCaprio, who plays Frank Abagnale in the film *Catch me if you can* said, 'Frank Abagnale is one of the greatest actors who has walked the earth'.

Abagnale was a lonely child. When his German mother divorced his father, Abagnale had to choose which parent to live with. Instead, he ran away from home and began his life as an international trickster. He got a Pan Am pilot's uniform by saying that his was stolen and that he had an urgent flight. This allowed him to stay in any hotel he wanted: Pan Am always paid the bill. What's more, he even pretended to be a footballer and played for a professional team for a year.

He broke the law constantly but he never went to prison until he was finally caught in the USA. Despite his crimes, Abagnale never had any enemies.

These days Abagnale doesn't need to trick anybody: he is a successful consultant. He advises companies on how to cheat their customers, and he also lectures at the FBI Academy. He wrote his autobiography in the 1970s and sold the film rights for $250,000.

Unit 4 Recording 2

**C=Mr Charming W=Woman M=Man
S=Sarah J=Judy D=Dog**

Dialogue 1

C: What a beautiful dress! Haven't I seen you before? You work in fashion, don't you?

W: Yes, I do. We met at a fashion show.

Dialogue 2

C: I've read all your books. You've just written a new one, haven't you?

M: Yes, I have. It's about a film star.

Dialogue 3

C: I love lobster! The food is delicious here, isn't it?

W: Yes, it is. But I prefer caviar.

Dialogue 4

C: You're Sarah, aren't you? No, you're Judy! Anyway, can I get you a drink?

S: *I'm* Sarah!

J: And I'd love a drink!

Dialogue 5

C: You were at the last party here, weren't you? Would you like something to eat?

D: Woof woof!

C: Yes, you would!

Unit 4 Recording 3

Speaker: Thank you for coming. It's good to see so many young entrepreneurs here. Today I'm going to talk about how to get rich. The American writer Scott Fitzgerald once said, 'Let me tell you about the rich. They are very different from you and me'. He's right. The super-rich have a number of personal qualities that make them different. But they aren't all good qualities. Here are some ideas for you entrepreneurs who want to get rich.

Unit 4 Recording 4

Speaker: Here are some ideas for you entrepreneurs who want to get rich. The first thing is, be mean. You shouldn't be too generous. John Paul Getty, one of the richest men in history, put payphones in the bedrooms of his house so that his friends couldn't make free phone calls.

Number two. You should start early. Really rich people know they want to be rich even when they are children. Matthew Freud sold mice to his schoolfriends. He said he would be a millionaire by the time he was twenty-five years old. He was right.

Number three. Don't be too extravagant. You mustn't waste your money on stupid things. Bill Gates doesn't wear a suit. He doesn't care about looking good because he doesn't have to look good. If you spend all your money on expensive holidays and presents, you will probably never be rich.

Number four. Be confident. You must believe in yourself. Everyone has great ideas but 99.9 percent of us never do anything about them. Anita Roddick, the boss of Body Shop, says 'It's all about having a good idea and having the confidence to sell it to the public'.

Number five. You have to work hard. Work long hours. This is the most important thing. No one ever got rich by sleeping half the day. Rupert Murdoch goes to five o'clock meetings. That's 5.00 in the morning. Bernie Ecclestone, the Formula One billionaire, went to his office at 6.00 in the morning. Every day. Even when he reached the age of seventy.

Number six. Think big. Be ambitious. You shouldn't think about the limits of your business. Sell yourself to the world, not only your home town. Of course there are lots of other ...

Unit 4 Recording 6

succeed fail reward punish buy sell produce consume advertise respond success failure reward punishment buyer seller producer consumer advertisement response

Unit 4 Recording 7

1 What is the opposite of succeed?
Fail.
2 What is the opposite of punish?
Reward.
3 What is a person who sells things called?
A seller.
4 What is the opposite of failure?
Success.
5 What is the opposite of reward?
Punishment.
6 What is the opposite of sell?
Buy.
7 What is the opposite of a consumer?
A producer.
8 'Advert' is short for which word?
Advertisement.

Unit 5 Recording 1

Play: cards, squash, chess, computer games, volleyball, a musical instrument, football
Go: fishing, skiing, jogging, swimming, dancing, sailing, surfing, cycling
Do: aerobics, exercise, gardening, athletics, karate, photography
No verb: reading, painting, cooking, drawing

Unit 5 Recording 2

Speaker 1

I've been taking classes in origami for three months. Basically, you learn how to make beautiful objects using paper. It's an ancient Japanese art and I really love it. It's very creative, and I've made lots of beautiful things already, like birds and other animals.

Speaker 2

Well, my hobby is cooking. I think it's actually quite creative. Certainly I've made up lots of my own recipes and people say I'm a good cook. I've been trying to open my own restaurant for the last few years but I don't have the money yet. But it's something I'll definitely do in the future.

Speaker 3

I think you have to be creative to look after children. We do all kinds of things: drawing, playing games, music. Y'know, even today, I've been playing with my three children this morning – that's why the room's a mess – and we've invented a new game. And tomorrow there'll be another new game.

Unit 5 Recording 3

1 I've been reading *Underworld* this morning.
2 I've been swimming.
3 She's known him all her life.
4 How many exams have you taken?
5 I've given up smoking!
6 How long have you been learning Chinese?

Unit 5 Recording 4

1 I saw the man.
2 She has a warm heart.
3 I like the red.
4 He ran after the car.
5 That's my part you've taken.
6 I got a tan last week.
7 Is that a bear in the picture?
8 It's been said already.

Unit 5 Recording 5

I=Interviewer   H=Hannah

I: Hannah, did it surprise you how you spend your free time?

H: Yeah, I didn't expect to see these results at all. Um ... I'm a film-maker so I think it's normal to spend a lot of time watching films at the cinema and on DVD, but a lot of other things surprised me.

I: For example?

H: For example, I spend eight percent of my free time shopping. Well, I can't stand shopping. It drives me mad.

I: Really?

H: Yeah, and the housework – I don't mind doing the housework, but it's not very interesting and I'd prefer to do less of that kind of thing. Also I noticed that I spend fifteen percent of my time watching TV and only ten percent reading, which surprises me because I enjoy reading and I always look forward to starting a new book.

I: You don't like TV so much?

H: Well, most TV is like junk food for the brain and I should watch less. Other things ... um ... I love cooking, and I try to cook a proper meal at least four nights a week. And I often invite friends over to have dinner so it doesn't surprise me that I spend seven percent of my time cooking and eating.

I: Is there anything you'd really like to change?

H: Um ... I never manage to do much exercise. I'd really like to go running every day just for half an hour but I never seem to find the time. So that's one thing I'd like to change.

Unit 5 Recording 6

A: Have you been to La Pescada, that new restaurant in Islington?

B: No. Where is it?

A: It's on a small street, just off Upper St.

B: And is it nice?

A: It's brilliant. I went there last night. It's Argentinian, and it has a great atmosphere – very lively. They play loud music, and serve Argentinian beers, with limes. The menu is very traditional, with lots of meat and fish. The chef is from Argentina, so he makes sure that all the meat is really fresh and good quality. They serve huge steaks, with a typical spicy 'salsa' – a sauce, and lots of delicious vegetables. And the best thing about it is that the prices are very reasonable. And the waiters are really friendly, and good-looking too! If you are in Islington, you must go. You'd love it!

Unit 5 Recording 7

A computer screen is rectangular. An egg is oval. A plate is round. A floppy disk is square. An elephant is heavy. A mouse is light. The Grand Canyon is enormous. Buckingham Palace is huge. An ant is tiny. The main road is wide. The back streets are narrow. Soap is smooth. A beard is rough. Toffee is sticky. Ice cream is soft. A stone is hard.

Unit 5 Recording 9

Pedro: I am going to tell you about Capoeira. Capoeira originated in Brazil, where it was started by the African slaves. They used it for entertainment, and also to fight against their white masters. It is a kind of martial art, which is also like a dance. Er, you need to be very fit and strong, and you should have good control of your body. You often have to use your hands to balance. Everyone sits around in a circle, singing and playing music, and two people fight in the centre. To fight the other person you kick with your feet, but ... er ... nowadays, there is no contact. As soon as you see the other person's hand or foot coming towards you, you have to move away quickly. You must be careful the other person doesn't kick you. If the other person kicks you, then you lose.

Afterwards, you can ... er ... relax and talk about the fight. And ... er ... we often spend the evening together, listening to music. I have been doing Capoeira for three years. I have improved a lot since I first started, and now I wear a green belt. In the future, I would like to become a trainer, and teach other people about this beautiful sport.

Unit 6 Recording 1

1 I got lost in the city because I hadn't been there before.
2 The evening went well because I'd planned it carefully.
3 I went to see the film because I'd heard it was good.
4 I was qualified for the job because I'd studied the subject at university.
5 I found the exam easy because I'd spent a lot of time studying before it.
6 It was a big day but I was tired because I hadn't been able to sleep the night before.

Unit 6 Recording 2

Speaker 1
This photo shows me walking along the Great Wall of China. It was early in the morning, so there was nobody there, except a man walking his goats. In the background, you can see the hills and the wall stretching out as far as you can see. Parts of the wall looked like they had been built in the clouds. I had already been in Beijing for one week, and before I left, I wanted to see the wall. I was very excited because I had heard that you can see this wall from the moon, and I wanted to see it for myself.

Speaker 2
This is a photo of the Grand Canyon. I went there with my family – all six of us. On the left of the photo, you can see one of the guides. I took this photo after we'd been walking for a few hours. We felt very happy to be there because we had heard about the Canyon, how beautiful it was. Some friends had told us how amazing it was but we'd never expected to see it ourselves. So it was very nice to see it in real life. It was very, very big. We walked for some hours and afterwards we just sat quietly. It was a very silent place, you see, and very beautiful.

Speaker 3
We took a train up, well, up the mountain and then we took a bus, and we were very high up ... erm ..., and then we walked to Machu Picchu. Far below us there was a river. We were very near the clouds and ... erm ... there were mountains covered in trees. We kept walking past a few stone huts and ... erm ... waiting to see the great ruin. We were very excited. We'd always wanted to see Machu Picchu. I'd heard that some people had started crying when they first saw the city because it's such an incredible sight. Anyway, eventually you get to a place where you can see all of the city. The stone ruins were so powerful and you think 'some people actually built this on top of a mountain'. It really was amazing. I took this photo when I first saw the city, just after we'd arrived.

Unit 6 Recording 3

Dialogue 1
S=Stefan W=Woman
S: I'd like two tickets to Dublin, please.
W: Single or return?
S: Return, please.
W: That's thirty-two pounds thirty, please.
S: Thank you. Could you tell me what time the next train leaves?
W: Two fifteen. But there are some delays to the service. You need to listen to the announcements.
S: Oh! Thanks.

Dialogue 2
K=Karina M=Man
K: Excuse me. How do we get to the National History Museum?
M: Um ... right. The quickest thing to do is to take the 31 bus to Grafton Street, and then ask again.
K: Is it far from Grafton Street?
M: No, it's a short walk from there. I think it's about five minutes' walk.
K: OK. Thank you.
M: But it's closed at the moment.
K: Oh! Thank you anyway.

Dialogue 3
S=Stefan W=Woman
S: Excuse me. Is there a post office near here?
W: Yes, there's one just down the road. Just go straight on and it's on your left.
S: Thank you.
W: But it's closed now. You need to go before 6 o'clock.
S: Oh no! Thank you.

Dialogue 4
S=Stefan W=Woman
S: Excuse me. Does this bus go to Temple Bar?
W: No, this one's for the airport. You need the 356.
S: OK, thanks.
W: But you need to go to the bus stop across the road.
S: Oh, OK.
W: There's one every hour.
S: Thanks for your help.

Dialogue 5
K=Karina M=Man
K: Two student tickets, please.
M: Have you got a student card?
K: Yes. One moment. Oh. I can't find it. I think I've left it at home.
M: Then I'm afraid you'll have to pay the full price. That'll be nineteen euros please.
K: Nineteen euros! OK. Thanks.

Unit 6 Recording 4

What time does the museum open?
Is there a bank near here?
Can you recommend a good restaurant?
How much is a return to the city centre?
Does this bus go to the airport?
Excuse me. Could you tell me what time the train leaves?
Excuse me. Do you know where platform 1 is?
Can you tell me the way to the station, please?
Just go straight on. It's on your left.

Unit 6 Recording 6

Dialogue 1
A: I read an amazing story about a family that was sailing.
B: Did you? What happened?
A: A whale jumped onto their boat.
B: Really? Where?
A: Near Australia.

Dialogue 2
C: A dog went home alone from India to Scotland.
D: Really? How?
C: It travelled by boat and, after months at sea, it ran home.
D: That's amazing!

Dialogue 3
E: This diver finds fifteen wedding rings a year.
F: Does he?
E: And he returns most of them.
F: That's interesting!

Dialogue 4
G: Karen Goode found a ring she'd lost ten years before.
H: Did she? How?
G: It was on the same beach.
H: That's incredible!

Unit 6 Recording 8

A=Acer P=Paul C=Cecille
A: Would you like to go on this tour?
P: You mean the bus tour?
A: Yes.
P: Yeah, OK. That sounds good.
A: OK, what about you?

C: Yeah, sure. Let's do that this morning.

A: OK. What about in the afternoon? I really like museums. I'd like to visit The British Museum or The National Gallery.

C: Oh, I've been to The British Museum.

A: Really? What's it like?

C: It's wonderful. It's full of different stuff ... erm ... jewellery, lots of ancient Egyptian treasures, paintings, statues. It's amazing.

A: Shall we go there then?

P: But you've already been?

C: Yes, but I'd like to see it again. Let's go there in the afternoon.

A: OK, and what about in the evening? Shall we go on the London Eye?

C: What's that?

A: Y'know, it looks like a big wheel. It's really popular. It's become a landmark. Lots of tourists go on it.

P: Mmm, how about going to Camden?

C: What's in Camden?

P: There's the market.

A: Er ... I think it's closed in the evening.

P: Oh, is it?

A: Er ... but it has a really nice atmosphere. Cafés and restaurants and things. Maybe we can eat there.

C: In Camden?

A: Yeah.

C: OK.

P: OK. That's fine by me.

Unit 7 Recording 1

Speaker 1

I have a friend in Italy, who taught all his five children to swim by throwing them in at the deep end – literally! He took them down to the swimming pool, where other children were swimming, tied a rope around their middle, and threw them into the water. He threw them in, pulled them up on the rope and then threw them in again, until eventually they learned how to swim for themselves. They all survived, and they are all good, strong swimmers now too!

Speaker 2

My art teacher at college had a strange way of teaching us to draw faces. It was learning by doing. He told us to sit opposite a partner, and draw their face without looking. He tied a scarf around your head, so you couldn't see the paper you were drawing on. Also, you had to keep the pencil on the paper all the time, so the picture was just one line. There were some very funny faces. But it did help you not to feel embarrassed.

Speaker 3

When I was learning the piano, my teacher told me to hold an orange in each hand as I played. It was supposed to help the position of your hand on the keyboard, but it was very difficult.

Speaker 4

They say that practice makes perfect. Well, my sister wanted desperately to learn to ride a bicycle, but nobody had time to show her. One day I found her sitting on the bicycle trying to balance it without moving. 'I am practising,' she said. 'When I can do it standing still, then I will be ready to start moving forward.'

Speaker 5

When I was studying Spanish with my flat-mate, she wrote the names of all the words she knew in Spanish on pieces of paper, and stuck them around the house so that she could learn them by heart. She wrote lists of verbs and tenses, and put them in the bathroom, and on the bedroom wall. Everywhere you went you saw Spanish on the walls. It was quite useful.

Unit 7 Recording 2

A=Aziz G=Gemma

A: Do you remember Mr Halsworth, our History teacher?

G: Yes. He was the short man, with those terrible glasses. He was really boring and we were always so naughty in his classes. We would throw paper at him!

A: That's right. He used to shout so much he would go red in the face.

G: Poor man. I remember Miss Matthews – the Music teacher. She was really beautiful, and she used to play us Mozart, and teach us songs from Africa. I remember her lessons were so relaxing, and enjoyable. She was inspiring.

A: Yes, she was lovely. And so patient. Not like Madame Bouchier, the French teacher! She was frightening! I didn't use to like her lessons at all. She used to tell me to sit at the front of the class, right under her nose, and ask me all the most difficult questions. And if you failed a test, or forgot to do your homework, she would punish you.

A: Oh, do you remember Mr Ford, the Religious Studies teacher?

G: Oh yes. He was great!

A: He was so open-minded, wasn't he? He used to teach us all about different religions of the world, like Rastafarianism, and he was also interested in astronomy, so we'd learn about the stars too. He was very knowledgeable.

G: Yes, and he never lost his temper, not even when we used to ...

Unit 7 Recording 3

1 He used to shout.

2 She used to play us Mozart.

3 He used to teach us.

4 I didn't use to like her lessons.

5 We didn't use to behave badly.

6 Did you use to work hard?

Unit 7 Recording 4

Part 1

D=Dave V=Veronika E=Ebo

D: In England, I would say no.

V: Really?

D: Generally, there's a feeling that old people are ... erm ... invisible. They aren't a part of society.

V: That's sad.

E: In Ghana, it's the opposite. We have a deep respect for old people. They're always involved in family decisions. They are ... erm ... if we have a problem, we go to old people for advice, to find out what to do.

D: What about in Sweden?

V: Erm ... in Sweden, I think we do respect old people. Certainly in the past.

E: In the past, you did.

V: I think so. Young people today, maybe less.

D: Yeah, I mean in England, kids just brush past them in the street. And it's a very youthful culture. Everything is aimed at young people ... TV programmes, cities. It's all for young people.

V: I thought England was very traditional.

E: Me too.

D: It is, but not in this way.

V: Do they have any rights?

D: What? Old people?

V: Yeah, like ... um ...

D: Yeah, they don't have to pay so much to go to museums, things like that. Travel is cheaper for old people. They can study for free, things like that.

E: You don't get any of that in Ghana, or anywhere else in Africa.

Part 2

E: I don't think we even have nursing homes in Ghana. I've never heard of them.

V: We do in Sweden, but they aren't common at all.

E: In Ghana, we would never send elderly people to a nursing home. Never, never, not in a million years. When people get old, they live with their children or their grandchildren, and ... er ...everyone is happy with this situation.

D: Really? I can't imagine it.

E: Yes, this is what happens and everyone expects it.

V: Old people are quite independent in Sweden. They live in flats. We don't live in extended families like you do, or like the Italians do, and some other countries, but ... erm .... yeah ... nursing homes aren't common.

D: Well, I guess the English are different again. But the nursing homes are pretty good. They provide a community, regular food, a routine for old people. Obviously, some nursing homes are terrible, but not all of them, and ... y'know ... they're allowed visitors. It's not like a prison.

Part 3

D: I think, for men it's 65, and for women it's 60. I think.

V: I think it's the same in Sweden. But I'm not sure.

E: In most countries in Africa, there is no age to retire. We keep working until we drop! Even if old people don't work full-time, they make themselves useful doing little jobs.

V: I think that's good.

E: Yeah, they always have a place in society, because they keep working.

V: That's good.

Unit 7 Recording 5

1 I could do it.

2 He wasn't able to stop.

3 I couldn't run fast.

4 They were able to play.

5 We couldn't see it.

6 Were you able to go?

Tapescripts

Unit 7 Recording 6

Narrator: This happened when I was about eight or nine. I went to a large school in the city centre. We didn't know anything about the countryside – all we knew about was London. So, one day my teacher decided to take the class to the countryside. It was a two-hour journey in the school bus, and when we got there, we looked at trees and nature and birds and things like that. It was a beautiful sunny day. Anyway, on the final part of the trip, in the afternoon, we went horse-riding. Now, it was the first time most of us had even seen a horse, and we had to get on it and ride. And I remember getting on this huge horse. They were really, really big. And everyone was moving really slowly on these horses. And, of course, what did my horse do? It decided to run off, with me on top of it. At first it didn't go too fast. But all of a sudden it started really galloping. So there I was screaming and shouting, with my arms around this horse, and it just wouldn't stop. I don't know how I didn't fall off. And the whole class was laughing at me. Eventually, I managed to stop it. And afterwards I was so frightened I was shaking for about an hour. It was the most embarrassing and frightening experience. I'll never forget it. I learned that me and horses don't go together, and I've never been on a horse since that day!

Unit 8 Recording 1

Dialogue 1
A: Where would you go with all that money?
B: To Hawaii.

Dialogue 2
C: She's got four brothers, hasn't she?
D: I didn't know that. I don't know her very well.

Dialogue 3
E: So who wants to do the shopping?
F: I'd do it, but I have to do my homework.

Dialogue 4
G: Is it possible to get some help? The job won't take very long with three of us.
H: You're asking for help? That makes a change!

Unit 8 Recording 2

Dialogue 1
Gabriel: Mexico City has too many cars, so it's really polluted. So, if I could change one thing, I'd have a law against all the traffic. I'd stop cars from going into the city centre.

Dialogue 2
Luciana: I'd improve the facilities for disabled people. People in wheelchairs have real problems because of the roads and pavements. Even in public buildings sometimes there are no elevators so they can't use the rooms on the higher floors.

Dialogue 3
Clive: There's no peace and quiet here. All the noise and mess is caused by these students. They scream and shout every night. So I would make some new laws against all the noise so we could get some sleep!

Dialogue 4
Olivia: Because of the stupid laws here, everybody builds these terrible buildings. They are really ugly, which means the city isn't so beautiful these days. If I was mayor, I would pass a law to stop these buildings.

Unit 8 Recording 3

W=Woman M=Man
W: The biggest change? I think it's probably been medical progress. The situation has really improved. Luckily, doctors and surgeons can cure so many diseases now that were just impossible when I was younger.
M: That's true.
W: Life-saving cures and operations have become more and more common. I'm sure in the future, disease won't be such a big problem, because we'll discover cures for most of the really bad diseases.
M: I don't know about that. There are still no cures for some of the most common diseases, like flu. And in developing countries, there isn't enough money to pay for some of the cures, so the situation hasn't changed.
W: Yes, that is a problem.
M: No, I think that the biggest change has been the change in lifestyle. It's got much worse.
W: Worse? How?
M: People work too much now, and unfortunately they don't have time to spend with their families. And when people have free time, they just watch the television. So not surprisingly, people are getting fatter. They are always too busy to cook properly, and so they eat fast food and ...

Unit 8 Recording 4

Roger: I stopped work a year ago, when we discovered Jack, our three-year-old son had a kidney problem. Before that, I just worked all the time. All I thought about was making money for my family. But when we discovered Jack was seriously ill, it changed our world completely. I decided to give up my job, so that I could spend time with him. Now I pick up the children from school every day, and we walk home through the park. It's been great to be with Jack, and now he has had an operation, which hopefully will mean that his life will go back to normal. As for me? Well, I won't be able to go back to my old job, so maybe I'll change career and start my own business. But for me it was the right decision. If I'd stayed at work, I wouldn't have spent time with Jack when he really needed me.

Tunde: My family wanted me to work in the family business, like my brothers did, but I was never interested in that. I had always dreamed of going to study in another country, to study Art. So when I finished school, I applied, and I was offered a place at the university in Paris. It was a big decision to come here, leaving my family and friends, and ... er ... coming to this country. Everything is so different here and I don't even speak the language, but it has worked out very well. I met my fiancée, Nancy, here, and we are planning to get married when I finish my degree. So I'm happy I came here. If I hadn't come to France, I wouldn't have met Nancy!

Sarah: My boyfriend was working nights as a lorry driver. We weren't very happy because we didn't really see each other. Then we went on holiday to Italy, and while we were there, we saw this old olive farm for sale. It needed lots of work doing to it, but it was beautiful, and we just fell in love with the house the moment we saw it. We came back to England, sold our house, left our jobs, and said good-bye to our friends. Two months later, we drove down to Italy to start our new life growing olives to make olive oil. It was very hard for the first year and we nearly changed our minds. We didn't have much money, and we knew nothing about farming olives or how to run our own business. But now things are much better, and we enjoy working together. I am glad we didn't have a change of heart. If we'd gone back to England, we wouldn't have been happy.

Unit 8 Recording 5

1 If I had known the test was today, I would have done some revision.
2 I wouldn't have missed the last train if I had left home earlier.
3 If I'd known it was you on the phone, I would've answered it.
4 If you'd asked me out to dinner, I'd have said 'yes'.
5 I wouldn't have felt so tired this morning if I'd gone to bed earlier.
6 If I hadn't gone on holiday to Greece, I wouldn't have met my husband.
7 I would have organised a party for you if I'd known you were coming.
8 I wouldn't have spent so much time with my children if I hadn't stopped work.

Unit 8 Recording 6

If I'd left home earlier, I wouldn't 've missed the train.

Unit 8 Recording 8

Dialogue 1
Man: Yes, definitely. I work on a cruise ship and when we have stopovers we get to see a bit of the country. Just for a day or two but it's enough to get a taste of what it's like. I've been all over the world ... to some really interesting places ... South America, the Caribbean and so on. You get to meet some interesting people too. I was talking to a passenger recently who turned out to be a doctor, some sort of famous doctor, who'd treated some really important people. So, yes, my job can be very interesting.

Dialogue 2.
Man: My wife and I are going to open a restaurant near where we live. It'll be an Italian restaurant as she's from Italy. We're a bit worried about it, of course, but it's something we've always wanted to do and it's now or never. Um ... at the moment, we're doing all the financial calculations but I'm planning to leave my job next month. It'll be a major change for both of us but we're

really looking forward to it.

Dialogue 3

Woman: I joined the gym about three months ago and it's made a real difference to my life. It was difficult at first ... you know there were times when I just wanted to go home and watch TV ... but it quickly became part of my daily routine. I feel so much better now. I've got so much more energy ... and I've made a lots of new friends too.

Dialogue 4

Girl: I think it depends really. Some people need a routine. Babies, older people ... perhaps. They like to do everything in the same way, in the same order. I don't know. I think life is probably a bit boring if you always do that, but it depends. My granddad had a very strict routine. He always ate at the same time and went to bed at the same time, and it worked for him, but it's not for everybody, is it?

Dialogue 5

Man: Well, I don't want to stay in my present job for too long, that's for sure. And I certainly don't want to settle down at the moment either. I'm always looking for new experiences ... new places to go ... new people to meet ... so yes, I think it's true to say that I like change!

Unit 9 Recording 1

Speaker: Good afternoon everybody. Today I'd like to tell you about our idea for a new business. We want to open a restaurant that serves food from all over the world. Our main idea is that the chefs cook food from fifty or sixty countries. The most important thing for us is that the food is great. We'll allow the chefs to choose the dishes and the menu will be very big, with something for everybody. We'll employ three chefs and six waiters. We won't make the waiters wear a uniform, and they will have one special perk: we'll let them eat free at our restaurant. To sum up, our restaurant will be small and friendly but with a great international menu. The name of the restaurant is World Food! Thank you for listening. Are there are any questions?

Unit 9 Recording 2

Speaker 1

I find her really annoying. She comes in at the end of the day, and gives you lots more work to finish by tomorrow. It makes it very difficult to organise your time.

Speaker 2

I am very pleased to work for Anya. She is a great boss, and very understanding. Like when my wife was ill in hospital, she sent her flowers. And when I was feeling worried about it, she sent me home for the day. I didn't have to ask, because she understands how you feel before you say anything.

Speaker 3

He can be quite aggressive. If someone forgets to do something, he really shouts. Sometimes he even throws things around the office. It can be very frightening.

Speaker 4

It's very exciting to work with Michael because he has so much energy and enthusiasm. He has a lot of new ideas for the business, and he involves people, so that their ideas are included too. Work never gets boring because he is always changing things.

Unit 9 Recording 3

I=Interviewer W=Mr Wilkins

I: So Mr Wilkins you've applied for a management position. Let me ask you a few questions.
W: Yes, fine.
I: Firstly, are you good at listening to people?
W: Yes, I think so. People often talk to me about their problems and ask me for advice, and things. So yes.
I: Their problems? That's interesting. And can you usually find solutions to difficult problems?
W: Well, actually, not always. No. I usually ask other people for their ideas. If there's a problem at work, for example, I ask my colleagues for ideas, and then try a few different ideas to see which one works.
I: That's good. So you listen to other people's ideas?
W: That's right.
I: And what do you think are your strengths and weaknesses?
W: Well, I'd say that my strengths are that I work very hard. I'm very motivated. And I'm good with people, so I get on well with my colleagues. My weakness is probably that I'm a bit disorganised. My desk is always a mess, and I tend to arrive late for meetings.
I: I see. And do you work well under pressure?
W: Yes. Quite well. I'm a calm person by character, so if there's a problem I don't panic. As I said before, I like to work hard, so if there's a lot of work to do, I'm happy to just keep working until it's finished. I'll get up very early in the morning, or just work all night until the job's done. That's not a problem.
I: OK. And do you like working on your own?
W: Umm ... that's a difficult one. I like working with people, as I said. That's the part of the job I enjoy best. But if there is a difficult document or report to write, then I work well on my own. Sometimes I'll work from home, so that there are no interruptions, so then I work on my own.
I: That's great. Well, thank you for taking the time to come and see us Mr Wilkins ...

Unit 9 Recording 5

1 In an international company it is useful to be able to speak more than one language.
2 Our company is very hi-tech so you need to be able to use a range of computer software.
3 A good salesperson can give good presentations.
4 I have to work accurately because mistakes are very expensive
5 People get very stressed when they continually work under pressure.

6 Many people work irregular hours in my company – some start early and some finish late.

Unit 9 Recording 6

Speaker 1

Air hostess: You have to be good at dealing with people. Some people get nervous about flying, or they feel ill. Or sometimes there are arguments between passengers, so you need to listen to people and solve these types of problems. Also, sometimes you have to persuade people to do things they don't want to do, like sit in a different seat... . Um ... I suppose ... it's useful to speak more than one language. And of course you have to like travelling! I travel thousands of kilometres every week.

Speaker 2

Office manager: I found that you needed to prioritise. There were so many things to do – you had to say, 'This is important. I'll do this first'. And then you had to delegate, find other people to do some of the jobs. We worked under a lot of pressure, and we worked irregular hours too. Sometimes we couldn't go home until midnight. That was fairly common. Other things: well, it was useful to be able to type fast. And we used a whole range of computer software. So, yeah it was kind of one of those jobs ...

Speaker 3

Medical scientist: You had to work accurately. And also you had to be very good with figures. You couldn't make mistakes. It was different when I was doing the job, but these days they use a lot of computer software. In fact most of the work is done by computer. And this helps with solving problems, because often you don't get the result you are looking for, and you don't know why.

Speaker 4

Bus driver: You need to be able to drive well obviously, and also to be patient. That's the most important thing. What else? Well, we sometimes get stuck in traffic jams. Y'know, it's a hot day and you're in the middle of the city, and you're stuck there for an hour. Well, they get angry. Other drivers. Passengers. So we have to deal with these people. And then sometimes we work irregular hours – at nights or early in the morning. That's a bit of a pain in the neck but y'know someone's gotta do it ...

Unit 9 Recording 7

1 She first learned soccer from her teacher at high school.
2 We went to a restaurant near the shopping centre. As usual, I paid the bill.
3 For my holiday I bought a return ticket to Paris.
4 There's a place on the freeway where we can stop and buy gas.
5 If you want to use the toilet, we can go to my flat. I live close to here.
6 I never get any mail, only stupid text messages on my cell phone.
7 Let's get some burgers and fries and go watch a movie.
8 A: How are you getting to the mall?

B: On the subway.

9 Excuse me. I'd like the check, and could you show me where the restroom is, please?

10 There's a restaurant by the underground station which sells great fish and chips.

Unit 10 Recording 1

J=Jack   A=Alice

J: Have you got a good memory?

A: I wish I had! I'm a disaster! I'm good at remembering things like appointments and meetings at work. That's fine. But I'm terrible with faces and names. It happens all the time that I meet people and I immediately forget their name.

J: Me too. I'm hopeless. I can never remember faces. The other day I was walking along the street and this man came up and said hello. And I had no idea who he was.

A: And who was he?

J: He was my boss's husband.

A: Oops.

J: Very embarrassing. What about dates? Do you remember people's birthdays, that kind of thing?

A: Well, I'm OK with birthdays because I write them all down in my diary. I wish I didn't have to, but ... y'know.

J: And phone numbers?

A: I can't even remember my own phone number half the time.

J: Personally, I wish I could remember things like writers' names or the names of songs. It happened quite recently that we were talking about books and I'd read an excellent novel and I wish I'd remembered the name because I wanted to recommend the book. But I just couldn't remember it.

A: What book's that then?

J: Um, I can't remember the title.

Unit 10 Recording 3

N=Narrator

N: Mother Teresa dedicated her life to helping street children and sick people in India. She started the Missionaries of Charity to help people in need. Her hard work and dedication inspired many other people to start caring for others. Now over one million people work for her charities in more than 40 countries.

N: Marie Curie was a brilliant scientist. Originally from Poland, she went to study in France and worked at the Sorbonne University with her husband, Pierre. Together, they discovered radiation. She won the Nobel Prize in 1903 and 1911.

N: Frida Kahlo was a gifted painter from Mexico. She was famous for her amazing and unusual paintings. At age 18, she was involved in a serious accident in which she nearly died. But she was determined to survive and made a remarkable recovery. Many people admired her for her colourful and lively personality.

N: Marilyn Monroe was a talented actress who was loved by people all over the world. She overcame many problems in her life to become one of the twentieth century's greatest cultural icons. Although she died quite young, she had already starred in thirty films during her career and is particularly remembered for her charm and beauty.

N: Rosa Parks, a black American, was a very brave woman. In Alabama in 1955, she refused to give her bus seat to a white woman. She was then arrested and sent to prison. People were so angry about this that they stopped using the buses for nearly a year. She encouraged many other black people in America to fight for their rights. Many of America's laws were changed because of her protest.

Unit 10 Recording 4

Narrator: Coco Chanel was born in France in 1883. Her father died when she was a child and her mother sent the children away to grow up with relatives. When she was a young woman Chanel met two rich men who helped her to start her business. She opened her first shop in 1913, where she sold perfume. Soon afterwards she opened a shop in Paris and began designing clothes. Her clothes and perfume business did very well until 1939, when she left France to go and live in Hollywood. In 1953 she returned to France. She dressed many famous film stars and she was still working when she died in 1971. She is considered one of the most influential designers of the twentieth century.

Unit 10 Recording 6

Dialogue 1

Man: So, thank you very much for coming, everybody. I hope you found the talks interesting and useful. If you want any more information, you can find us on our website. The address is in the programme, so do send us an email. Thank you and goodbye.

Dialogue 2

F=Father   D=Daughter

F: OK, you've got everything? Passport, ticket, money.

D: Yeah, I think so. Let me just ...

F: Have you got the address where you're staying?

D: Yes.

F: Your mobile?

D: Yeah, it's right here.

F: So you'll give us a call when you arrive.

D: Yeah, it'll probably be late this evening.

F: OK, have a safe trip.

D: Thanks, Dad.

F: And we'll see you in a couple of weeks.

D: Two weeks. OK, bye.

F: Bye, darling.

Dialogue 3

M=Man   W=Woman

M: Are you off now?

W: Yep.

M: Have a good weekend.

W: You too. Bye.

M: Bye.

Dialogue 4

M=Man   W=Woman

M: Thanks for everything. I really enjoyed it.

W: You're welcome. Come back any time.

M: Thanks a lot.

W: Maybe see you next weekend. There's a party at Joe's.

M: Oh OK, yeah, sounds good. Alright then, thanks. Bye.

W: Take care.

Unit 10 Recording 7

Leaving on a jet plane

All my bags are packed
I'm ready to go
I'm standing here outside your door
I hate to wake you up to say goodbye
But the dawn is breaking
It's early morn
The taxi's waiting
He's blowing his horn
Already I'm so lonesome
I could cry

CHORUS
So kiss me and smile for me
Tell me that you'll wait for me
Hold me like you'll never let me go
I'm leaving on a jet plane
Don't know when I'll be back again
Oh babe, I hate to go

There's so many times I've let you down
So many times I've played around
I'll tell you now, they don't mean a thing
Every place I go, I'll think of you
Every song I sing, I'll sing for you
When I come back, I'll wear your wedding ring

(CHORUS)

Now the time has come to leave you
One more time
Let me kiss you
Then close your eyes
I'll be on my way
Dream about the days to come
When I won't have to leave you alone
About the time I won't have to say

(CHORUS)

Unit 10 Recording 8

1 Ouch!
2 Yuk!
3 Shh!
4 Mmm!
5 Phoo!